The rebirth of private policing

Until recently, commentators have ignored private policing and have been preoccupied instead, with the activities of public police officers. In consequence, there has been much discussion of the role of the police but little debate about policing, an activity undertaken throughout history by a mixture of public, private and quasi-public agents. Contrary to models of police history which see a complete break between earlier private models of provision and the new police, Les Johnston claims that there is no clean break between the new and old forms of policing.

In the first part of the book, Johnston reviews the history of private policing and examines the various ideologies of privatization. He goes on to look at current developments in private policing, including such areas of topical concern as the activities of the private security sector, and the increasing effects of privatization on police forces. Lastly, Johnston's argument forces us to re-assess the conventional distinction between public and private authority so often taken for granted in social and political theory.

Les Johnston has written extensively on policing and also on social theory. He is Deputy Director at the Centre for Police and Criminal Justice Studies, University of Exeter.

The rebirth of private policing

Please remember that this is a library book,
and that it belongs only temporarily to each
person who uses it. Be considerate. Do
not write in this, or any, library book.

Les Johnston

London and New York

First published in 1992
by Routledge
11 New Fetter Lane, London EC4P 4EE

Simultaneously published in the USA and Canada by
Routledge
a division of Routledge, Chapman and Hall Inc.
29 West 35th Street, New York, NY 10001

© 1992 Les Johnston

Typeset by
NWL Editorial Services, Langport, Somerset TA10 9DG

Printed and bound in Great Britain by
Mackays of Chatham PLC, Chatham, Kent

British Library Cataloguing in Publication Data
Johnston, Les. *1948–*
    The rebirth of private policing.   1. Police.
    I. Title
    363.2

Library of Congress Cataloging in Publication Data
Johnston, Les
    The rebirth of private policing / by Les Johnston
    p.   cm.
    Includes bibliographical references and index.
    1. Law enforcement.   2. Police, private.   3. Police –
    contracting out.   4. Privatization.   I. title.
    HV7921.J64   1991   91–13442
    363.2'89 – dc20   CIP

ISBN 0–415–05192–4
       0–415–05193–2 (pbk)

Contents

Preface

Ten years ago, anyone suggesting that police services in Britain might be subjected to privatization would have been thought insane. Today, whenever one converses with police officers, the topic of privatization invariably crops up. Circumstances, it would seem, are changing rapidly. In Chapter 3 of this book, I construct a hypothetical case of privatization in 'Profitshire Constabulary'. When it was written this fictional scenario seemed, if anything, rather far-fetched. Yet, less than 6 months after its completion, a senior British police officer was proposing something very similar to my 'Profitshire' model, in arguing for the right of police forces to set up private security companies: 'I would like to see North-umbria Police Security Ltd. competing on equal terms without subsidies, with the money it made ploughed back into public policing. What is wrong with making money?' (Sir Stanley Bailey, Chief Constable of Northumbria: *Daily Mail* 18 September 1990).

It is important, however, to get the privatization issue into some sort of perspective. In particular, two things need to be emphasized. First, privatization takes a wide variety of forms. Here, I have defined the concept in broad sociological, rather than narrow economic terms. In that sense, my concern is not merely with 'contracting out' to private security, but also with the multifarious forms of (historical and contemporary) policing undertaken by private citizens. Inevitably, this perspective requires us to differentiate between 'policing' (a complex and variable set of social functions carried out by a variety of agents) and 'police' (a specific group of personnel). Unarguably, this book is about policing, rather than about police. Second, it is necessary to locate private policing in its historical context. In doing this, I try to provide a corrective to models of police history which see the emergence of the 'new police' (after 1829) as signalling a complete break with earlier, private modes of provision. In fact, there is no clean break between the 'old' and the 'new' policing. Public policing certainly came to dominance in the period from about 1880–1950. But private policing, in its various forms, continued to exist. In that sense its resurgence during the last 20 years, indicates a renewal, or 'rebirth', of private activity, alongside public modes of provision. In different historical periods, policing consists, then, of varying mixtures of public and private elements.

The book is organized into three parts. Part II consists of six chapters, each dealing with some substantive area of private policing. Though these focus, primarily, on Britain and North America, I have tried wherever possible (given the dearth of comparative material on the topic) to provide information on developments in other countries. Each one of these chapters can be read independently, so readers can, if they wish, 'dip into' chapters for information on a particular topic (e.g. the structure of the private security sector, autonomous 'self-policing' by citizens, privatization in public police forces). Part I places the topic in its historical and political context, reviewing past forms of private policing and assessing some dominant, ideological justifications for privatization. Part III places the issue in a wider perspective. Here, I make two points. First, recognition of the present resurgence of private policing has major implications for the sociology of policing which has, by and large, adopted rather limited theoretical perspectives. Second, that resurgence also has implications for how we conceptualize power and authority. Policing, conventionally defined, is an archetypal public (state) function, police officers enjoying a legitimate capacity to exert coercive power with authority. Yet, the existence of private policing, especially when private agents interact with public agents, and/or have powers delegated to them by the state, calls into question the distinction between 'public' and 'private' authority. In fact, the rebirth of private policing forces us to reassess the conventional distinction between 'public' and 'private' spheres, so often taken for granted in social and political theory.

Les Johnston
Exmouth,
January 1991

Acknowledgements

In the course of writing this book I have received help from a number of people to whom I now express grateful thanks without, of course, implicating them in any of its shortcomings. To begin with I should acknowledge two intellectual debts. The first is to Clifford Shearing and Philip Stenning of the University of Toronto. Though I have never met either personally, their substantial output of research on private policing in North America is, inevitably, an important influence on anybody concerned with the topic. Nearer to home, Nigel South has been ploughing a relatively lone furrow for almost a decade and he, more than anybody, has opened up the issue of private policing for debate amongst British academics. Anyone interested in looking at a rare example of empirical fieldwork in the private security industry could do no better than consult Nigel's doctoral thesis (South 1985). A number of people have made constructive comments on draft versions of some chapters, and others have helped by giving encouragement at various stages. In particular, I would like to thank Derek Griffiths, Robert Reiner, Lee Weavers and Richard Williams. I am also indebted to Talia Rodgers of Routledge, first for tracking me down at the British Sociological Association Conference in 1988, and thus, setting the wheels in motion; second, for the valuable (and valued) support and encouragement she has given me over the last fifteen months.

Writing a book of this sort obviously depends upon the accumulation of written material. Here, I would like to thank library staff at Polytechnic South West (Exmouth), the University of Exeter, and at the Police Staff College, Bramshill, Hants. I am particularly grateful to the Commandant for giving me permission to use Bramshill College Library's invaluable resources. I am also grateful to those who have responded to my 'begging letters' requesting information and documentation on a variety of topics. Here, I am especially indebted to Barry Adam, Chris Corns, Professor Alfred Heijder, Mr Aubrey Johnston (New Zealand Department of Statistics), Daniel Mason, Mr F. de Mot (Belgian Ministry of the Interior), Frank Pearce, Wesley Skogan, Yaffa Tzubery (Ministry of Police Jerusalem), John Wildeman, the New Zealand Department of Justice, and the New Zealand Police (especially Inspector R.R. Honan).

Many people have given me ideas and information – sometimes without knowing it – which have been used in this book. I have benefited enormously from teaching various cohorts of students on the MA degree in Police Studies at the Centre for Police and Criminal Justice Studies, University of Exeter. In this case, I have learned much more from them than they have learned from me. For the same reason I thank students on the BA Social and Organizational Studies (Police) degree at Polytechnic South West (Plymouth). Several people also granted me interviews, giving freely of their valuable time. Here, I would like to thank John McClellan, Markku Pesonen (Managing Director of Suomen Teollisuuden Vartiointi Oy, Helsinki) and Kalle Lehmus (Helsinki Police).

I would also like to acknowledge the financial assistance given to me by the Faculty of Arts and Design, Polytechnic South West, whose research committee awarded me a grant in aid of this research; and by the British Council which supported teaching/research carried out in Finland during September 1989. I am also grateful to the University of Manchester for the award of a Hallsworth Research Fellowship (October 1990–September 1991) to support research on 'Spatial and sectoral dimensions of policing'. Some of the work carried out in the early stages of that research project has helped in the final drafting of Chapters 6 and 9 of this book.

Last, but not least, I thank my wife (the other) Les Johnston who, together with Robert, has tolerated my daily incarcerations in 'the bunker' during the last year with stoical fortitude.

Part I

Historical and political background

Chapter 1

Private policing
Before and after the 'new police'

In recent years there has been an avalanche of literature devoted to the analysis of historical patterns of social control in capitalist societies, much of it claiming to identify certain 'master tendencies' arising during the last three hundred years. In a valuable analysis of this literature, Cohen (1985) itemizes some of these 'master tendencies': notably, the movement from arbitrary and decentralized control (eighteenth century); to rational and state-centred control (nineteenth century); and, finally, to hybrid forms of statist decentralization in the current period. Yet, having himself been a leading figure in the field for more than 20 years, Cohen is increasingly cautious about the identification of distinct 'master tendencies' in the process of social control, arguing in his later work for greater recognition of the fragmented nature of the phenomenon (Cohen 1989).

I shall return to the issue of historical patterns of social control in more detail in the final chapter. For the moment, however, the question of whether the process is best seen as consisting of unitary stages, or of more diffuse and fragmented patterns, provides a useful backcloth to the present chapter. For although this chapter is directed to the history of policing, it addresses that topic in a somewhat unconventional way. Historians of policing have, in the main, been preoccupied with analysing the emergence and impact of public police forces during the nineteenth century. My concern, however, is to locate that emergence and impact alongside a history of private modes of policing which have persisted, in a variety of forms, into the twentieth century: forms which, as I indicate in later chapters, show every indication of further expansion in the present period.

CONCEPTS OF 'POLICE' AND 'POLICING'

To begin with, however, it is necessary to consider the concepts of 'police' and 'policing', the former being a relatively modern concept, the latter an old one (Steedman 1984: 8). Prior to the eighteenth century, if the word 'police' was used, reference was, in effect, being made to the broad social function of 'policing': 'the general regulation or government, the morals or economy of a city or country' (Palmer 1988: 69; cf. Ascoli 1979: 7 for citation of Dr Johnson's definition). Here, the word is derived from the Greek *polis* (the root base of 'polity', 'politics', 'policy'). 'Policing' thus referred to a socio-political function (rather than merely a formal legal one) exercised in civil society (rather than merely within the confines of the state). It was only in the mid-eighteenth century that the word 'police' began to be used, in its continental sense, to refer to the specific functions of crime prevention and order maintenance. From then, it was but a short step to defining 'police' in terms of a specific personnel. In England the word was first used in this sense by John Fielding in a pamphlet of 1758, though its first statutory use was in relation to the Thames River Police in 1800. After the formation of the 'new police' in 1829, of course, the equation of 'police' with 'personnel' was taken for granted.

The problem is that over time the concepts of 'police' and 'policing' have been conflated, historians and sociologists assuming that the two mean the same thing. This is the point behind Steedman's observation that historical analysis has tried to apply modern definitions of the police to past practices, with disastrous effects. Take the case of the 'Metropolitan version' of police history (the view that 1829 signalled the beginning of a steady process of centralization, co-ordination, and nationalization of policing in England). The problem here is that half a century after the foundation of the new police, municipal governments still defined policing in broad socio-political terms. At the local level, ratepayers still saw themselves as employing police as 'poor law officers, inspectors of nuisances, market commissioners, impounders of stray cattle and inspectors of weights and measures' (Steedman 1984: 8).

In effect, long after the emergence of the new police, the role of the uniformed officer was concerned, not merely with narrowly repressive functions, but with matters relating to the general 'regulation' of populations (Donzelot 1979). As Steedman indicates, the range of such work increased considerably after the

1856 County and Borough Police Act and the Local Government Act of 1858, police forces performing regulatory functions within the general structure of the 'administrative state'. Primarily for reasons of cost and convenience, a variety of social functions were devolved on to local police forces, the 1856 Act breaking new ground by empowering magistrates to require the police to engage in work other than keeping the peace. During this period, then, the police undertook a wide variety of duties. As well as being engaged as poor-law relieving officers, their duties involved them in the inspection of lodging houses, the inspection of weights and measures, the collection of the county rate, the surveying of roads and bridges, the supervision of market trading, the impounding of cattle, and the inspection of nuisances. In this respect, officers were employed very much as an 'administrative police' by munici-palities, though interestingly enough, despite the real variability of police work, a rudimentary conception of the appropriate police role was already prevalent amongst rank-and-file officers. (Whereas some administrative duties, such as inspection of weights and measures were unpopular because officers were brought into conflict with the 'non-criminal' middle classes, others such as the policing of vagrancy, were seen as more in line with the 'genuine' police role of dealing with 'criminal' populations.)

In fact, the period saw something of an 'inspection fervour', with suggestions that the police should be appointed as factory inspectors and, after the 1870 Education Act, as truancy inspectors. Indeed, '[c]arried away by the vision of a thoroughly policed and inspected society, some, including county chief constables, suggested that the homes of the poor should be inspected by the police, for cleanliness and against overcrowding' (Steedman 1984: 54). Many of those forms of policing which did appear were, therefore, concerned with the 'social' or 'moral' regulation of the poor. In Plymouth, the 'Sanitary Police', formed from the 'Water' or 'Dockyard Police', enforced the residential and working restrictions contained in the 1864 Contageous Diseases Act, on the local population of prostitutes. Though this force was resented by the Plymouth City Police, it enjoyed considerable support from middle-class residents, medical and military professionals, and the local press (Marsden 1990). Here, as elsewhere, the principle of policing was very much in line with that proposed in Colquhoun's *Treatise on the Police of the Metropolis* (1796), the aim being to 'give the minds of the People a right bias' (cited in Philips 1980: 177). To be sure, the moral concern expressed by writers like Colquhoun was, simultaneously, a concern about 'dangerous classes' of criminals, and many commentators have noted that the discourse of criminal pathology was conflated with discourses of sanitation, disease and moral pathology during the period (Hobbs 1988). Nevertheless, the prevalence of such 'social' or 'moral' policing (whatever its criminogenic undercurrents), together with the 'administrative policing' already described, demonstrates that 1829 did not signal a simple rupture in the structure and practice of local policing in England. Certainly by the 1880s centralization had begun to tie the interests of local forces to the concerns of the central state to an increasing extent. Equally, by that time chief constables had begun to reject the idea of the police serving as an executive arm of local government. Yet, although the variety of roles performed by the public police was slowly reduced from what it had been before, the forms through which policing and regulatory functions could be exercised remained more diverse than police history has allowed for.

Just as police history has simplified the impact of the new police on 'moral' and 'administrative' policing, so it has simplified the impact of the new public forces on private forms of social regulation. It is certainly true that the formation of new police forces after 1829 'signalled the change from a law-enforcement system dependent on unpaid JPs, parish constables and *ad hoc* watch forces, to one reliant on bureaucratic, uniformed, paid police forces' (Philips 1989: 114). Yet that generalization obscures the extent to which private provision, albeit more limited in scope, survived the formation of public forces. It is to the consideration of private forms of provision between the eighteenth and early twentieth centuries that the rest of this chapter is directed. During the course of it, I review selected examples from England and, to a lesser extent, from North America.

VARIETIES OF THE PRIVATE FORM

'Thief-takers', informers, and others

The history, structure, and organization of criminal justice can usefully be examined across three dimensions: the public and the private; the formal and the informal; the central and the local. With the risk of being over simplistic, it can be claimed, with some justification, that criminal justice during this period veered towards the 'private', 'informal', and 'local' side of that dichotomous classification.

This view is borne out in McMullan's (1987) account of crime control in sixteenth- and seventeenth-century London. Here, control developed in a fragmented way, there being various forms of accommodation between central state, local state, citizens, and the criminal fraternity, including patronage, nepotism, and private initiative. During this period law enforcement in England rested on local settlements, districts engaging in various forms of self-policing. These modes of control reflected the fragmentation of the country into independent shire-states. London, however, posed different problems from other localities, having a growing and mobile population, an expanding crime problem, and a number of unregulated areas. These 'wayward districts' often had the character of medieval 'liberties' (places granted special status independent of city or state control by virtue of having been ecclesiastical franchises). Some harboured law breakers under feudal rights of sanctuary which, though having been legally terminated in the sixteenth century, sometimes persisted into the eighteenth. Enforcement agencies found it difficult to penetrate such areas and, in effect, 'formal state control was an elaborate, negotiated and tenuous artifice', order depending effectively upon a 'fluid system of patron–client power blocs' (McMullan 1987: 123).

In this context law enforcement, policing, and punishment were open to purchase and negotiation. Policing, moreover, lacked any central command structure, and any attempt at central co-ordination met local resistance. In consequence, disorganization, coupled with the corruption arising from a speculative market in police services, led the city to encourage self-policing on a greater scale. Citizens were encouraged to spy on each other for reward, and to inform on their accomplices when arrested, in return for pardons. Fundamental to this informal economy of crime control was the principle of 'set a thief to catch a thief': 'In policing terms, informers and thief-catchers were recruited from criminal worlds and sent back to survey them' (McMullan 1987: 134). Such practices, however, exerted a rudimentary degree of co-ordination and centralization over criminal justice, since the activities of informers and thief takers were authorized by the state. Justices of the peace encouraged victims to seek out intermediaries to recover their property, and the state's trade in warrants and pardons linked the judiciary to the private thief-taking sector. What we have here, in effect, is an early form of public–private partnership in crime control: or, to take a more cynical view, an early version of the 'commercial compromise of the state' (South 1987).

The London example gives an insight into the structure of the English criminal justice system in the seventeenth and eighteenth centuries. First and foremost, the system was an amateur one. The only full-time state employees who enforced the law were revenue officers dealing with customs and excise. Criminal justice was mainly in the hands of parish constables (elected annually), along with justices of the peace and their deputies. Neither were paid, both offices being civic responsibilities rather than professions. However, justices charged fees and constables could reclaim costs incurred during their year of service.

This system was different from that found in absolutist states, such as pre-revolutionary France, where the monarch had access to a professional and centralized bureaucracy (Emsley 1983). In England, by contrast, suspicion of central state control meant that law enforcement was somewhat *ad hoc*. The military could be used against rioters and organized criminals, such as smugglers, but its intervention was unpopular with both soldiery and people alike (McLynn 1989: 18). Eighteenth-century England, unlike France, had no military governors and policing was a local function organized through relatively autonomous counties and parishes.

The problem was that this system posed increasing problems. First, it was being overwhelmed by the volume of law being generated by the expanding state, much of it aimed at the revocation of traditional rights, such as wood gathering. A second problem concerned the central state's lack of effective control over certain parts of the realm. Some industrial areas were, effectively, lawless. In Southwark, for example, groups of vigilantes calling themselves 'shelterers' carried out a form of private 'anti-policing', defending people from arrest and 'trying' law officers. Areas which had been settled by squatters, such as the Kingswood Forest area of Bristol, were also havens for allegedly 'ungovernable people' (Brewer and Styles 1980). Finally, the system showed signs of chronic corruption. Some justices began to use their positions as a source of livelihood, gaining fees for the issuing of warrants and licences. So-called 'trading justices' set up 'justice shops' in large towns, selling licences for alehouses and protecting brothels in return for bribes. At the same time, the system of parish constables was breaking down. In part, this was due to the ambiguous role of the constable as both law enforcement officer and member of the community (Sharpe 1984). But the position had become increasingly problematical for the occupant, with the demands placed upon him by the expansion of the legal apparatus. Amateur constables, most of whom would have been tradesmen continuing to run their businesses on a daily basis, increasingly tried to escape office, either by paying a fine or by paying a deputy to perform their duties.

Private prosecutions and felons associations

Probably the most striking difference between this system and our own, however, was that there was little or no attempt at criminal detection. Crime was brought to the courts when victims prosecuted offenders. Officials did not go out to find it. Justices dealt with the evidence, but detection and apprehension of suspects was left to victims, who often went to great lengths to regain stolen property (Beattie 1986).

Obviously the system permitted considerable victim discretion as to whether and in what terms an offence was reported. Discretion was often coupled with informalism, justices encouraging informal settlements between victim and offender to keep less serious cases out of court. Some private and informal arrangements, such as those involving the payment by the victim of a 'reward' for the return of stolen goods, were also commonplace. The most famous exponent of this practice was the notorious 'thief taker' Jonathan Wilde, but the system was not peculiar to England and Cohen (1988) describes a similar form of private settlement ('theft-bote') occurring in eighteenth-century Massachusetts.

Reliance on private prosecutions had its attendant dangers. For one thing, the system was arbitrary and capricious. However, a later American example suggests that the system could also have certain benefits. In Philadelphia private prosecution, though costly, was widely used by working people from the seventeenth century until the formation of a public police force in 1854. People entered litigation for a variety of reasons: to gain justice; to intimidate a neighbour; to extort money; to prevent prosecution against themselves. Yet the system ensured a degree of popular control over criminal justice, giving people the 'freedom to police themselves' (Steinberg 1986: 243). Not surprisingly, legislators wanted to dispense with a system which maximized popular consumer power. Yet, interestingly, many of those arrested and prosecuted by the newly formed police force continued to resist state monopolization of criminal justice 'by prosecuting policemen themselves, establishing informal methods of adjudication with magistrates, and simply fighting back' (Steinberg 1986: 244).

In English rural areas, of course, informal mechanisms of social regulation, such as dismissal or chastisement by an employer, pressure from a priest or landowner, arbitration, or ostracism, enabled the criminal justice system to be bypassed as often as not (Sharpe 1984). In fact, large landowners, who controlled central government through parliament and local government through the magistracy, did not want a formalized/centralized system of criminal justice which would undermine their power base. After all, 'what the eighteenth century gentry and aristocracy valued was the discretion which the system left them free to exercise' (Philips 1980:158).

Even when formal prosecution was enacted, however, cost proved a disincentive. This problem encouraged some people of property to band together in 'associations for the prosecution of felons' so that costs of apprehension and prosecution could be shared. These associations developed rapidly after about 1760–70, and the 1839 'Royal Commission on a Constabulary Force for England and Wales' identified approximately 500 of them. In fact, recent evidence suggests that the number was greater, estimates varying between the 750 to 1,000 identified by Shubert (1981) and King's (1989) figure of 1,000 to 4,000.

Felons associations, which usually consisted of between twenty and sixty members, were primarily concerned with crimes against property. Philips's (1989) analysis of the surviving records of 213 associations in twenty-six English counties between 1760 and 1860 found only two cases of prosecution for murder, the bulk of the thirteen death sentences he discovered having been passed for property offences (horse theft, sheep stealing, burglary, robbery, and stealing from a shop). Associations were local. Most were restricted to a geographical area of no more than 10 or 20 miles, and there was little co-ordination or co-operation between different bodies. Associations provided two basic services. They offered rewards for information leading to arrest and conviction. (Shubert (1981) lists rewards ranging from £21 for murder to £10 for arson.) They also provided assistance to members in the prosecution process and would occasionally prosecute on behalf of non-members, too poor to do it for themselves. Some also undertook posse and patrol activity, the most famous being the Barnet General Association established in 1813.

Rude (1985) gives two examples of organizations set up by West Country capitalists. In Bristol in 1777, leading merchants combined to protect two ships and a warehouse threatened by arson, whilst in 1802, woollen manufacturers, having raised subscriptions to the value of £2,500, met at Bath to take common action against threats made by workers to destroy new machinery. Most groups, by contrast, arose in order to deal with problems of theft. Brewer (1980), for instance, describes an association of florists set up to counter flower thefts. But most were formed to deal with problems of burglary, sheep stealing, and horse theft. As in America during the same period – when an 'anti-horse thief' movement appeared (Brown 1975: 125–6) – a surprisingly large number of associations were formed to deal with that crime (see Davey 1983: 24; and Philips 1989: 114–18).

The demise of the associations after about 1840 raises the question of their place in the history of policing and social regulation. Here, there are two diametrically opposed views. Shubert (1981) argues that the governing classes, by joining associations, sought to remove the element of discretion from the prosecution process. This, he says, contradicts Hay's (1975) thesis that the judicious use of discretion by magistrates (seen in the widespread granting of pardons to offenders) was an ideological tool used by the rulers to ensure deference from the ruled. For Shubert, by contrast, felons associations represented 'an attack on this system of flexible justice. Their concerns were those of Beccaria, Romilly and other legal reformers that the law be applied rigorously and consistently in order that criminals be deterred' (Schubert 1981: 37). Philips (1989), however, argues that this interpretation is far too simplistic. Certainly, many felons associations included in their articles stipulations that members who refused to carry through prosecutions would be excluded from the society. However, this penalty was rarely enforced, so the deterrence principle was adhered to only inconsistently. Nor, says Philips (1989), is there any evidence to indicate that asssociation members were generally in favour of Benthamite reforms of criminal law, policing, and prosecution. In the case of police reform, for example, what we find is a complex relationship between associational membership and attitude towards the 'new police'. London Associations, by and large, supported the police reforms, but many subscribers – especially those in rural associations – saw no reason why they should also have to pay rates to support the protection of other people's property. All in all, then, Philips contends that there is no simple connection between support for felons associations and support for an emerging public police force.

The question of the role of felons associations in policing history can, however, be addressed differently. For as well as examining members' attitudes towards changing patterns of policing, it is useful to consider associations as representing a specifically private strain of social regulation. This strain, despite its relative decline in the 1860s, was sometimes transformed into alternative private-regulatory forms. (Some associations, for example, became insurance companies.) But more importantly, in functional terms, it presaged things to come. Here, Philips's comment that felons associations are 'the modern analogy . . . of privately run security services or other forms of "private police"' (Philips 1989: 118) is a perceptive one.

Vigilantes

The felons association acted as a private adjunct to an English criminal justice system perceived as arbitrary, patchy, and inefficient. In America, during that same period, vigilantism offered an equivalent element of private provision, though in circumstances where the criminal justice system was even more sparse in its provision than in England.

Brown, the foremost writer on American vigilantism, defines the classical vigilante tradition in terms of 'organized, extralegal movements, the members of which take the law into their own hands' (Brown 1975: 95–6). The first American vigilante movement appeared in 1767, and from then, until about 1900, vigilantism was a constant factor in American life. Typically, vigilantist ideology subscribed to the view that, on occasions, it was necessary to 'break the law in order to uphold it', the vigilante being committed to 'circumventing the law of the land, but never [to] harming or destroying it' (Burrows 1976: 13).

'Vigilance committees' possessed defined goals, rules, and regulations. Their duration varied, but few persisted beyond a year, and most had exhausted their energies within a period of weeks or months. At least 326 movements have been documented for the period from 1767 to 1910. Most contained a few hundred people (a large proportion of the community in many frontier towns), though groups varied in size from the dozen or so members found in Pierre, South Dakota in 1880, to the 6,000-plus belonging to the San Francisco vigilance committee of 1856 (Brown 1975: Appendix 3). Membership reflected the social structure of American communities at the time. Leaders tended to be drawn from an elite of businessmen, professionals, and affluent farmers, the middle layer of farmers, craftsmen, tradesmen, teachers, and lower professionals providing the rank-and-file.

Often, this economic class difference, was reflected in ideology. Like English subscribers to private forms of justice, local vigilante leaders usually paid the highest taxes. And, like their English counterparts, 'they had the customary desire to whittle down the tax rate and keep local expenses in check'. In that sense, there was a persuasive economic rationale for a form of justice which was 'cheaper, as well as quicker and more certain, than regular justice' (Brown 1975: 117).

The economic motive was related to several others, all of which tended to encourage the vigilante solution. Because of the sparse pattern of settlement, law enforcement was highly localized in the township, and poor transportation made fugitives difficult to catch. Problems of law enforcement were matched by inadequacies in the system of justice itself. Outlaws would bribe officials, pack juries, and intimidate witnesses making conviction difficult. Yet the very sparseness of the population made the establishment of an adequate policing and judicial system difficult, since substantial expenditure of funds could easily bankrupt a town lacking any substantial base for taxation.

Alienated and marginalized elements of the lowest sections of society – 'outlaws' and 'lower people', rather than the 'honest poor' – were the main targets of vigilantism. Outlaws rejected the respectable values of life and property adhered to by the elite, and in a frontier society where social bonds were fragile and weak, such rejection threatened the brittle social fabric. Fearing the take-over of newly settled areas by such alienated elements, vigilante or 'Regulator' movements responded with vigour against groups of horse thieves, robbers, counterfeiters, arsonists, murderers, slave stealers, and land pirates in areas such as East Texas in the 1830s, Northern and Southern Illinois in the 1840s, and Northern Indiana in the 1850s (Brown 1976). Punishment was usually harsh and speedy. Whipping and expulsion were common punishments in the early years, but as time passed hanging became the customary sentence. (In accordance with this the meaning of the term 'lynching' changed from whipping to killing during the 1850s.) In total, it is estimated that organized vigilante groups executed more than 700 people between 1767 and 1910, though if the activities of unorganized lynch mobs, Ku-Klux-Klansmen and others are included, the total for the period probably exceeds 6,000.

The first American vigilante movement, the South Carolina Regulators, emerged in 1767 to stem the tide of crime arising in the 'back country'. This was accomplished successfully, but like later vigilante groups, the South Carolina Regulators did not know when to stop. Not only did their activities became more brutal, arbitrary, and sadistic, they turned their attention more and more to issues of lower-class morality – idleness, vagrancy, vice, and domestic disorder. Moreover, having regulated lower-class morality, they then turned to the regulation of local elites, in some cases settling old scores for good measure. Fearful of a sustained threat to the political order, the governor decided to meet fire with fire, recruiting a band of 'Moderators' to restrict the activities of the Regulators. Eventually, the two groups reached a compromise and order was restored, the Regulators disbanding in 1769.

The South Carolina example indicates that vigilantism was directed at both moral and criminal transgressions, as well as to activities arising in both public and private domains. Examples of 'morally sanctimonious vigilance' (Burrows 1976: xv) were especially associated with the 'Bald Knobbers' in Missouri who, in 1885–86, sought to curb the evils of liquor, gambling, and prostitution. (It was they, incidentally, who penned what is surely the most graphic vigilante warning, attaching it to a slip of paper on the body of an executed victim: 'Don't fool with the wrong end of the mule'.) A century before, in New Jersey, vigilantism had also penetrated the domestic sphere, wife beaters and child abusers being subject to regulation:

> an odd Sect of people have lately appeared there, who go under the Denomination of Regulars: there are near a Dozen of them, who dress themselves in Women's Cloaths and painting their Faces, go in the Evening to the Houses of such as are reported to have beat their wives: whence one of them entering in first, seizes the Delinquent, whilst the rest follow, strip him, turn up his Posteriors and flog him with Rods most severely, crying out all the time 'Wo to the Men that beat their Wives'.
>
> (*New York Gazette* 18 December 1752, cited in Burrows 1976: 37)

Examples of this sort were commonplace a century later when the 'White Cap' movement spread across the nation. White capping most frequently inflicted beatings upon 'drunken, shiftless whites who often abused their families' (Brown 1975: 24) and was, in effect, a spontaneous movement for the moral regulation of poor rural whites. It also served as a link between the first and second Ku-Klux-Klans, and there is an interlacing of moral and criminal fears with racist (and sexist) practices in many of the southern vigilante movements of the late nineteenth century (see Ayers 1984: 259–60)

These examples indicate the diversity of the vigilante phenomenon, some writers differentiating between vigilantism concerned with crime control and that concerned merely with the control of social groups (Rosenbaum and Sedeberg 1976). That differentiation is also reflected in Brown's distinction between classic vigilantism (that directed against horse thieves, outlaws, and the rural lower classes up until 1900) and neo-vigilantism (that directed at urban Catholics, Jews, Negroes, radicals, and labour leaders). The clearest case of neo-vigilantism arises with America's largest movement of all, the San Francisco Vigilance Committee of 1856. Five years previously, a vigilance committee had operated in response to crime problems in the city (Stewart 1964), but by 1856 crime was under control. Though the 1856 vigilantes spoke of a crime problem, there is no evidence to suggest that crime had increased significantly during the period and, in reality, the vigilantes were concerned with a different set of issues: political corruption and fiscal reform. In effect, the aim of the movement was to wrest control of government from the dominant group of Irish Democrats. This was quickly achieved and within months of its formation the committee was able to lay down its arms, some of its leaders being elected to office as 'People's Party' candidates at a later election.

There are both similarities and differences between the American vigilante movements and the English felons associations (Little and Sheffield 1983). In both cases, local elites formed self-help organizations in order to produce cheap and speedy criminal justice. However, whereas the law was frequently exceeded by vigilantes, felons associations retained a strong formal attachment to the rule of law. Both examples demonstrate, however, that organized self-policing may arise during periods of social transition. In one case that transition took a spatial form, frontier development exposing the sparseness of the formal, criminal justice system. In the other case transition was structural, capitalist industrialization and urbanization generating the preconditions of acute disruption in the system of order maintenance. The critical point was that, in each case, a process of social transition engendered private provision, though the precise form which that provision took was affected by the socio-cultural and legal tradition of the society. What these examples demonstrate, then, is that self-help is a common adaptive form in times of social transition; a form which may emerge, submerge, and re-emerge alongside public forms at different historical periods. This fact is borne out both by the successive waves of vigilantism occurring in twentieth-century America and by the current re-emergence of private solutions in America and Britain.

Subscription and volunteer forces

The coexistence of public and private forms is also evident at the level of organized and uniformed forces, many public forces developing from, and operating alongside private bodies. From as early as the sixteenth century, wealthy Londoners had paid young, healthy retainers to watch over their property (Draper 1978), and consequently, the first organized forces arose from private initiatives. Colquhoun's Marine Police Establishment (1798), consisting of sixty armed men, cost £5,000 its first year. Four-fifths of this cost was borne by the West India Company, though the investment was a sound one, the force saving £100,000 worth of cargo during the period (Clayton 1967). Likewise, the Bow Street Runners (1750) 'were perhaps closer to being a private police force than the noble precursor to the Metropolitan Police' (South 1987: 81), offering protection to local brothels and inns in return for considerations. In that sense, 'the private police force formed, in Britain, the original nucleus of the civil police proper' (Bowden 1978: 250). Furthermore, the railway boom enabled twelve railway police companies to be established between 1837 and 1859, thus providing the foundation for some of the quasi-private forces in operation today (see Chapter 6).

In addition to that there were a variety of voluntary and subscription forces in operation throughout the English country-side, some established under the 1833 Lighting and Watching Act, some through private subscription (Emsley 1987: 183). Some of these forces, such as that formed in the Stoke and Burnham hundreds in Buckinghamshire, used local agricultural labourers for patrol (Storch 1989), but most employed professional police officers sent from London. Often these subscription forces deve-loped out of felons associations, as was the case with the Barnet Association, the best-known subscription force. Here, the six constables 'actively patrolled, watched the beershops, aided the delivery of the post, repaired gaps in fences, and watched for stray livestock' (Storch 1989: 230). The force at Stow-on-the-Wold was so successful that by 1837 twelve Metropolitan officers were employed (Davey 1983), and in at least one case, at Blofield, Norfolk, the force was transformed into a regular, publicly paid one.

In fact, even at the turn of the century, despite the relative consolidation of public policing, private provision continued. One initiative, described by South (1988), was the voluntary Women's Policing Movement. This arose from several, sometimes contra-dictory, sources including 'self-help' for women, the Suffragette Movement, and the legacy of Victorian moralism. Most of the bodies involved were privately financed and, between the 1890s and the 1920s, tried to pressure government to adopt the principle of women police by engaging in public patrol.

When the war broke out, a large number of uniformed volunteer bodies appeared, often organized by society ladies. By the 1920s the Women's Police Service operated in several major cities, usually for government departments, but sometimes for factories (e.g. Nestlé) and other private bodies, such as churches, for whom they helped rid the streets of undesirable females. Such 'moral policing' had also been provided for by a 1914 convention of the National Union of Women Workers where concern had been expressed about the dangers to young women of the mobilization of soldiers. The Voluntary Women Patrols which ensued were supported by a mixture of organizations: the Mothers' Union, the Church Army, the Girls' Friendly Society, the YWCA, and the National Union of Women's Suffrage Societies. The stated aim of patrols was to restrain the behaviour of women and girls who congregated around army camps, in order to safeguard them 'from the results of the very natural excitement produced by the abnormal conditions now prevailing' (*The Times* 13 October 1914, cited in Lock 1979: 22). Such female police provision was supported by voluntary donation at first, though later Home Office subsidy was granted so that women could be trained to aid police work in London. Police funds were then used 'to employ a private, secondary force of moral guardians who, for example, reported on the behaviour of the members of the audience in London cinemas' (South 1988: 19). Similarly, patrols were encouraged by vigilance committees, church organizations and the London Council for the Promotion of Public Morality.

The emerging private security industry

At the same time, the private security sector was developing. The first burglar alarm (a mechanical device linking a set of chimes to a door lock) was invented in the eighteenth century by an Englishman called Tildesley. However, the modern alarm industry really began in 1852 when Augustus R. Pope, a Boston inventor, filed a patent for the first electronic burglar alarm which could prevent unauthorized opening of doors and windows. Pope sold the patent to Edwin Holmes in 1857, who in turn marketed the device amongst the New York wealthy, adding refinements such as security lights. By the early twentieth century several companies were competing for domination of the New York alarms market, and in 1905 AT&T, the leading telephone company, bought out Holmes's organization. Within a short time, the American burglar and fire alarm business had become a closed industry, with a few companies controlling the market, something which continued until the passing of antitrust legislation in the 1960s (McCrie 1988).

The example confirms both the speed of expansion of the American security industry and the extent of its concentration. In England, by contrast, development was more sedate. Private detectives had appeared in the eighteenth century, but the biggest boost to their activity was given by the 1857 Matrimonial Causes Act, which enabled them to establish a role for themselves in divorce. In time, some agencies expanded into other areas of work, especially infiltrating factories and unions on behalf of employers, and in 1901 Garnier's detective agency was established as one of the first multi-purpose organizations.

The guarding industry began to emerge in the inter-war years. In 1926 Arnold Kunzler founded Machinery and Technical Transport which provided couriers to safeguard the passage of cash, bullion and other valuables by road, rail and air. In 1935 the first patrol services were offered by Night Watch Services Ltd, a company formed by the Marquis of Willingdon and Henry Tiarks, a merchant banker, to protect Mayfair residents from East End undesirables and Mosley's fascists. The company employed fifteen uniformed watchmen on bicycles, armed with truncheons, torches, and whistles. After a lull during the war years it reappeared, to offer, at first, only static guard services, though without great success, since for most people 'the idea of one's own private night watchman did not catch on' (Clayton 1967: 13–14). In 1947 the company changed its name to Security Corps, and after succumbing to Home Office criticism that the name was too militaristic, became Securicor. From then on the company developed quickly. Bowden suggests that by the end of the 1950s 'as an efficient, sophisticated, centralized and streamlined security organization, it compared very favourably with the fragmented, undermanned and inefficient civil police service' (Bowden 1978: 254). Certainly, by then, Securicor had begun to benefit from the civil police's abandonment of guarding, escorting, and cash-transfer duties.

In America private security, like vigilantism, had developed rapidly because of the delay between the establishment of settlements and the arrival of federal law enforcement. (Train robbery was not legislated as a federal crime until after the First World War: Lipson 1988.) In many cases private police forces, such as that at Fords (Weiss 1987), emerged to defend corporate capital against trade unionism. One of the first and most effective of private forces was the railroad police (Dewhurst 1955), an organization which numbered 10,000 by 1929. Like the The Coal and Iron Police (the notorious 'Pennsylvania Cossacks'), the railroad police employed 'hard men' to protect corporate property and handle industrial relations. In effect, states such as Pennsylvania handed over wholescale policing powers to company forces (Morn 1982: 168).

In addition to company police, other agencies were emerging. Henry Wells founded the American Express Company in 1850 and, together with William G. Fargo established the Wells Fargo Company 2 years later. By the end of the 1850s both Adams Express and American Express were using their own cars on the railroads because local police lacked jurisdiction beyond their areas and federal provision was absent. Other companies such as Brinks Incorporated (1859) and the Pinkertons (1850) emerged at the same period. Pinkerton offered the first comprehensive detective agency, combining files, special agents, and criminological techniques, and within a short time, a number of railroad companies, together with the US Post Office became clients. Apart from involvement in labour disputes (notably at the Carnegie Steel Company and in the Pennsylvania coalfields), the activities of the Pinkerton agency ranged from the detection and pursuit of outlaws (such as the James gang and Butch Cassidy) to political espionage (operating behind Confederate lines in the Civil War). Indeed, so pervasive was the activity of the agency that one commentator observes, 'the Pinkerton law enforcement dynasty provided America with something we have always boasted we didn't need and never had: a national police force' (O'Toole 1978: 28)

Self-policing and community regulation

Policing functions are not, of course, merely exercised through formal associations, committees, and forces. Social regulation has been, and continues to be, exercised by informal self-policing within communities. Consider an English example from rural Gloucestershire in the 1920s:

> We knew ourselves to be as corrupt as any other community of our size – as any London street, for instance. But there was no tale-bearing then, or ringing up 999; transgressors were dealt with by local opinion. . . . We certainly committed our share of

statutory crime. Manslaughter, arson, robberry, rape, cropped up regularly throughout the years. Quiet incest flourished where the roads were bad. . . . Sometimes our sinners were given hell, taunted and pilloried, but their crimes were absorbed in the local scene and their punishment confined to the parish.

(Lee 1962: 205–6)

The regulation and containment of crimes such as incest within the community need not, however, be seen as an exclusively rural phenomenon. Roberts, describing Edwardian Salford, paints a similar picture to rural Gloucestershire:

Such a sin, of course, had to be recognized in whispered tête-à-tête; but I don't recall a single prosecution: strict public silence saved miscreants from the rigours of the law.

(Roberts 1973: 44)

There is more than a hint, here, of police exclusion from the community, and Roberts' account casts serious doubt upon the consensual model of police history. As he says, 'one spoke to a "rozzer" when one had to and told him the minimum'. Certainly, 'the public' (the middle and upper classes) 'held their "bobby" in affection and esteem – which he repaid with due respectfulness'. But such a view was never shared by the urban working class (Roberts 1973: 100)

Samuels' (1975) account of the nineteenth- and early twentieth-century 'quarry roughs' of Headington Quarry, Oxfordshire, makes much the same point, though here, resistance to the police was more vigorous than in Salford. In Quarry, the police were the hereditary enemies of the local poachers, and always patrolled in pairs. Poachers trained their dogs – usually lurchers and mastiffs – to look out for the police and drive them off. Quarry was a 'no-go area' for law enforcement, much like the 'China' area of Merthyr Tydfil had been in the early nineteenth century. Here, the inhabitants represented the worst fears of respectable society: 'an alien, organised, hereditary, non-industrious, and immoral criminal class' which, though rejected by society, was sufficiently united by self-interest and family bonds to resist 'those outsiders who came under the banners of "Reform", "Respectability", and "Control"' (Jones 1982: 109). 'China' was, in effect, a 'frontier' town, where residents prevented the police from making arrests, and where 'community law' intervened to upbraid wife beaters and punish adulterers, as in the American examples described previously.

Whereas 'China' was an urban area with sufficient social cohesion to deny entry to the new police, other urban areas with less cohesion (Deansgate in Manchester, Thomas Street in Birmingham) became, in Jones's phrase, 'police property', by virtue of their continued subjection to regular searches. However, there is undoubtedly a degree of historical continuity between the no-go areas of today and those of a century ago. This is clearly demonstrated in Davis's (1989) analysis of 'Jenning's Buildings', a group of slum tenements, housing Irish and other casual labourers and their families, in mid-nineteenth-century London. Here again, the police faced problems in controlling the slum, only entering in groups, and being forced to tolerate the continuation of much illegal activity. What is interesting about this example, however, is the extent to which police strategy sought to utilize communal self-policing in the pursuit of order maintenance. In this case, the Metropolitan Police used collaborators, or middlemen (those who supplied labour, ran businesses in the tenements, loaned money, or collected rents) who, by exercising their authority, were able to maintain a degree of order in the Buildings without police intervention. By using powerbrokers, whose authority derived from their control over jobs, housing, and money, the police were able to ensure that disorder was kept within reasonable bounds; a strategy which, Davis maintains, has been continued up to the present day in the community policing of areas like Broadwater Farm.

The examples described here confirm Clarke's (1987) suspicion that a relatively small number of police officers was able to maintain social order in late nineteenth-century England, only because populations were able to manage instances of anti-social behaviour without their intervention. These examples also raise a question about the police's management of informal control mechanisms in communities, an issue which is addressed in Cohen's (1979) account of policing inter-war Islington. Here, again, the police sought to win consent through the penetration of civil society, and to this end, packaged themselves as a neutral body. Though some sections of the community still saw them as a coercive force, the police tried to defuse working-class resistance by 'turning a blind eye' to minor illegalities on the streets. This was hardly a solution, however, as it merely accentuated the problem of choosing between law enforcement and order maintenance. So a second solution was reached whereby in certain localities statutory norms of order were used only as a last resort. In their place 'a system of informal, tacitly negotiated and particularistic definitions of public order were evolved'. These made some working-class usages of social space legitimate, whilst outlawing others. For example, well-dressed young women on the streets in daylight might be regarded as respectable housewives, whilst at night they risked being outlawed as prostitutes: 'The new norms in effect imposed a system of unofficial curfew, informal out-of-bounds, to define what were the wrong people, wrong age, wrong sex, in the wrong place and the wrong time' (Cohen 1979: 131).

Cohen's account, like Davis's (1989), points to the relationship between the formal, external policing of a neighbourhood and its informal, internal control mechanisms. Where his analysis fails, however, is in assuming that some balance is readily achieved between these two elements. In fact, such balance is difficult to achieve as the police apparatus is pushed by contradictory forces: on the one hand, to eradicate those informal processes, because their very informality isolates them from the formal sphere and makes them 'dangerous': on the other hand, to utilize them for the positive benefits they might bring to order maintenance. To a large extent, this contradiction corresponds to the difference between 'hard' and 'soft' policing styles, and ideally, the police hope to achieve some functional balance between the two. In practice, however, despite arguments to the contrary (Gordon 1984), the extent to which police (state) penetration of informal (civil) institutions is productive of order, is always problematical.

Chapter 2

Ideologies of public and private provision

In the twentieth century, policing and public security, unlike some other areas of public service, have tended to be immune from ideological debates about the alleged benefits and disbenifits of public versus private provision. Despite the continued existence of private initiatives after 1829, it has generally been assumed that policing is an inherently public good, whose provision has to reside in the hands of a single, monopoly supplier, the state. This view has persisted until recently. It has been shown in the previous chapter, however, that disputes about the desirability of state involvement in policing were widespread in the nineteenth century. In that sense, immunity from ideological dispute is a relatively recent phenomenon and there is no reason to assume, in an era of widespread privatization, that the public model of policing provision will remain for ever sacrosanct.

The purpose of this chapter is to examine ideologies of public and private provision. In doing this, it is necessary to make several qualifications. First, the chapter does not provide a definitive review of such ideologies. Its aim is merely to outline and comment on some pertinent areas of debate. Second, although the chapter does contain references to policing, its main object is to differentiate between competing sets of ideological principles, regarding the provision of goods and services in general. It is particularly important to articulate those issues because the relative public domination of policing has insulated that activity from any discussion of the principles of provision for more than a century. It is especially worrying, at present, that changes in the balance of policing provision (towards 'privatization') may be taking place without much opportunity for that discussion to occur. Third, the chapter should be seen as 'servicing' later parts of the book, in so far as the substantive areas of private provision discussed in later chapters, are invariably contained within, justified by, or criticized in terms of the ideological principles outlined here. Any understanding of the discourse of privatization depends, therefore, on some familiarity with those issues of principle. At the same time, it should not be assumed that any policy outcome (for example, the expansion or contraction of public or private provision in a given area) can be 'read back' as a simple effect of the application of its 'corresponding' ideological rationale. After all, outcomes are as likely to arise from the 'unprincipled' and pragmatic realities of economic and political horse trading, as they are from the realm of 'applied political ideology'.

The chapter is divided into two sections. In a short first section I outline the socialist defence of the principle of public provision, and consider its assessment of the relationship between public and private sectors. In the second section I consider a number of variants of liberal, market-based theories of service provision. Given the centrality of these to advocates of privatization, the bulk of the chapter is devoted to that side of the debate.

SOCIALISM AND PUBLIC PROVISION

Socialism is a heterogeneous mix of ideologies, ranging from gradualist versions of social democracy, to the various radical Marxisms. In this section I outline some key aspects of the socialist view of public provision. Given that heterogeneity, however, it should be emphasised that this account serves a heuristic function only, and is not meant to provide an adequate description of the different socialist positions.

Socialists have a profound suspicion of the free market, seeing it as unjust, individualistic, inefficient, undemocratic, and likely to give rise to social divisions and conflicts. By contrast, public provision is assumed to have certain essential benefits:

1 It maximizes social values and promotes social cohesion.
2 It enables goods and services to be allocated according to need. In the case of welfare, for example, removal of the profit motive prevents those in need from being exploited by unscrupulous providers.

3 Public control facilitates planning and the regulation and standardization of goods and services. This, in turn, makes it more likely that equity between recipients is achieved and efficiency in provision is ensured.
4 Public provision allows the principle of distributional justice to be applied, thereby enabling existing (market-based) inequalities – of material resources, status, and power – to be challenged.
5 Public provision of services ensures maximum public accountability and maximum commitment to the public interest by those responsible for delivery.
6 Public provision is not subject to the pathological effects of market anarchy. Planned provision can ensure that unprofitable services, for which there is a genuine social need, are made available through arrangements such as cross-subsidy.

Two things can be said about this list. In the first place, as I have suggested already, policy outcomes should not be seen as a simple reflection of the application of a set of principles. The reasons for Labour's nationalization of certain industries in the post-war period (and its non-nationalization of others) are multifarious and, as many commentators have suggested, bear a complex relationship to the ideology of public provision (Eatwell 1979; Miliband 1973). Second, although all of these principles have been deployed at various times to justify intervention in economic and welfare policy, their deployment has been neither consistent nor universal across all areas of the policy spectrum. In the case of criminal justice, for instance, despite the state's actual domination of this field, there has been remarkably little attempt by left-wing theorists to construct public policies consistent with the principles of equity and social justice, described above. (For a rare exception, see the discussion of 'socialist justice' in Jefferson and Grimshaw: 1984.)

It should also be said that laying down sets of principles is one thing: deriving policies and objectives from them is another. Anyone familiar with the history of Labour Party politics in Britain will recognize that the principles described above can be transformed into a number of different, and sometimes incompatible, policies. Consider, for example, debates within the Party prior to the foundation of the National Health Service. Here, there was a major dispute between Bevan and Morrison over whether a public health service should be administered at the national or the local level. In the early 1930s the Socialist Medical Association had published plans for a free and comprehensive service, managed by local government, with a planning tier at regional level. Morrison, the champion of local government, was broadly sympathetic with this view, fearing that a national body would whittle away local authority functions. Bevan responded in two ways. First, he maintained that a locally based service would merely perpetuate existing discrepancies in the quality of provision between rich and poor areas. Equity, in other words, demanded national administration. Second, he insisted that a national body would be more financially accountable, rational, and efficient than a local one. The example confirms two things: that general principles can sanction a variety of policies; and that critical policy outcomes can owe as much to considerations of organizational rationality and financial efficiency, as they do to issues of socialist principle (Klein 1983).

At this point it is appropriate to examine how socialists perceive the connections between public and private spheres. Consider first the classical reformist view, presented by Marshall (1950) and Titmuss (1958), a full discussion of which can be found in Hindess (1987). Here, public intervention in welfare is seen as a corollary of the development of citizenship rights. Both authors maintain, however, that there are conflicting principles at work in welfare states. On the one hand, there is a private sphere of class and market relations. On the other hand, there is a public sphere, based upon citizenship and social values. For Marshall, the uneasy balance between these principles (encapsulated in the 'post-war compromise') produces a 'democratic-welfare-capitalism' whose elements are interdependent and, ultimately, complementary. Marshall regards the compromise as sustainable and desirable, so long as the balance between the elements is maintained. Titmuss, by contrast, takes the view that the moral values of the public sphere should dominate over the amoral private sphere. In his opinion, the economic values of the market need to be segregated from the social values of the public sphere, though his fear is that the altruism of the latter is constantly subverted by the encroachment of the former. Though Titmuss pursues a more radical, redistributive politics than Marshall, both writers are in agreement that citizenship has a socially integrative function and that any undermining of it by market forces will tend to threaten social stability.

Here, then, we are presented with the view that private–public relations involve (at best) tension or (at worst) incompatibility between competing ethical principles. This view is rather different from the Marxist characterization of relations between the state and the market, where contradictions are seen in structural, rather than ethical terms. In this case, the public sphere is conceived as an essential functional component of the capitalist system yet, simultaneously, as a structurally unstable element within that system. This combination of views is well expressed in Castells's analysis of the 'urban crisis'. Here, the city is conceived as a spatial unit reponsible for certain essential capitalist functions (the reproduction of labour power and of capitalist social relations). As these functions have not been provided by individual capitalists in the past (who saw no profit in doing so, and whose actions were, in any case, conditioned by the exigencies of capitalist competition) facilities such as housing, education, transport, and public security have, by and large, been provided by the capitalist state. The 'urban crisis' occurs because there is an inherent contradiction between capital's need to provide for 'collective (but unproductive) consumption' and its need to allocate resources productively, for profit. The upshot of this contradiction is 'the fiscal crisis of the state' and the growing politicization of urban problems (Castells 1977).

Though there are fundamental differences between reformist and Marxist approaches to state–market relations, they share one important assumption with advocates of the free market – the belief that the legal character of property (whether it is constituted as 'private' or 'public') has, in itself, necessary social consequences. Thus, the socialist case for public provision, outlined above, rests upon the view that private markets produce certain *inevitable* consequences (inequality, injustice, waste . . . , etc.) merely by virtue of being private. It will soon become apparent that liberal approaches rest upon a simple reversal of that same assumption.

LIBERALISM AND THE STATE

Libertarianism versus the minimal state

Libertarians are committed to individual property-based rights and a belief that individuals should have maximum freedom. This makes them difficult to classify in normal political terms. Like the 'left' they favour the repeal of censorship laws, and oppose state interference in matters of personal sexual behaviour. Yet their defence of private property and the free market links them with the 'right'.

Anarcho-capitalists, such as Rothbard (1978), deny that the state has any role to play in the provision of facilities, suggesting that all services should be organized privately. This follows from the axiom that 'no man or group of men may aggress against the person or property of anyone else' (Rothbard 1978: 23). For Rothbard, even a minimal state threatens liberty because, by its very definition, it enjoys a monopoly of coercive power. According to this view, although individuals have moral obligations not to abrogate other's personal and property rights, they have no moral obligation to obey the state, which, far from serving a collective good, itself abrogates personal rights. Rothbard looks forward, then, to the abolition of taxes ('forcible theft') and to the withdrawal of the state from all existing activities: 'War is Mass Murder, Conscription is Slavery and Taxation is Robbery' (Rothbard 1978: 24–5). Even the functions of internal and external security – assumed by other liberal theorists to be an inherently public monopoly – can, it is maintained, be provided by private firms, funded by customers' voluntary payments. As for law courts, they could be replaced by private arbitration companies, something which, it is argued, is already developing in the USA with the emergence of bodies such as the American Arbitration Association (Friedman 1973).

Under such a free-market order, systems of law would be produced for profit on the open market, 'just as books and bras are today' (Friedman 1973: 159), and there would be competition between different brands of law, just as there is between different brands of soap powder: 'If you wanted to ban alcohol, you could buy a strip of land and ban it there' (Hayward 1989: 13). Policing, like any other commodity, would be purchased on the open market, consumers paying monthly premiums to police agencies or insurance companies for protection of their person and property. The existence of the profit motive would, it is argued, ensure efficient protection of the public, also enabling consumer choice to dictate police priorities.

Significantly, the model also adopts a radical 'victimology'. For one thing, many activities currently defined as illegal (the sale of heroin, prostitution) would be de-criminalized in a libertarian system, so that 'crimes without victims' would be rare. In the absence of legal involvement in these areas, there would be less opportunity for organized crime to feed off illegal profits. More important, however, the system would place priority on the victim's (consumer's) needs, rather than on the needs of an abstract 'society'. Instead of placing the emphasis on jailing the criminal in the interests of society, the libertarian system would compel the criminal to make restitution to the victim. The present system, where the victim 'is not recompensed but instead has to pay taxes to support the incarceration of his own attacker', would, in Rothbard's view become nonsensical, once libertarian principles reigned. For in a libertarian world, the focus would be 'on the defense of property rights and therefore on the victim of crime' (Rothbard 1978: 45–6)

The main charge directed at this view of society is of course, an ethical one: that the system would degenerate into private feuding and judicial chaos, heralding a situation of private justice and social inequity. Anarcho-capitalists respond to this charge in two ways. Friedman maintains that although competing private protective agencies might adopt different legal codes and different definitions of criminality, in order to attract customers, they would have to produce an efficient system of dispute settlement and a common approach to criminality. If they failed to do so, they would be undercut by competitors. Rothbard, by contrast, responds with the blunt denial that stateless society raises any ethical issues at all, the solution to the problem of political ethics already being encapsulated in the theory of liberty itself (Barry 1983: 120). Rothbard would therefore recognize no conflict of interest between National Front members wanting to march through the streets of Lewisham, and local ethnic groups wishing to prevent such activity. For if the streets of Lewisham were privately owned, the owners would decide upon their legitimate use and, by definition, no ethical issue would arise. For Rothbard (1978) , then, the issue of free speech is an issue about the rights of property holders to utilize their resources as they think fit.

The libertarian view is a fundamentally individualistic one. As there are no public goods and services (though Friedman makes some concessions about defence), there being no state and no taxation, those unable to purchase welfare and other services by private means would have to rely upon charity. (Libertarians assume that one of the effects of a stateless society would be to generate more and more charitable activity to help the 'deserving poor'.) As for crime and deviance, without a public sphere, there could, by definition, be no such thing as a crime against the public, and libertarian penal policy would take the form of compensation to victims. How compensation would be extracted from offenders refusing to engage in arbitration mechanisms, is less certain.

Such extreme methodological individualism does, however, expose certain theoretical tensions. For one thing, the theory assumes that individuals will accept a libertarian code of law, though it denies both the social conditions of existence of legal codes and any degree of social determination of that acceptance. In effect, we are presented with a set of unconfirmed assertions about spontaneous processes, without any convincing explanation of the mechanisms which underpin them. Furthermore, Rothbard's evasion of ethical questions by *a priori* argument is, as Barry (1983) suggests, legitimate only if one accepts the fundamental arguments about property and liberty from which deductions are made. In the absence of such acceptance, political argument becomes impossible; a high price to pay for theoretical consistency. That problem is exacerbated by the reductive conception of politics adopted by libertarians. As Newman (1984) suggests the libertarian solution to the 'collectivist fallacy' is the 'abolition of politics'. But, in fact, only government is abolished, since libertarians cannot permit any recognition of politics and power outside government: least of all, in the market place itself.

Finally, the argument that co-operation between protection agencies would prevent the generation of private armies and private justice is, at best, speculative. In fact, other liberal critics have recognized that were such speculation to be faulty, private agencies might present an even bigger threat to individual liberty than that allegedly presented by the state. It is this last issue which is addressed in Nozick's work. Nozick, in contrast to anarcho-capitalist writers, argues for a minimal state. The functions of this state would be limited to protection against force, theft, and fraud, and to the enforcement of contracts. In short, it would be a protection agency with no right to intervene in the economy, or to seek to promote social justice, since any extension into those areas would be deemed to threaten liberty.

Nozick begins by postulating a Lockean state of nature, a hypothetical society where no state has yet emerged. Here individuals face one another as equals, all enjoying the same rights to engage in non-aggressive behaviour and to defend themselves against others' aggression. Recognizing that 'in union there is strength' (Nozick 1974: 12) groups of individuals, in these circumstances, are likely to form mutual-protection associations and individuals will have the right, if they so wish, to pay a fee in return for protection. A society with plural protection agencies is still not a state, but Nozick argues that the same 'morally unobjectionable' transactions which produced protective agencies, will eventually give rise to one.

The problem identified by Nozick is that private enforcement is likely to produce constant feuds, conflicts over compensation demands, and endless retaliatory actions. Furthermore, since some agencies would be weaker than others, individuals would have different chances of having their rights enforced. Under these circumstances, one dominant protection agency is likely to emerge. Eventually that agency will insist upon monopoly rights, in order to eliminate unfair and inconsistent procedures between competing bodies. The 'ultraminimal' state emerges, then, when a monopoly agency prevents others from operating in its jurisdiction.

At this stage, the monopoly supplier only offers protection to those who pay for it. Those not paying would, unlike subscribers, be unable to enforce punishments or demand compensation, a situation which would, again, amount to unequal treatment between different categories of people. Nozick argues that this problem can be overcome if the monopoly supplier, by providing protection to those who would not pay for the service themselves, effectively compensates those individuals for depriving them of their right of membership of alternative agencies. Once this is achieved, a 'minimal' state exists.

The concept of compensation is critical for Nozick's argument, serving as an ethical justification for the monopoly state's abrogation of some people's rights not to pay for a service they do not want. In effect, the rights violation of the state is traded off against the compensation offered to non-subscribers. In consequence, it can be claimed that there is no violation of rights because non-subscribers are compensated by receiving free protection. In this manner, Nozick is able to deal with two moral objections simultaneously: the view that it is wrong to leave some citizens unprotected; and the view that it is wrong to force people to pay for a service they do not want. Both objections can be tackled if non-subscribers are 'deemed to have paid for their protection by means of the compensation payments to which they are entitled because of their loss of self-enforcement rights' (Green 1987: 45). By these means, Nozick attempts to provide a moral justification for the emergence of the minimal state through a form of 'invisible hand' theory (Nozick 1974: 118–19). In short, the state has emerged from anarchy by a series of morally justifiable transactions 'as a successful market response to consumer needs, like cornflakes' (Sampson 1984: 193).

A number of criticisms have been directed at Nozick's position. Anarcho-capitalists suggest that there is nothing to prevent the minimal state from developing into a maximal one. Certainly, Nozick insists that it is illegitimate for the state to carry out functions other than protection, but writers such as Rothbard would insist that, legitimacy notwithstanding, expansionism is an inherent feature of all states. This issue is particularly problematical for Nozick because he adopts a conventional definition of the state, regarding it as an organization with a monopoly of coercive power. Barry suggests that this creates a contradiction in the argument: 'if the state does act as a state it must violate rights and if it does not it would not be a state by his conventional definition' (Barry 1983: 113). A second problem concerns the question of compensation. Again, anarcho-capitalists would maintain that rights violations cannot be compensated, as compensation is a subjective process: we do not know what a person would accept for their loss of right to enforce the law, nor indeed that they would consent to compensation at all. A third problem concerns how the minimal state is to be financed. Nozick insists that taxation is a violation of individual rights, but justifies it for the purposes of the minimal state, thereby failing 'to account for the necessity of taxation in terms consistent with the inviolability of the basic Lockean rights' (Gray 1986: 77).

Oddly, however, the most serious problem with Nozick's moral philosophy concerns the *ad hoc* way in which moral principles are used. He justifies the claim that the dominant agency will compensate independent non-subscribers (thereby giving moral justification to the state) on the grounds that 'generally people will do what they are morally required to do' (Nozick 1974: 119). But if people follow moral principles why do protective agencies ever need to arise? Seemingly, Nozick envisages a peculiar world where individuals break moral codes and commercial agencies invariably abide by them. Apart from the naivete of this view, there is, as Sampson suggests, an obvious contradiction: 'Only if moral rules are violated can a protection agency emerge; only if they are obeyed will it become a state' (Sampson 1984: 200).

Hayek and the limited state

Hayek, unlike the other authors discussed so far, has had a significant impact on mainstream political debate in the last decade. In Britain the main vehicle for his ideas has been the right-wing Institute for Economic Affairs, an organization which has had tangible influence on the construction of Conservative policy. For Hayek, freedom, the paramount political value, has two characteristic features. First, it is defined negatively. Freedom is simply the absence of coercion. A person without choice or material resources remains free, provided that coercion is absent. Second, freedom and coercion are defined as individual attributes: 'freedom refers solely to a relation of men to other men, and the only infringement on it is coercion by men' (Hayek 1960: 12). This means that any infringement of freedom must be the intentional result of another individual's behaviour.

Both of these points have important implications for Hayek's assessment of the relative merits of the market and the state. He claims that there are two types of social order. 'Made' orders consist of elements constructed by the issuing of commands. A typical example would be an army or a factory. There are, however, a number of elements of social activity (language, law, custom, etc.), which though intentional, are not the product of any single plan. A typical example of such spontaneous activity would be that occurring in the market. The 'road to serfdom' arises whenever governments try to intervene to direct the spontaneous market order in some desired direction. In that respect, communist and social democratic governments have all tried to treat the spontaneous market order as if it were a 'made' order. This approach fails because of its 'inability to conceive of an effective co-ordination of human activities without deliberate organization by a commanding intelligence' (Hayek 1960: 159). Here, Hayek is fond of quoting Adam Ferguson's dictum that society is 'the result of human action, but not of human design' (cited in Newman 1984: 138).

Hayek's argument rests upon two assumptions about the allegedly essential characteristics of the state and the market. On the one hand, state intervention, beyond the making of general procedural rules, inevitably contains the seeds of coercion, because planning ('intentionally') constrains spontaneity. On the other hand, market mechanisms, precisely because they are the spontaneous result of no individual intention (the 'invisible hand') are, by definition, non-coercive.

However, Hayek is not merely a philosopher of minimal government. Indeed, he denies that the principle of liberty justifies the restriction of government activity merely to the maintenance of law and order; admits that 'no government in modern times has ever confined itself to the "individualist minimum"'; and accepts that there is no reason why government should not, on occasions, intervene in social welfare activity (Hayek 1960: 257–8). At the same time, he insists that there are good reasons for non-intervention. For one thing there are epistemological obstacles to government activity. Take the case of economic planning. An economy consists of a multiplicity of actors, each with individual preferences. Effective planning by governments, however, assumes an unrealistic knowledge of those preferences: a 'knowledge ... which is dispersed among a great many people', the ordering of which 'cannot be established by central direction' (Hayek 1960: 160).

Hayek's point is that government activity is feasible so long as it does not contravene such epistemological obstacles, and justified so long as it does not involve the adoption of coercive powers over individuals. In this latter respect, government has to be bound by the rule of law: that is by general rules which are aimed neither to benefit, nor to discriminate against, categories of people. Having said that, he maintains that much government activity exceeds the appropriate limits. For example, state involvement in welfare – which, in principle, may not contravene the pursuit of liberty – has, in practice, contradicted the rule of law. For instead of being constrained by general principles, the welfare state has used coercive government power for redistributive purposes. As this requires 'a kind of discrimination between, and an unequal treatment of, different people [it] is irreconcilable with a free society' (Hayek 1960: 259–60).

Hayek objects to all conceptions of social or distributive justice on two grounds. First, being forms of social planning, they are epistemologically untenable. Second, all attempts to direct economic and social policy along predetermined lines undermine spontaneity and contradict the rule of law. As for the accusation that market outcomes, such as inequalities of income and wealth, are themselves unjust, his response is simple. The concept of justice does not apply to mere 'states of affairs'; only to intentional human conduct. Accordingly, market processes 'can be neither just nor unjust, because the results are not intended or foreseen' (Hayek 1976: 31, 70). Or, to put it bluntly: 'we must recognize that we may be free and yet miserable' (Hayek 1960: 18).

Contrary to Nozick, Hayek sees the state not so much as a minimal state, but as a 'limited' and 'enabling' state. Such a state provides the basic conditions for spontaneous market activity to flourish: a legal framework ensuring rights of property ownership, property transfer, and contractual stability; a system of national security; a basic framework of law and order. In addition to this, he accepts that the state has a duty to provide its citizens with some absolute level of protection against deprivation, though such basic welfare provision should not be used for furthering principles of social justice. Here, he is neither against state involvement, nor even against certain forms of state compulsion, only against state monopoly (Barry 1979: 115). Thus, whilst state responsibility in guaranteeing basic services for the poor, the aged, the disabled, and the unemployed, is recognized, the state need not be the monopoly supplier of these services. Nor, indeed, provided that it ensures provision by some responsible body, does the state, itself, have to supply them at all.

A number of observations can be made about Hayek's position. First, like other liberal writers, he suffers the consequences of methodological individualism. There seems, for example, little justification for restricting the definition of coercion to individual behaviour with coercive intent. There are, after all, many schools of political thought which would accept the coercive potential of supra-individual agents. Equally, his conception of economic agents as deployers of free choice in a spontaneous market place is flawed. For one thing, such a view denies the social conditions of existence of an individual's range of choice in a given context. For another, it rests upon an essentialism which he, himself, undermines. On the one hand the market is perceived as an essentially spontaneous order. On the other hand, governments persist in breaching the rule of law, thereby confirming that, in reality, spontaneity is a chimera. Ultimately, as Hindess suggests, the Hayekian case for liberalization is more a matter of faith than anything else (Hindess 1987: 132).

A second issue concerns Hayek's relationship to conservatism. In Britain, some assessments of the so-called 'new right' (Gamble 1979; Levitas 1985; King 1987) have interpreted free-market policies of the last decade through formulae such as 'free economy/strong state'. Often, it is maintained that the values of free-market liberalism espoused by writers such as Hayek, contradict statist conservatism as embodied in Thatcherism. Given the choice between 'freedom' and 'order', the 'new right', it is said, opts for order every time. Certainly, there is some truth in this argument. Hayek is very much a 'conservative liberal', much removed from the anarchic model of liberalism discussed earlier. And there is, undoubtedly, a tension between his expressed desire for free innovation, and the 'quasi-religious awe' with which he regards the cultural and constitutional framework surrounding such innovation (Sampson 1984: 181). Strictly speaking, however, the substance of his argument exposes no such contradiction. Since state intervention is assessed according to its character, rather than according to its volume (Hayek 1960: 222), he accepts that such intervention, even in the economy, may be vital. Indeed, he lists circumstances (e.g. governmental failure to control picketing rights) where non- intervention may be positively damaging to the free market (Hayek 1960: 278). In this sense his position is entirely consistent with a robust policy of state intervention in industrial relations, as well as in other areas of social policy.

None the less, he does have serious difficulty in justifying those forms of state intervention which he does consider legitimate. Certainly, strict libertarians, as well as rejecting Hayek's justification for overtly coercive state functions (national defence, law and order) would also object to many of the 'non-coercive' activities he permits (the provision of parks and civic amenities, subsidies to the arts, etc.), on the grounds that their very dependence on the extraction of taxes makes them, also, coercive. In truth, Hayek provides little theoretical justification for defining such activities as public functions and 'the contents of [his] agenda of government do seem a little arbitrary' (Barry 1979: 111).

This factor of arbitrariness indicates a degree of pragmatism in Hayek's writing. Certainly, his acceptance of welfare intervention seems to rest upon purely practical considerations. The fact that 'he prefers welfare to the workhouse' (Newman 1984: 152) is interpreted by Sampson as a piece of conservative opportunism: he prefers it, only because it is a barrier against insurrection. This suggests 'an odd lack of confidence in his own persuasive arguments' (Sampson 1984: 183). More seriously, however, it is an opportunism with theoretical costs. In a chapter on 'Coercion and the state' (1960: Chapter 9) Hayek refines his concept of coercion in order to consider justifications for state intervention. In the course of this chapter it becomes clear that coercion is a matter of degree, the degree of its occurrence in any particular case being affected by relevant social conditions. In a series of examples Hayek considers the social circumstances whereby monopoly may, or may not, be coercive. If, he says, a famous artist (enjoying a monopoly of talent) refuses to paint him for less than an exorbitant fee, it would be absurd to call this coercion. But in circumstances where the services of a monopolist are crucial to one's existence (Hayek gives the example of the owner of a spring in an oasis), coercion may arise.

This argument has devastating implications for Hayek's position. On the one hand, it is necessary for him to provide some theoretical basis for demarcating those circumstances where state intervention is justified, from those where it is not. In that sense, the example concerning the spring is crucial. Here is a case where the social conditions of monopoly justify state intervention in order to alleviate certain social disbenefits. On the other hand, this particular argument destroys two key elements of the Hayekian model. First, it demonstrates that coercion, far from being defined in terms of a strict methodological individualism (one individual's intentional infringement on the freedom of another) is infected by a social dimension. The concept of coercion is not entirely encompassed by individuals and their subjective intentions, but sometimes consists of a relationship between individuals and a variety of social conditions. Second, this covert redefinition of coercion introduces a substantive element – what Newman (1984:

34) calls an element of personal autonomy – into what had previously been a rigidly formalized and procedural model of freedom. Here, it seems, in order to ensure substantive (rather than merely formal) freedom, intervention by the state may be justified. The problem for Hayek is that that justification opens the flood gates of substantive criticism on an otherwise formal discourse.

Public interests and public goods

A third liberal approach to state–market relations is offered by public choice theory, a theory which has had considerable impact on public policy. Proponents of this view share, with other liberals, a rigid individualism. Collective entities, such as society, are regarded as reducible to individual actions, 'goods' and 'bads' being defined in terms of individuals' subjective preferences. Social actors are perceived as individual, egoistic, rational maximizers, able to calculate the costs and benefits of particular courses of action.

Generally speaking, public choice theory assumes that the pursuit of individual utility leads to a desirable social order. According to this view, ethics is no more than 'unanimity' between individual subjects (Barry 1983: 102) and all notions of 'public interest' or the 'common good' are rejected, together with the social practices which are justified in their name (welfare economics, distributive justice, and the like).

At the same time, however, unlike the positions discussed previously, public choice theory does not assume that institutions emerge in a spontaneous manner, through the 'invisible hand'. Prisoners' dilemma games, indicate circumstances where the outcome of each actor pursuing selfish interests is, in aggregate terms, irrational. Accordingly, many public choice theorists emphasize the need for appropriate mechanisms of government and rule enforcement to be designed, so that a framework can exist within which orderly economic activity can occur. This presumes, in effect, a positive role for the state in underpinning social order.

The prisoners' dilemma also has implications for the provision of public goods. Public goods have two characteristics which distinguish them from private goods. First, they have the property of non-excludability; individuals and groups cannot be prevented from using them. (It is difficult to prevent people, if they are so inclined, from using the service provided by a lighthouse.) Second, they are indivisible; their use cannot meaningfully be divided amongst individuals and groups. (One cannot extract a quantity of clean air from the atmosphere and market it.)

The problem with public goods is that they are vulnerable to 'free riders': if one cannot be excluded from the benefits of clean air or lighthouses, one is tempted not to pay for them. Since the rational optimizer has no incentive to contribute to the production of public goods, there is, in effect, a collective-action problem. This can only be resolved by the intervention of some coercive body (the state) which extracts taxes from citizens, therby ensuring the production of public goods.

The problem for public choice theorists, however, is that state intervention has got out of hand. This has given rise to a situation where goods which could be supplied by the market are, increasingly, provided by the publicly funded bureaucracies of 'big government'. Savas explains the growth of government in the United States in several ways. First a form of 'fiscal illusion' arises. Government spending always seems a good bargain for the individual, costs remaining invisible because they are aggregated. Such invisibility is, then, exploited by politicians who can buy the votes of potential beneficiaries and engage in practices of 'logrolling' (vote trading) whilst, all the time, hiding behind the veil of fiscal illusion. Simultaneously, monopolistic government agencies seek to expand public employment. Savas takes an example from urban policing:

> Over a twenty-five year period the number of [New York] police officers rose from 16,000 to 24,000 but the total annual hours worked by the entire force actually declined slightly. The entire 50% increase in manpower was completely devoted to shortening the workweek, lengthening the lunch hour and vacation period and providing more holidays and paid sick leave. Inefficient staffing was legitimized by a state law that called for an equal number of police officers on duty on each shift, despite the fact that crime statistics showed few criminals working in the small hours.
>
> (Savas 1982: 24)

Emphasis on the 'budgetary imperialism' of public bureaucracies is common to all public choice analysis. Such an emphasis follows from the belief that politicians and bureaucrats are, despite their public responsibility, just as self-seeking as the rest of us. The only difference is in the incentives. When politicians or bureaucrats pursue 'the public interest', they do so by spending other people's money, not their own. As a result there is 'little personal incentive to make sure that government expenditures are efficient or wise' (Shaw 1987: 23).

Public sector bureaucracies are, therefore, criticized in two respects. First, bureaucrats have a variety of motives, all of which lead them to seek expansion of their empires (increased salary, increased pension benefits, greater personal prestige, more power, greater patronage) (Niskanen 1971). Second, they have little incentive to operate efficiently since the public sector, unlike its private counterpart, lacks reliable measures of efficiency and is not faced with threats from external competitors. This means that 'because of their grasp of technical knowledge, bureaucrats can increase the supply of their service beyond the political demand for it, get away with inefficiency and enhance their own salaries (Green 1987: 102).

This situation is made possible through the 'bilateral monopoly' enjoyed by bureaucrats and politicans. Bureaucrats aim to maximize budgets. Politicians aim to maximize votes. The consequence of this monopoly is a systematic oversupply of public goods beyond what would be optimal, given consumers' rational preferences. Niskanen (1971) and Tullock (1979) suggest, in fact, that both the budget and output of bureaucratic monopoly suppliers are likely to be twice that of an equivalent private competitive supplier. The problem is exacerbated, moreover, by bureaucratic monopoly over information as to the real costs of goods and services:

> governmental agencies do not have to reveal the cost of a unit of output at different levels of production. This means, in effect, that bureaucracies have a monopoly of information about the costs and benefits of what they are doing.
>
> (Hoover and Plant 1989: 61)

In consequence, both citizens, as well as potential critics, remain in a state of 'fiscal illusion'.

The policy recommendations of public choice theory are, to some extent, predictable. Monopolistic public bureaucracies should be reduced to a minimum; competition between agencies should be increased, in order to encourage efficiency; vouchers might be issued to consumers in order to give them a choice of services in a competitive market; the size of large bureaucracies should be reduced and they should be encouraged to take out contracts with private firms for the provision of certain services; in certain cases user fees, which could be retained by the operating agency, might be introduced (Shaw 1987; Tullock 1979; Self 1985).

Two types of criticism can be directed against the public choice position. First, there are objections to the substantive content of the theory. Self (1985: 67–8), for example, criticizes Niskanen's generalizations about bureaucratic behaviour: bureaucrats do not necessarily expand their budgets, sometimes preferring a quieter life; the existence of parliamentary committees and agencies of financial scrutiny, suggests that political controllers are not always impotent, due to lack of information about bureaucratic activities.

Substantive criticism apart, there are also theoretical difficulties ᴧ ᴧh the position. At the most general level, Hindess (1984) has demonstrated that there are serious theoretical shortcomings in all rational choice models of action, including the public choice version. In the particular case of public choice, however, there is a major problem concerning the concept of 'public good'. This is particularly well demonstrated in Savas's account of 'the nature of goods and services' (Savas 1982: 29–52). In this account, Savas tries to provide a theoretical justification for establishing the 'sensible limits to government', by identifying the nature and characteristics of particular categories of goods and services. By categorizing goods and services according to their 'natures', a typology is produced ('private', 'public', 'common-pool' or 'collective'). This is then used to show that some goods, now provided by government, can more sensibly be provided by non-governmental means. What Savas suggests is that only certain kinds of goods (those consumed collectively and from which exclusion is impossible) have attributes which require 'some sort of collective action'.

Ostensibly, this typology is meant to justify determinate forms of production or provision of goods. In that sense, the production–provision aspect, itself, is a dependent variable. The problem is, however, that when Savas talks about particular cases, the production–provision dimension enters into the typology as an explanatory element. Consider the example of fire protection.

Here, he suggests, is an example which demonstrates an important principle about the typology: that goods and services can, at different times and in different places, occupy different locations. Nowadays, fire protection is a collective good. In the last century it was a toll good; and even sometimes a private good, private companies protecting their own subscribers and nobody else.

Savas's demonstration that goods can be located across varying dimensions of the cross-cutting typology at different times is both interesting and useful. The problem is that in demonstrating such fluidity, he undermines the project which the construction of the typology was intended to justify. For what the case of fire protection proves is that goods are not defined by reference to their 'essential natures' at all, but rather by the form of production which determines their mode of consumption. In the past, people consumed fire services individually and exclusion was possible because of that private mode of provision. In the present the situation has altered. All this confirms is that many categories of good have no 'essential nature' at all and, in consequence, that Savas's typology is, essentially, a complex tautology.

So what may be said in conclusion about the public choice position? First, typologies of goods, such as Savas's are not necessarily worthless. Indeed, there is much to be said for exploring the historical and spatial fluidity of different forms of provision of goods. The critical fact, however, is that the location of goods in the public or private domain is a product of political decision, not of some allegedly essential quality of the goods themselves. This suggests a second point. Justification for public or private provision of goods and services has to be seen as a political problem to which there can be no general answer, either in terms of the inherent nature of goods or in terms of the allegedly essential qualities of the public or private spheres.

CONCLUDING COMMENTS

This last point is the crux of the matter. In the course of this chapter I have summarized a number of arguments about the appropriate roles of the state and the market. I have also indicated that in each of the positions outlined, one can find varying degrees of ambiguity, inconsistency, contradiction, and confusion. Behind these specific problems, however, there lurks a more general question about the recognition of social and political conditions in the analysis of state–market relations. What this chapter has demonstrated is that competing political ideologies (socialist versus liberal), because they seek, above all else, to defend the principles of public or private provision against attack by their adversaries, are unconcerned about the social and political environment within which goods and services are produced and allocated. The problem is, however, that that environment has significant effects on the character of production and allocation.

Hindess (1987) suggests that the tendency of the protagonists in this debate to deploy essentialist forms of argument (the view that the market is 'essentially amoral', or the state 'essentially wasteful'), ignores a variety of social, political, and organizational factors, whose effects are variable according to different circumstances. The simple opposition between 'market' and 'plan' (and the accompanying view that any combination of the two is unstable or untenable) takes no account of the different social contexts in which either might operate. The problem is that oppositions of this sort 'all too often mask extremely complex and heterogeneous sets of conditions'. Markets, for example, always operate under specific, and varying, institutional conditions: different legal frameworks; different political and administrative controls; different organizational environments; different categories of market actor (large corporations ... one person businesses ...). Unless these conditions and their effects are considered, 'arguments for or against market provision are of little value' (Hindess 1987: 150–1).

If this view is accepted, then the simple defence of pro-market or anti-market principles is inadequate to the task of assessing relations between the public and private spheres. Moreover, it is apparent that the 'public–private dichotomy' constructed from those competing principles, provides a very poor account of the reality of service provision in capitalist societies. There is rarely, if ever, a clear exclusivity between public and private provision. Most public services in Britain, from the National Health Service to the municipal library, or the local swimming pool engage in private (fee-paying, or other) activity. This suggests that the conceptual distinction between public and private spheres is less absolute than it might first appear, a fact which is becoming increasingly significant in the realm of policing.

Part II

Private policing: current developments and their policy implications

Chapter 3

Privatization and public policing

A recent article in the journal of the Institute of Economic Affairs proposed that the Church of England should be privatized, the clergy becoming a 10,000 strong sales force paid according to the number of customers enticed through the church doors (Hamilton 1990). The suggestion that the church be judged by some ecclesiastical equivalent of the standards of commercial theatre ('bums on pews') might seem offensive to some, but it merely reflects the fact that the philosophy of privatization, once accepted, has few logical bounds. For if it is assumed that public ownership breeds inefficiency in industry, the same assumption can, presumably, be applied to public service as a whole (Steel and Heald 1984). It is for this reason that advocates of privatization believe that the policy can prove helpful to any part of the public sector (Pirie 1988). And it is for the same reason that both church leaders and chief constables might do well to heed the words of John Moore, whose much-quoted statement of Government intent on privatization included the chilling reminder that 'No state monopoly is sacrosanct' (Moore 1983: 91).

PRIVATIZATION AND PUBLIC POLICY

Though this chapter is concerned with privatization in police organizations, analysis of that context demands some under-standing of the points at issue in privatization policy as a whole. In this section I consider two of those issues. First, how is the policy to be assessed? Second, how is privatization to be conceptualized?

The question of assessment is, predictably, controversial. Vehement criticism of the way in which privatization policy has been implemented during the last decade, has come not only from the political left, but also from the liberal right. Consider an example. Moore's statement makes it clear that the main object of privatization is to reduce monopoly and encourage competition. If competition is not achieved, he maintains, 'an historic opportunity will have been lost' (Moore 1983: 92). But there is good reason to suggest that many of the privatizations which have occurred have merely replaced large nationalized organizations with large privatized ones. Neo-liberal economists complain, therefore, that, Thatcherism has mistaken oligopoly and duopoly for genuine competition, as in a telecommunications industry dominated by British Telecom and Mercury Communications (Veljanowski 1989). Indeed, some critics suggest that denationalization policy has taken precedence over the encouragement of competition to the extent that 'The conflict between privatization and liberalization . . . is no longer a conflict, but a rout' (Kay *et al.* 1986: 29).

Such comments suggest that the concept of privatization (and its connection to 'denationalization', 'liberalization', and the like) requires clarification, a point I shall return to below. But what of the empirical evidence on privatization? Does such evidence help us to make a clear assessment? Unfortunately the answer to this is probably not. Certainly, there are authors who, drawing on empirical studies, claim that private enterprise performs more successfully than public enterprise (Pryke 1986). Equally, there are authors who are more guarded about the comparative performance of the different sectors (Millward 1986). Part of the problem is that interpretation of the evidence is as much a political as a technical exercise. This is well demonstrated in the case of local-authority competitive tendering, made compulsory for certain services after the 1988 Local Government Act. Here, local authorities claim that more than £100m was saved in the 6-month period after August 1989. But trade-union evidence indicates that this is an inflated figure, since the cost of the process was itself more than £55m. And whilst the unions claim that more than three-quarters of contracts have been won in-house simply because private firms are not up to the task, advocates of privatization complain that local authorities engage in anti-competitive practices, packaging contracts in such a way as to benefit in-house applicants and deter private bidders (Wolmar 1990).

In view of these difficulties, it is hardly surprising that the most common conclusion drawn from empirical evidence is a rather bland one: 'there are efficient and inefficient public enterprises and efficient and inefficient private enterprises' (Kay *et al.* 1986: 15). This observation is confirmed in Ascher's detailed analysis of local authority contracting-out and competitive tendering. Her point is that the success or failure of privatization policy is conditional upon a number of social, political, and organizational factors. In particular, she suggests that privatization of local services works best where demand has come from the bottom-up, rather than from the top-down. Imposition of such policy from the centre (as in the case of the various NHS reforms) is likely to be unsuccessful, because different localities have different priorities and will want to make different trade-offs between cost and quality, or effectiveness and efficiency (Ascher 1987: 269). In short, privatization may offer scope for improvement in local services, but this is conditional upon its mode of implementation.

These comments raise two issues. First, there is a conceptual one. If privatization not only has top-down and bottom-up forms, but also relates to 'liberalization' and 'denationalization', there is a clear need to clarify the concept. Second, there is the question of how far different forms of privatization benefit and empower individuals allegedly exercising free choice.

As for the first of these, the conceptual issue, there is considerable confusion. Some writers simply side-step the issue altogether. Pirie (1988), for instance, lists no less than twenty-one types of privatization, though says nothing about the relationship between the different types in the context of privatization as a whole. Other writers adopt a slightly more systematic approach to the issue, distinguishing components of privatization such as 'charging', 'contracting out', 'denationalization', and 'liberalization' (Steel and Heald 1984), but again, there is little attempt to disentangle the conceptual elements with any degree of rigour.

One exception to this is found in Saunders and Harris (1990). In their view privatization, far from being a unitary phenomenon, has a number of forms, each of which has different implications for both producers and consumers of state services. Commentary on privatization has, they suggest, ignored such variable forms and their varying implications. Accordingly, they construct a typology of privatization across two dimensions. The first relates to whether privatization transfers power and responsibility from the state to producers and investors, or to consumers. Obviously, they say, any privatization will affect both producer and consumer groups. Nevertheless some privatizations are mainly concerned with changing the conditions of ownership (e.g. by sale) while others are concerned with changing the conditions of consumption (e.g. by allowing clients to buy services, thus turning them into consumers). The second dimension concerns the nature of change in the government role: specifically whether ownership passes into private hands (the government entirely giving up its right to determine the use of resources), or whether there is merely a change in control (the government passing on certain of its powers to other agencies).

On this basis, Saunders and Harris (1990) construct a four-fold typolgy of privatization:

1 Denationalization and demunicipalization benefit producers by selling ownership of state assets to private agents. Though this has considerable impact on producers, who are subjected to profit-and-loss accounting, it has little effect on consumers, who still pay large, anonymous organizations for their gas charges and telephone calls.
2 Commodification benefits consumers by selling them state assets (e.g. council house sales). As with denationalization, there is a change of ownership, though in this case it has a major impact on consumers.
3 Liberalization involves no change in ownership, the state retaining responsibility for providing and financing services, but non-state agencies engage in the organization of provision (e.g. deregulation of bus services; 'opting out' by schools and hospital trusts; 'contracting out' by local authorities). This has a major impact on producers (since state employees may lose their jobs, or experience deteriorating conditions of service), and it may affect standards of service to consumers. But, fundamentally, it does not change the consumer's status *vis-à-vis* the supplier. Consumers, as before, pay a community charge for refuse collection, and it makes relatively little difference to them whether the supplier is a local authority or a private contractor.
4 Marketization again involves a change of control rather than one of ownership. This time, however, it involves the replacement of state provision by allowances made to consumers enabling them to buy the services they want in the market. The classic example of this would be educational vouchers.

This typology confirms that any assessment of privatization has to be conditional. One cannot make a blanket statement about the costs and benefits of privatization policy without first examining both the form of privatization under consideration, and the context in which it is implemented. Conventional assessment of privatization rarely takes this form, however. Proponents of the policy assume that it maximizes effectiveness, efficiency, and freedom, irrespective of the political and organizational context. Opponents, by contrast, assume that the profit motive invariably leads to more highly priced, poorer quality services. In fact, the truth is likely to be more complex and more variable than either side allows for.

Saunders and Harris's (1990) typology has both strengths and weaknesses. Though they fail to take account of informal and voluntary modes of provision (forms of privatization which are especially significant in the policing context), they do recognize that there has been little examination of the effect of privatization on consumers. The experience of council house sales suggests, however, that the social and political impact of privatization in the sphere of consumption is likely to be of considerable importance. Above all else, however, their typology confirms Le Grand and Robinson's (1984) point that privatization is not just the simple replacement of the state by the market. Nor are private and public provision in some sort of zero-sum relationship, the more one grows, the more the other shrinks: a point which is very evident in the policing context. It is to that context which I now turn.

PHASE ONE: 114/83 AND THE 'PRIVATIZATION MENTALITY'

Recently, a major report on British policing expressed concern about the 'privatization mentality' which has, allegedly, come to dominate official thinking about the police service (JCC: Avon & Somerset Constabulary 1990). Certainly, it is true that in spite of commitment by the three Thatcher administrations to 'law and order' policies, the police service has, since the early 1980s, been subjected, more and more, to demands for greater value for money. This has come about in a number of ways: through the application of the Financial Management Initiative to police budgets; through the increased influence of the Home Office and the enhanced role of the Inspectorate of Constabulary (Weatheritt 1986); through the attempt to develop measures of police effectiveness and efficiency, together with statistical techniques and information systems appropriate to such development (Sinclair and Miller 1984); and through the involvement of the Public Accounts Committee and the Audit Commission in efficiency exercises (Rawlings forthcoming).

The key statement of intent was found in Home Office Circular 114/83: 'After this rapid growth [of police expenditure] a period of consolidation is desirable' (Home Office 1983). The Circular indicated that the combination of constraints on public expenditure, together with a police workload which showed 'no sign of diminishing' meant that the service had to 'make the most effective use possible of the substantial resources now avaliable to it'. Accordingly, the Circular specified a number of key principles which would provide the basis of future assessment of the effectiveness and efficiency of forces. Looked at in hindsight, it can now be seen that these principles, at least in the way that they have subsequently developed, fall into two overlapping categories: policies concerned with management, and policies relating to the employment of civilians.

Police management has often been characterized as unsystematic and *ad hoc* (Butler 1984). During the 1980s there has been an attempt to introduce rational principles into the management of police organizations, the most influential of which has been *Policing By Objectives* (PBO) (Lubans and Edgar 1979). Indeed, Circular 114/83 itself expressed a desire for police forces to 'set realistic objectives and clear priorities'. The idea was that after internal consultation between management and rank-and-file officers, and external consultation between police and community, clear force objectives would be established. These could then be implemented, reviewed, and evaluated in a rational manner. To some extent PBO was seen by the Home Office as a 'cure-all' for some of the problems of the early 1980s; it acceded to demands for greater police accountability by conceding public consultation, rather than external control of police policy; and it seemed to offer a means of subjecting police practice to some degree of rational scrutiny. There were good reasons for doubting, however, that a theory whose roots lay in the commercial private sector would work in practice, given what we know about the nature of police organizations (Johnston 1988). Such scepticism seems to have been confirmed by recent evidence, one survey noting that despite the implementation of the policy by no less than forty police forces in England and Wales, 'there appeared to be, at best, a token commitment to Policing By Objectives' (JCC: Devon & Cornwall Constabulary: 1).

There is also evidence that similar difficulties have arisen with attempts to subject management to greater financial scrutiny. Consider the issue of performance indicators, a key element of the 'privatization mentality' and a clear attempt to exert greater central control over police resources. Circular 114/83 had indicated that some measures of police performance would have to be developed, though, at this point, it was left to individual forces to devise them. Unfortunately, there is evidence to suggest that many forces failed to grasp this opportunity (JCC: Avon & Somerset 1990) or failed to understand what was required of them. The Devon & Cornwall survey, after asking forces about any measurements of performance which they had developed, or were developing, concluded that there existed amongst them 'a degree of confusion ... as to precisely what constituted a "measurement of perform- ance"' (JCC: Devon & Cornwall 1990: 50). This was reflected in the variable methods used, some forces, for instance relying entirely on Home Office data; some carrying out public opinion surveys; some doing activity analysis; and some trying to develop their own matrix of indicators.

The problem is, however, as the Avon & Somerset report implies, such variation is anathema to a Home Office dedicated to increased central control of police resources, and it is possible that future performance indicators may be imposed on the police service from the centre. To some extent, of course, such a centralization has already emerged with the growing influence of the Inspectorate. Here, two methods of evaluation have become important; first, the 'matrix of indicators', an information base used for carrying out force inspections derived from various force returns; second, the use of computerized financial information systems to compare performance across different forces.

Of course, this centralization is a complex one, for as with other public services (such as education and health), the police service has experienced centralization in some areas, coupled with decentralization in others. There has, for example, been both financial devolution (linked to the idea of 'cost centres') and operational devolution (linked to the principles of PBO) in a number of forces. The idea of devolving financial and operational responsibility to subdivisional levels, coupled with a willingness to accept elements of consumerism into the evaluation of police services (most recently through the publication of Inspectors' reports on individual forces for the first time) indicates the positive side of the 'privatization mentality'. At the same time, however, it has to be borne in mind that the decentralization of day-to-day financial *administration* is coupled with a thoroughgoing centralization of elements of financial and operational *policy making* at central state level.

The second element emphasized in 114/83 was civilianization, the Circular stipulating that bids for increased establishments would not normally be approved if existing officers were occupying posts which could be more economically and properly filled by civilians. Circular 105/88 further emphasized that the Inspectorate, in gauging the success of a force's policy on civilianization, would pay particular attention to the numbers of 'accountable' civilians employed (i.e. those either directly replacing police officers, or releasing officers for operational duties, as distinct from those 'non-accountable' personnel merely engaged in duties such as catering or cleaning), and went on to specify twenty-five categories of work suitable for civilianization (Home Office 1988a).

As a consequence of these developments it is now possible to find civilians employed in a wide variety of posts including scenes of crime officers, coroners' officers, photographers, press and public relations officers, control room assistants, front office counter assistants, fingerprint officers, and gaolers. In some areas of work civilian involvement has been relatively uncontroversial. Two-thirds of forces now have administrative support units. These units, largely staffed by civilians, have taken over routine clerical tasks and the preparation of prosecution files, in order that police personnel might be released for operational duties. A review undertaken by management consultants in the West Midlands Constabulary suggested that these procedures had increased the operational availability of constables by 26.6 per cent. In other areas, however, the employment of civilians is more controversial. Some of this concern reflects a view that civilians are encroaching on tasks which are part of the essential police function. The Police

Federation, for example, has expressed concern about civilians being employed in the production of crime prevention surveys, and as gaolers, front office clerks, control room operators, and driving instructors (*Police* January 1989). The Federation has also expressed concern that the speed of civilianization might contribute to the disintegration of the traditional police mandate, encouraging the emergence of a two-tier police service: specialized operational personnel engaging in public order functions, civilians making a major contribution to crime prevention and community-related activity (Mason 1988).

There are, however, doubts that civilianization is the panacea implied in the 'privatization mentality'. For one thing, there is a huge wastage rate amongst civilian staff. It is not unusual for a force to lose between one-quarter and one-third of its civilian support staff in any one year. This high turnover is due to low pay, poor career structures, and the promise of better job prospects elsewhere. The problem is particularly evident in areas such as computing where forces find it difficult to attract qualified personnel. Yet, if they choose to train staff in computing skills, those individuals, once qualified, are likely to be attracted by better job prospects in the private sector. Some forces have responded by paying competitive salaries for specialized civilian personnel. But this defeats the whole point of civilianization and already, in some forces, it is cheaper to use police officers than civilians to run computers. Increasingly, therefore, the various associated costs of civilianization (training, appraisal, relocation, redeployment, wastage, etc.) appear to suggest that it may not continue to be the cheap alternative which it was once thought to be. It is significant that one American study also concludes that 'using civilians may not lead to cheaper police protection' (Heininger and Urbanek 1983: 205).

The issue of civilianization raises two critical questions. First, there is the issue of how far the process can be pushed without compromising policing effectiveness or fundamentally changing the police role. It is, for example, feasible to civilianize all front-desk personnel and, already, more and more members of the public come face to face with civilians, rather than police officers, when entering a police station. In itself, this may be an efficient deployment of resources. Moreover, it can be applied to other areas of activity, such as the taking of statements, with equal justification. Yet, there is room for doubt as to whether the insulation of police officers from routine access by members of the public is a good thing for police–public relations, and hence, for effective policing.

There is also the question of whether civilianization is merely the 'thin end' of a more robust wedge of privatization. This view is certainly justified if it is seen as part of a general process towards the increased provision of police services by private agents of different sorts. In that sense, civilianization of traditional patrol functions, either by the expansion of the Special Constabulary, or by the creation of 'street wardens' is already on the immediate horizon. Equally, once the economic rationale for civilianization is accepted, it is not difficult to imagine the process as a 'step on the way' to the full privatization of certain functions. After all, if low-grade administrative functions can be done more cheaply by civilians, why not contract them out to private companies? If this can be done, why not go further and privatize traffic wardens? And if, as the Audit Commision Report on 'The management of police training' suggests, there is scope for civilianization here (*Police Review* 1 December 1989), why not follow the example of nurse training and contract out large elements of the syllabus to the polytechnics? Such examples beg the question of what prospects exist for widespread privatization of police services.

PHASE TWO: FUTURE PROSPECTS

At the end of 1989 officials of the Police Federation, the Prison Officer's Association, and the Fire Brigade's Union held informal discussions about the possible privatization of elements of the three services and agreed that the meeting should be seen as a basis for future talks (*Police Review* 22 December 89). Such developments reflect growing concern in public sector unions that the emergency services could be subjected to privatization initiatives.

It is in the ambulance service, however, that such developments are most evident. Here, there are already clear indications that a two-tier service is emerging. Partly, this has been precipitated by the industrial dispute of 1989–90, but in fact, such developments were already well under way; initially as an extension of the principle of contracting out in the NHS; more recently through the opportunities for self-government contained in the NHS reforms.

The most radical example of privatization can be found in the Northumbria Ambulance Service (Davenport 1989; 1990) which, alongside those in Norfolk and Lincolnshire, has applied to establish itself as an NHS Trust under the reforms. Here, four independent companies have been established to offer commercial services, both to other parts of the health service and to the public. Each service is based upon a particular form of ambulance-worker expertise: 'Communicom' offers telecommunications services, mobile telephones, radios and message-paging services: 'Communifleet' uses the service's garages to provide a 24-hour car-servicing facility for members of the public, and will, in future, offer driving lessons and MOT tests: 'Communiaid' offers first-aid training and consultancy to local employers: 'Communicaire' offers a private ambulance service by luxury car, or jet air-ambulance, to those seeking it. Having decided to opt for self-government in 1991 under the NHS reforms, the service in Northumbria will, in future, have much more opportunity to benefit from income generated by such commercial ventures.

In Northumbria 40 per cent of non-urgent cases are now handled by the private sector and the front-line ambulance fleet has been reduced from more than 200 to seventy-seven. Though some form of basic training is given to bus and coach drivers who carry non-emergency patients, the changes have provoked anger from health service unions, critical of the two-tier service. Nevertheless, that model is winning favour with the Department of Health. In Wiltshire, as in Northumbria, a distinction has emerged between specialist services provided by trained paramedics and services provided by private and voluntary means. In Wiltshire's 'Medicar' system, 47 per cent of all patients are now carried in private cars by 150 volunteers, paid only on a mileage rate. Regular trips by large numbers of patients are contracted out to taxi and coach operators, and stretcher cases not needing close medical supervision are contracted to outside agencies, such as the Red Cross (Whitfield 1990). From April 1991 the London Ambulance Service will operate on similar lines to Northumbria and Wiltshire, non-emergency services being run on business lines through the thirty-one District Health Authorities.

Clearly, there is scope for similar initiatives in other emergency services. Both the Institute for Economic Affairs and the Adam Smith Institute have suggested that the fire service might be transferred to the private sector on the grounds that it would be both cheaper and more technically innovative (Pirie 1988). After all, it is said, other countries provide fire services privately. The practice is commonplace in the USA, where 90 per cent of provision is through volunteer fire departments; and in Denmark and Sweden the majority of the population get fire protection from private companies under contract to government (Savas 1982).

In an attempt to ward off demands for full privatization, a recent report from the Chief Fire Officer's Association offers a hostage to fortune by proposing that the fire service and the paramedic wing of the ambulance service should merge into a single organization. This is justified on the grounds that Britain is unique in the western world in not having such unified emergency provision. More to the point, however, it would as Sir John Wheeler of the Home Affairs Select Committee put it, allow for the full contracting out of the non-emergency 'coach service for elderly ladies', currently provided by the health service (*The Times* 20 April 1990).

Such developments beg the question of how the process could proceed in the police context, and already forces are speculating, in private, about sponsorship. Mason (1991) notes that the Gibraltar police, a force organized very much on British lines, has vehicles supplied by the National Westminster Bank which bear not only the word 'police', but also the legend 'Sponsored by Nat West Bank'. Sponsorship is, however, only one form of income generation; and income generation is only one form in which privatization might develop in the police context, given the diversity of police services. For present purposes three categories of privatization will be distinguished, though it should be said that these, to some extent, overlap and interpenetrate.

1. Load shedding through commercial and voluntary provision

Classically, 'load shedding' occurs where both the funding mechanism and the delivery of a service are shifted into the private sector (Fixler and Poole 1988). Under the heading of 'load shedding', however, I also include those instances where publicly funded police organizations have some of their functions usurped by voluntary action (e.g. vigilantism) and circumstances where police agencies actively encourage such voluntary action (e.g. Neighbourhood Watch).

For the moment, I shall say nothing about privatization of this sort, as it is discussed in detail in subsequent chapters. Suffice it to say that the police service has expressed serious concern about some of this activity – notably the provision of street patrols by vigilante groups or private security personnel, and the replacement of sworn constables by private security guards at public installations, such as docks and defence establishments. Alan Eastwood, Chairman of the Police Federation, has referred to cases of this sort as 'straws in the wind', though the analogy of the 'dripping tap' is, perhaps, more accurate since private provision has been growing for a considerable time, and is likely to expand further in the foreseeable future.

2. Contracting out, agencies and internal markets

Contracting out is the principle form through which 'liberalization' (Saunders and Harris 1990) is likely to occur in police forces. Here, the police authority hires the provider of the service, but retains overall funding responsibility (cf. Fixler and Poole 1988: 111). Services already contracted out in certain police forces include relatively uncontroversial activities such as catering, cleaning, and vehicle maintenance, design and organization of building works, building maintenance, laundering, publishing, bookbinding, and the repair of radios and other equipment. Some examples are more sensitive. Concern has been expressed, for example, about the competence and integrity of personnel engaged in security work, a West Midlands Constabulary report finding that 20 per cent of applicants put forward by 'Burns International Security' to guard Police Headquarters had criminal records (*Daily Telegraph* 9 April 1990). Similar sensitivity arises with respect to the possibility of contracting out computer and information services to facilities companies, though as Hulbert (1988) points out, the privatization of naval dockyards such as Devonport, indicates that the precedent of private involvement in the processing of sensitive intelligence and information is already set.

At present, contracting out has been, is or likely to be, extended into two immediate operational areas. First, there is the clamping and storage of illegally parked vehicles which has been contracted out in parts of London since February 1988 (Fraser 1988). More recently, the Association of London Authorities and the London

Boroughs Association expressed lack of confidence in the police's handling of parking enforcement and approached the Home Office with a view to taking over that activity, the police agreeing to transfer responsibility to them for authorized on-street parking. These developments have, so far, enabled the transfer of significant numbers of traffic wardens out of central London (MacLean 1989). A second area to be contracted out (the escort and supervision of prisoners) is discussed in Chapter 5.

Contracting out is sometimes combined with the establishment of new organizational forms for service delivery. In 1989 the Home Office appointed County Natwest, a merchant bank, to study the prospects for running the Police National Computer, the Directorate of Telecommunications, and the Forensic Science Service on commercial lines. In the case of the Police National Computer, the report recommended the contracting out of day-to-day operations and development work to the private sector, though it did not recommend wholescale privatization, preferring instead to retain the Home Office as sponsor. This proposal is linked to the 'Next Steps' strategy of management reform in the Civil Service (Efficiency Unit 1988: see also Fry *et al.* 1988). One of the objects of this strategy is to exploit the commercial potential of public sector departments, not through total privatization (since at present, this is seen to be politically impossible), but by establishing them as agencies under a chief executive. In April 1990 Richard Luce, the Civil Service Minister, announced that eighteen further departments would be granted agency status bringing the total number of agencies up to thirty. By the end of 1991, Luce said, half of the civil service (including the 80,000 people running the social security Benefits Agency) will consist of executive agencies at 'arm's length' from government (*Independent* 3 April 1990).

In the case of the Forensic Science Service, the developments create a commercial market in which police forces will pay for services consumed. Officials have already made it clear that this implies greater selectivity, on the police's part, of cases chosen for forensic work, irrespective of rising crime rates (Kirby 1989b). Inevitably, these developments have provoked immediate criticism from the police associations. Although the object is to create an internal market in forensic science services (and it is clear that the agency will be expected to meet demands from the fire service and from defence organizations as well), it should not be assumed, however, that the model is based upon some notion of a decentralized, consumer-led, free market. On the contrary, the agency proposals, though imbued with the 'privatization mentality', are quite consistent with the further expansion of central state control of services. This is made very clear in Cozens's suggestion that the agency model provides the best available means of facilitating the national co-ordination of police services (Cozens 1989). The reasoning here seems to be that the development of such 'strong, independent operating units within a clearly defined strategic framework' provides a form of central co-ordination, apparently less political in form, than a system dominated by the Home Office or the Association of Chief Police Officers (ACPO). Such a view is entirely consistent with proposals to place funding for common police services, such as forensics, under Home Office control, thereby creating a centrally co-ordinated 'free market' in those services (*Police Review* 14 July 1989).

Attempts at 'liberalization' of police services through the establishment of agencies and markets are likely to continue in the immediate future. At present, the Home Office is considering the agency option, amongst several others, in its plans to create a national magistrates' courts service in England and Wales. Pressure is also mounting on the Government to end police control of criminal records after recent criticism of the inaccuracy of files and the haphazard disclosure of information. A report of the Home Affairs Committee noted that more than half a million searches of criminal records were ordered by Whitehall in 1989 for 'vetting' purposes (a 20 per cent increase on the previous year) and proposed that the National Identification Bureau, at present run by the Metropolitan Police, should be replaced by a statutory agency (House of Commons 1990b).

3. Fees, charges and selling services

Potentially, the generation of income from fees and charges offers the most likely model of privatization of public police services. The police are not permitted to charge for services which they have a legal duty to provide, but police authorities have the right under s. 15 (1) of the 1964 Police Act to levy charges for 'special services'.

(Although the Act does not define a 'special service', effectively, they are services which the police have the power, but not the duty, to provide). Typically, such charges are made for police presence at sports fixtures and other public events. Debate arising from a recent legal case (Harris v Sheffield United), coupled with the fact that nothing in the Act precludes events such as political meetings from being defined as 'special', has opened up the ethical question of whether, and in what circumstances, charges are appropriate. So far, legal judgment has applied the principle of 'public benefit' to particular cases, though in practice, charges seem to be applied on a somewhat *ad hoc* and arbitrary basis by police authorities (Weatherill 1988).

Such arbitrariness was demonstrated in the 1989–90 ambulance workers' dispute. Here, some police authorities charged 'income-generating rates' for the supply of police personnel, whilst others only asked health authorities to pay the lower 'mutual aid' rates which obtain when one police force assists another. During this dispute there was, therefore, wide variation in police charges: from £8.20 per constable per hour in Hertfordshire, to £21.00 in neighbouring Bedfordshire (*Police Review* 19 January 1990).

At present, however, the policing of public events is more of a loss-making than an income-generating exercise. This is especially evident in the policing of football matches where the stipulations of the 1964 Act only permit charges to be levied on police services provided inside the ground, those provided outside (traffic control, etc.), being part of normal duties. In fact, many police forces have added to that overall loss by failing even to charge realistic rates for these services. The cost of policing London football grounds during the 1987–8 season exceeded £8m, though only one-eighth of this was recouped from the twelve London clubs. Recently, the Metropolitan Police have introduced new charges, aimed to reflect the real costs more accurately. (That trend is likely to be followed nationally. In the 1989–90 season charges to football clubs rose by 50 per cent over the previous season's total.) Significantly, in London, the police have also encouraged some clubs, such as Tottenham Hotspur and Chelsea, to increase the proportion of private security officers employed inside the ground, thereby enabling the numbers of police personnel to be reduced. Here, then, it would appear that should police authorities seek to levy realistic rates of payment, clubs will turn to the, cheaper, private sector. In that sense, there would seem little likelihood of police forces generating income from public events policing, unless conditions can be created where they can compete on more equal terms with the private sector.

Another recent development has been the introduction of the ACPO 'Unified Intruder Alarms Policy' (Rees 1989; JCC: Northumbria 1990). This policy is aimed, primarily, at reducing the police time spent on responding to false alarm calls. Estimates suggest that as many as 98 per cent of call-outs can be for false alarms, each response costing about £50. The policy defines strict criteria governing the installation, operation, and management of systems and stipulates that police response will be withdrawn from any premises producing more than six false alarms in any 12-month period. It also enables forces to charge applicants for the registration of alarm systems with the police. Northumbria Constabulary intends to charge a £20 registration fee and £50 for a false call-out. Again, the policy is unlikely to generate substantial income, though, if implemented across the country, it is likely to produce considerable cost savings. Moreover, cost questions aside, the alarm policy is important in two respects. First, it points to a change in the police role, indicating a movement away from the protection of property to the conditional protection of property (JCC: Northumbria 1990: 21). Second, like the previous example, it raises questions about the potential for competition between public and private sectors. MacLean (1989) suggests that because the policy is, in effect, a tax on crime prevention, it may persuade customers to turn to the private sector, the police having priced themselves out of the market.

Potentially, a more fruitful source of income generation may be found in sponsorship. The Cornwall Ambulance Service recently set up a £3,000 deal for crews to wear badges advertising a communications firm, and already, there is speculation about parallel developments in the police service. At the 1989 International Police Exhibition and Conference, Raymond Kendall, Interpol's Secretary General (and a former Metropolitan Police Commander) suggested that the police should accept private funding for campaigns against specific crimes or offers of technical equipment. Kendall argued that European police forces were considerably behind the Americans in such developments. Commenting on these suggestions, an editorial in *Police Review* (29

September 1989) considered the pros and cons of sponsorship. Under such deals, forces would presumably sponsor products in return for benefits. Computer firms, for instance, might offer free installation, servicing and consultancy. The process offers obvious short-term benefits to forces and, because of the large police market, might encourage competition and higher standards of goods and services in the long term. However, sponsorship also has negative aspects. It could expose police officers and members of police authorities to the dangers of corruption. It might lead to an undignified scramble for sponsorship by forces. It might tarnish the image of forces where sponsored goods prove defective. Above all, it might compromise the independence of forces from private, commercial pressures.

This last concern is the most serious. As yet, sponsorship activity has tended not to be linked directly to operational policing, the bulk of it involving support for community crime-prevention projects. However, examples already exist of what is, effectively, sponsored policing. The policing of Heathrow Airport by the Metropolitan Police and the policing of the Channel Tunnel by Kent Constabulary both involve funds being provided by private bodies for operational policing (JCC: Avon & Somerset 1990). And in a future where police resources are likely to be squeezed by government, it is possible that sponsorship may encroach more and more on operational activities, and on the autonomy of chief officers.

Another form of income generation might involve selling police services. In the light of the previous discussion, the question arises of whether specialist services could be marketed in ways parallel to the commercial activities of the Northumbria and Wiltshire Ambulance Services. Here, there are two issues. First, what services could be marketed? Second, what sort of commercial mechanism would be required to carry out the marketing function? To some extent, the second question is easier to answer than the first since, as far as it is possible to ascertain, there is nothing in the 1964 Act to prevent a police authority from establishing a commercial company, provided that it is financed from non-public funds. (Whether, in practice, the Home Office would try to dissuade any police authority from doing so is, of course, a matter of political judgement.) As to the question of marketable services, it is clear that some police skills and resources could be sold without raising too many ethical problems, and without fuelling excessive political controversy. Here, for instance, one can think of the marketing of garage services, telecommunications skills, driving tuition, dog training, and the hiring of police premises for conference and residential purposes, as obvious examples. Other areas, however, are more contentious. The provision of specialized alarm, security, and crime-prevention advice to commercial companies, or the sale of specialized detective skills to businesses and private individuals, are areas which could be seen as part of normal police duties according to the 1964 Act.

Colin Moore of Devon & Cornwall Constabulary addressed this issue at the 1989 Superintendents' Association Conference (*Police Review* 6 October 1989). Moore, speculating on the future, identified several possible models of policing. One of these, 'commercialization', involved the police service charging for some of its 'non-public' tasks and offering the private sector person-alized services, such as checking premises or transporting cash. A similar proposal, whereby the police might develop a commercial wing for selling 'non-public' services to the private sector, has also been put forward by Sir Peter Imbert. Whether the stipulations of the 1964 Act can be circumvented by drawing a demarcation between 'public' and 'non-public' tasks (the former, normal police duties; the latter, open to commercial exploitation) is open to question. (One is reminded here of the similarly tortuous distinction between 'operational' and 'non-operational' matters.) Nevertheless, Moore's model clearly foresees a situation where police forces engage in income-generating activity by selling services to the public. Furthermore, his proposals, reflecting professional concern about the expansion of the private security sector, suggest that the police should engage in limited competition with the industry.

The commercial model, although radical, is still, however, a reactive and defensive one. Fundamentally, it is a response born out of a fear that police budgets will be restricted, more and more, by governmental demands for efficiency. And although there is recognition of the threat from the private security sector, the 'commercial' model envisages only limited competition with that sector. It is possible, however, to push the strategy even further. The 1988 Local Government Act requires local authorities to undertake certain activities, only if they can do so competitively, and one of the areas listed where they may compete, is in the provision of security. So what are the prospects, especially in the light of growing police concern about the private sector's expanding role in the provision of street patrols (Boothroyd 1989), of a more offensive strategy: one where the police, instead of merely complaining about the erosion of their traditional role by the private sector, engage in direct competition with that sector for domination of the market?

Let us construct a hypothetical model of such activity. 'Profitshire Constabulary', having undertaken the successful marketing of garage and telecommunications services for several years, decides to expand its activities by selling security services to the community. The Chief Constable reports to the Police Authority that his hard-pressed force is unable, because of financial constraints, to offer the level of protection that members of the community demand. Indeed, he says that the disparity between public demand and the police's ability to meet that demand is leading to a loss of public confidence in the local police. In order to deal with this situation the Chief Constable suggests that, following the precedent which has already been set in marketing garage and telecommunications services, the force should establish a company for the sale of security services to the community. Personnel employed here would be engaged, primarily, in local crime prevention and community-policing work, increasing the visible police presence on the streets through foot patrol – precisely the function demanded by most members of the public. The arrangement would enable individuals, groups of individuals, residents' associations, and local councils to purchase extra police services. In order to meet the conditions of the Police Act, assurance is given that such provision will be offered only in addition to those services provided as part of normal police duties. There is, in other words, both a guarantee that commercial services are extra services which would, otherwise, be unavailable to those members of the public wishing to consume them; and an assurance that such services would not lead to any reduction in normal provision.

The Chief Constable informs the Police Authority of two possible means by which personnel could be recruited to this company ('Profitshire Constabulary Security Services'). One would involve the company using civilians, effectively in the role of security guards, for the patrol of residential streets and the protection of premises. Such personnel would be carefully vetted by the police, though lacking police powers they would have to call upon regular police officers when the exercise of constabulary powers was required. The second and preferred option would be for the company to use 'civilians for police purposes', according to the terms of the 1964 Act. In effect, civilians would be recruited, trained, and granted constabulary status in much the same way as Special Constables are now, though unlike Specials they would be paid employees of the company. The advantage of this model over the first would be that employees possessing constabulary status, together with the legal authority accompanying it, would enjoy enhanced levels of public legitimacy.

The Chief Constable concludes by saying that the formation of a company along these lines would enable the police to meet a growing public demand which conventional police services could never hope to satisfy. Furthermore, as well as generating income, it would enable the police to put the brakes on the private security sector's erosion of the traditional police role. The company would be able to market itself as a body with impeccable standards of recruitment, training, efficiency, and public accountability: the very features, conspicuous by their absence in the private sector. Such standards of excellence would be likely to attract consumers who might, otherwise, have been drawn to the private security sector.

Clearly, such a scenario might seem unrealistic. After all, one can think of numerous practical obstacles to implementing it. There would be certain resistance from the Police Federation, fearful of 'policing on the cheap'; and the Home Office would see the development as signalling the demise of the unpaid Special Constabulary, and, therefore, as being in direct conflict with Government plans for its expansion. Nevertheless, whether the scenario is feasible or a mere flight of fancy, it does enable us to address a number of important issues relating to the commercialization of the police role.

One of these concerns the question of whether public police forces can create conditions under which they could compete effectively with the private sector in the provision of police services. Considerable doubt has been expressed about this by those subscribing to what South (1989) calls the 'complementarity' view of public/private police relations. This thesis maintains that public and private policing organizations co-exist with one another in a relatively complementary fashion, each aware of the other's strengths and limits. Accordingly, there is scepticism about the possibility of public police bodies competing effectively with the private sector on its own ground. Doubt is cast upon the ability of police organizations to market themselves successfully, and upon the commercial capacities of police managers. Furthermore, since police forces give officers a higher standard of training and pay than that found in the private security sector (whether they be fully trained constables or merely, in the present scenario, civilians with police powers), there is bound to be a lack of real competitiveness, since the private sector will always be able to undercut the more expensive police product. Any suggestion that consumers will pay more for better services is regarded with scepticism. Finally, it is noted that once the police engage in the provision of private services they inevitably open themselves up to the threat of civil claims for damages (South 1989: 88–9).

A second problem concerns the impact of such commercial undertakings on normal police practices and policies. Let us say, for example, that 'Profitshire Constabulary Security Services' is contracted to undertake residential street patrols by a local tenants' association, concerned at the high rate of burglaries in their locality. Are we to believe the assurances of the Chief Constable that the provision of such private services will have no impact on normal police deployment policy in the particular subdivision concerned? Or is it likely that the local superintendent, cognizant of the extra (private) resources being channelled into the subdivision, will take those extra personnel into account when calculating deployment priorities? The problem here is that the finite supply of police resources, coupled with the infinite demand on police time, makes it unlikely that public and private elements of provision can, in reality, be demarcated. The likelihood of such demarcation is further reduced by the fact that police managers enjoy considerable autonomy in the determination of operational priorities: an autonomy which, because of its invisibility, is relatively exempt from external scrutiny. The provision of private services by a public agency, therefore, opens up complex questions, not only about the relationships which should pertain between commercial and public priorities, but also about the mechanisms available for assessing those connections. In effect, the introduction of commercial provision through public-sector police agencies adds manifold complications to the already muddied area of police accountability.

A third set of problems concerns the impact of commercial criteria on police–public relations and on public assessment of police services. At present, members of the public relate to the police as clients. Such a relationship is very different from that obtaining between the provider and the consumer of a service. Arguably, this may have benefits for the public, since consumer status should lead to greater choice. Hence, dissatisfaction with 'Profitshire's' security provision will, presumably, force consumers to look for an alternative supplier. And, in principle of course, competition between suppliers should improve the overall quality of security provision. As with any commercial solution, however, there are problems. Choice can only be exercised if one has the capacity to pay. So there is the danger that some people's security needs may remain unsatisfied; or that they might only be satisfied by the hard-pressed public sector. In this connection, some have expressed concern about the possible emergence of a 'two-tier' system of policing: private provision of 'normal' police services for well-heeled suburbanites, the public police function being restricted to control of the urban 'dangerous classes'.

Whether or not this is an exaggerated image of the future of police–public relations, however, commercialization of services does change the relationship between police officers and members of the public. This is particularly true in an operational context, for if one sets up a dual system of policing with two levels of constable (one responsive to public demand, the other to public demand on a commercial basis) the relationship between citizen and constable is altered. At present it is not a commercial transaction. Once it becomes so there are serious implications for what one might call the 'judicious exercise of discretion', as well as for the public's perception of how that discretion is exercised. It is not merely that police officers become more prone to accusations of graft and corruption, something which, whatever the current state of police conduct, is relatively rare. It is that the commercialization of services inevitably, generates new forms of public assessment of the police. To put it bluntly, once people pay for *some* police services, it is likely that they will begin to assess *all* police services as consumers, rather than as passive clients. This may be no bad thing; but it is almost certainly something for which police organizations are unprepared, despite the likelihood of their growing commitment to commercial ventures. In the commercial world 'the customer is always right'. This is a maxim which, one suspects, the police will find very difficult to swallow.

Chapter 4

The private security sector I
Structure and control

PRIVATE SECURITY IN BRITAIN

Defining the boundaries of private security, like defining the boundaries of policing, raises complex conceptual issues upon which several writers have commented (see, for example, South 1988). Though I shall discuss some of these conceptual issues later, the approach taken here, being primarily a descriptive one, enables me to present a broad review of the industry in a single chapter. It should be borne in mind, however, that statistical data on the industry are notoriously unreliable, particularly in the light of conceptual debates about where the precise boundaries of the sector should be drawn. For that reason, the data presented in this chapter should be seen less as objective facts, than as broad indications of general trends.

The contract security industry can be divided into three categories (see Jordan & Sons Ltd 1989):

1 Physical/mechanical: i.e. the provision of locks, safes, strong rooms, grilles, shutters, security glass, anti-bandit screens, vehicle security etching, cash bags, boarding-up services, etc.
2 Electrical/electronic: i.e. manufacturers, surveyors, and installers of alarms, detectors, control panels, CCTV, signalling apparatus, video motion detection, access control and electronic locking systems, security cameras, cash-handling aids (e.g. smoke and dye canisters), etc.
3 Manned (and womanned) services: static or patrol guarding services, cash transportation (bank collection, wage packeting), key holding and responding to alarms, alarm monitoring, CCTV; and audio surveillance remote monitoring, etc.

Several things can be said about this classification. First, it indicates the complex and fragmented nature of contract security. This fragmentation can, of course, work against consumer interests since, as McAinsh (1988) suggests, suppliers are inclined to claim benefits for their product sector (e.g. alarms) over that of others (e.g. physical means). Second, the classification is incomplete. For one thing, it does not cover private enquiry agents (of whom I shall say more in the following chapter); nor does it include the many specialist 'security consultants' whose activities range across the three categories. (An interesting example here is Rover's recent appointment of John Stalker to head a team of investigators examining the leakage of information from the company. Stalker announced 'I have tied up with a firm from the West Country called Cogitaire who specialise in computer analysis problems. I have also hired a few ex-policemen, including a former detective chief superintendent.' He went on to add that this specialist work 'could not be done by a police force or Rover's own in-house security' (*Daily Express* 21 September 1990).

Although the present chapter will concentrate on the structure of the contract sector, it also has to be recognized that a huge in-house security sector operates alongside it in factories, banks, hotels, universities, government departments, local authorities, and the like. In the USA General Motors, alone, has a force of 4,200 plant guards, a body larger than the municipal police forces of all but five American cities (O'Toole 1978). In Britain there is no reliable calculation of the numbers of in-house security personnel. The most frequently cited figure – a very rough-and-ready one – is that 50,000 such personnel existed in 1971, and 60,000 by 1978. (This is based on Shearing and Stenning's (1981) somewhat creative manipulation of Home Office (1979) figures.) Generally, it is assumed that in-house security personnel outnumber contract personnel by a ratio of about 3:2 (South 1988). It has to be recognized, however, that the ratio varies according to one's definition of in-house security, for as South indicates the term 'security' is often used by companies as a convenience label for staff with multiple roles: 'security' plus health and safety duties, cleaning responsibilities, etc. Suffice it to say that the in-house sector is a substantial one. Morover, it is one which is undergoing expansion in certain areas. One growth area is in the development of risk-management strategies. (At least one British university, backed by private enterprise and the Home Office, is offering postgraduate degrees in the subject.) Another is the in-house investigation of commercial fraud in banking and insurance, about which I shall say more in the next chapter.

Estimates of the numbers employed in private security in Britain vary. Twenty years ago two British criminologists asked: 'Who would have thought that by 1970 a quarter of a million uniformed men would be operating in our society under the control of private companies?' (McClintock and Wiles 1972: 9). Unfortunately, the authors offered no empirical evidence in support of this estimate which, for the time, is almost certainly exaggerated. (Another contributor to the same book puts the figure at only 40,000, 25,000 of whom were employed in cash guarding and the patrol of private property, the remainder in the manufacture, maintenance, and installation of alarms, locks, safes, and other equipment (Randall and Hamilton 1972).) Two decades later there is still an astonishing absence of empirical research on this question. All that can be said is that best estimates of numbers employed vary between the 100,000 suggested by MATSA (Managerial Administrative, Technical and Supervisory Association) and GMB (General, Municipal, Boilermakers and Allied Union), and Bruce George MP's figure of 250,000. In the absence of statutory regulation, estimation of numbers of firms is also difficult. One can, for example, trawl through local editions of Yellow Pages to get an indication of the numbers of companies and range of services offered. (In the London edition, alone, 400 such firms are listed for the city centre.) Alternatively, one might accept IPSA's (International Professional Security Association) estimation that up to 20,000 firms exist in Britain (4,000 belonging to reputable trade associations, another 12,000– 16,000 independent of them).

Though precise estimates of total employees are unavailable, it is certain that employment has expanded significantly over the last two decades. The same is true of the market as a whole. According to Randall and Hamilton (1972) the industry, whose sales had been below £5m per annum in 1950, had achieved a turnover of £55m by 1970. By 1976 the turnover amongst non-manufacturing members of the British Security Industries Association (BSIA) (which claims to account for 90 percent of the industry's business) had risen to between £120m and £130m (Home Office 1979). Since then, it has continued to expand steadily:

	1981	1982	1983	1984	1985	1986
£m	357.5	418.3	476.4	520.1	581.5	712.9

(Jordan & Sons Ltd 1987; 1989)

Jordan & Sons Ltd (1989) estimate total market size in 1987 to be £807.6m, an increase of 13.3 per cent on the previous year's total. According to their calculations this compares with increases of 22 per cent (1986), 11.8 per cent (1985), 9 per cent (1984), and 13.9 per cent (1983).

The British market continues, increasingly, to be dominated by a few large companies. The extent of that domination can be illustrated by comparing figures from the 1987 and 1989 editions of Jordans's survey of the contract sector:

Percentage market share

	1985	1987
Racal Chubb	25	30
	(as Chubb & Sons)	
Securicor Group	15.5	20
Group 4 Total Security	7.5	10
Total	48	60

The largest and fastest growing section of the market is in alarms, access control, and CCTV. Between 1986–7 the alarms market grew by 12.8 per cent, CCTV by 17 per cent, and access control by 33 per cent (Jordan & Sons Ltd 1989). Though in Britain, as in the USA (Vines 1988), the alarms sector is likely to remain the market leader, areas such as CCTV are expanding rapidly. Here, the market doubled between the years 1983–7. It continues to expand at 40 per cent per annum and in 1990 it is predicted that retail expenditure on it will total £230m (Hobson 1990). Such expansion is due, in part, to the speed of technical development and the sophistication of new equipment. Specialist systems such as the audioscope (consisting of a rigid optical probe) permit simultaneous visual and audio surveillance during covert operations. Others, such as the 'Trojan system', can be concealed in office furniture. One specialist suggests that the advent of CCTV will inevitably lead to the reduction of the human element in security (Tomkins 1986) and use of the equipment on the London Underground has already provoked the accusation that it will lead to the withdrawal of uniformed police and security guards. Nevertheless, systems continue to proliferate in clubs, discos, shops, banks, petrol stations, on buses, in pedestrian subways, and on council estates. Police forces use them on the roads ('hoolivans') and in the air ('helitele'). The versatility of CCTV – the fact that it can be used to monitor everything from sea fronts (Bournemouth) to shopping precincts (Plymouth, Wolverhampton), and from hospitals (Glenfields, Leicester), to multi-site college campuses (Polytechnic South West) – means that despite concern about implications for civil liberties (Liberty 1989), its continued growth is inevitable.

The manned security sector accounted for 38.3 per cent of the total market in 1987 (41 per cent in 1985), the size of the market increasing by 10.2 per cent between the years 1986–7. Two companies dominate the guarding element of manned security: Group 4 with 24 per cent of market share and Securicor with 21 per cent. (Reliance and Securiguard come next with 9 per cent each.) The transport element is dominated by Securicor (55 per cent), the rest of the market being divided up between Group 4 and Security Express/Armaguard (15 per cent each), Brinks-Mat (10 per cent), and the rest (5 per cent).

As I have already said, it has been suggested that there may, eventually, be some contraction of labour-intensive security due to the expansion of the electronics market (South 1988). This may be true, though as South admits, prediction is difficult. For one thing, markets may be affected by external factors. For example, if public police forces adopted the 'Profitshire' model described in the previous chapter, manned security would gain a new lease of life. After all, it is likely that public demand for the 'extra' uniformed presence on the streets that such an initiative would offer, would be substantial. In that respect, MATSA's suggestion that 'the classic nightwatchman is a thing of the past' (cited in South 1988: 31) to be replaced by electronic surveillance is somewhat premature. Moreover, although manned security appears to be shrinking as a relative proportion of the total security market, it continues to expand in absolute terms. Security is not a zero-sum game.

It is in the manned sector, however, that wages and conditions are most problematical. A letter from the West Yorkshire Low Pay Unit (*Independent* 30 September 1989) described a group of twelve security guards earning £1.50 per hour and working 60–70 hours per week (including public holidays) without overtime payments.

King (1988) surveyed advertisements for nineteen contract companies in the London Evening Standard over a 2-week period and found average wage rates to be £2.73 per hour. By his calculations (even assuming 'generous' overtime payments of time-and-one-quarter after 40 hours), this would produce gross earnings of £177.40 for a 60-hour week consisting of twelve-hour shifts, and including nights and weekends. This compares with the average manual worker's wage of £184.10 for 43.1 hours. It is easy to see, therefore, why in London and the South East many contract companies have a staff turnover of 400 per cent per annum (Fendley 1988). King's point is that the industry is both ineffective and inefficient because companies pay low wages in order to undercut their competitors when tendering for guard contracts. The irony in this observation is that 2 years after King's article was written, Reliance Security Services, the company which employs him as marketing executive, was involved in just such a contractual relationship with the Ministry of Defence when providing guards at Deal Barracks.

The British market is highly concentrated, though despite this, several smaller firms are expanding rapidly. (The fastest growing, Britannia Security PLC, has been acquiring small, locally based companies for some time.) Nevertheless, despite justified concern about the growth of small 'cowboy' guard operations, employment is concentrated in a few major companies. In the late 1970s, 84 per cent of employees worked for just nine companies (Home Office 1979), and overall, the picture is of an unbalanced structure: on the one hand, a large number of localized companies employing small numbers of personnel, and competing for guarding and cash-carrying contracts; on the other hand, a few large, highly diversified, technologically developed, multinational corporations, employing vast numbers of people.

Some indication of the extent of diversification can be given by considering three well-known companies. The activities of Securiguard Group PLC cover cleaning and maintenance, security, communications, and personnel services. The company began in 1967 under the name of Academy Cleaning Services. In 1979 there was a major expansion into security with the formation of Securiguard Services Ltd. Between 1983 and 1987 four manned guarding companies were acquired: Property Guards of Liverpool (1983), Concorde Armoured Services of Bucks and Hants (1984),

Consolidated Safeguards of London (1985), and City Security Guards of New York (1987). In 1987 the company also expanded into personnel services, acquiring He-Man, Action Secretaries, and Portman Recruiting Services. The recent acquisition of two American companies (Premier Management Group and the Spence Protective Agency) means that US interests now account for about one-fifth of group turnover. The group employs 12,500 staff, over 3,000 of whom are in one of the fourteen nationwide locations of the UK Security Division. (That division recently won the contract for guarding the Royal Marine base at Taunton.) The Security Division remains the largest activity, accounting for 40 per cent of turnover in 1988 (though diversification is confirmed by the fact that in 1987 that figure stood at 57 per cent). Securiguard is one of the top three providers of manned security in the country, offering static guards, mobile patrols, and keyholding. CCTV, access control systems, and integrated security systems are offered through the Technical Systems Division. Pre-tax profits for 1988 stood at £3.2m, a substantial increase on figures for 1987 (£1.57m), 1986 (£1m), and 1985 (£715,000). Average wage per employee in 1987 was £4,427. (All details obtained from Tirbutt 1989; Jordan & Sons Ltd 1989.)

Modern Alarms Ltd installs and rents security alarm systems. The company was founded in Birmingham in the mid-1960s. In the first year it had fifteen employees and an annual turnover of £50,000. By 1988 it had 1400 employees and a turnover of £60m. The company no longer concentrates solely on alarms, having diversified into other areas of electronic security. In particular, it sees CCTV as a potential growth area since, according to the group's Managing Director Mike Hawker, it reduces the cost of manned surveillance to consumers and also provides a useful information tool for managers wishing to check on the integrity and efficiency of their staff. Latest technological developments combining CCTV with alarm technology and access control, also enable the company to offer integrated security packages to consumers. In 1987 the average wage per employee was £9,723, reflecting the fact that the company includes 700 service and installation engineers amongst its staff. This figure places the group in sixteenth position (from the ninety to one hundred companies surveyed) in Jordans's league table of wage rates for the industry. (All details from Green 1989a; Jordan and Sons Ltd 1989.)

Securicor Group PLC is a huge multinational enterprise involved in a variety of different businesses: cash carrying, cash processing, security guards and patrols, express parcels services, electronic surveillance, mobile communications. It also has interests in alarms, cleaning services, hotels, vehicle dealerships, insurance, and travel. In 1988 the group had 36,331 employees (30 per cent of whom worked outside the UK), a turnover of £382m (an increase of 14 per cent on the previous year), and profits of almost £21m. This placed it at number 245 in *The Times* '1,000' list of companies. (Group 4 Securitas, the next major security company was, by comparison, much smaller, having a mere 6,789 employees, a turnover of £81m and profits of £1.3m, figures which placed it at number 818 in the list.) Subsidiaries include Pony Express International Ltd, whilst an associate company is Telecom Securicor Cellular Radio Ltd (in which the group has a 40 per cent stake). Security Services PLC, the security division of the corporation has invested heavily in Europe, having centres at Courbevoie (near Paris) and in Luxembourg (covering the Benelux region). At Courbevoie 250 staff are employed to collect and process £26m of cash per month. Company pre-tax profits were up by 40 per cent (at £38.2m) for the year ending 30 September 1989, though still £5m below market estimates. Cellnet's contribution to profits had risen dramatically during that 12-month period (from £2.6m to £19.25m). The group is a member of BSIA, and justifiably proud of its careful screening of potential security employees, and its rigorous training programmes. Each time Securicor recruits a guard, it costs the company between £1,000 and £1,200 for recruitment costs, screening costs, and a week's residential training. (All details from Green 1989b; *Independent* 7 February 1990; Jordan & Sons Ltd 1989; South 1988; Allen 1988.)

PRIVATE SECURITY OUTSIDE BRITAIN

USA: In contrast both to Britain and to the other countries discussed below, there is an sizeable body of empirical research on private security in the USA. (There is also a considerable volume of work on private security in Canada undertaken by Shearing, Stenning, and others from the Centre of Criminology, University of Toronto.) In the USA, the Department of Justice has sponsored several major research programmes on the industry, the most important of which have been the 'Rand' and 'Hallcrest' reports (respectively Kakalik and Wildhorn 1972; 1977; Cunningham and Taylor 1985).

In 1970 the USA had a roughly equal proportion of public and private police (Wildeman 1988). However, the ratio between public and private personnel has been variable. Rand claims that in 1950 the USA had 199,000 public police officers and 282,000 private security personnel – a ratio of 1:1.42. In 1960 there were approximately 260,000 public police and between 302,000 and 357,000 private security personnel. By 1970, the huge investment in public law enforcement which had occurred in the late 1960s reversed the balance, public police officers (at 396,000) slightly outnumbering private security personnel (at 382,000) – a ratio of 0.96:1 (Kakalik and Wildhorn 1977, vol. 1: 16; 1977: 38).

The numerical dominance of public police was, however, short-lived, due to the dramatic expansion of private security during the 1970s. Hallcrest estimated that by 1982 the 1.1m people (excluding Federal Government civil and military security workers) employed in private security outnumbered the combined (650,000) local, state, and federal sworn law-enforcement personnel by a ratio of nearly 2:1. This total of 1.1m employees consisted of 448,979 in-house personnel (including 346,326 guards, 20,106 store detectives, and 10,000 investigators) and 640,640 employed in contract security (including 541,600 guards, 26,300 armoured car/courier operatives, and 3,000 security consultants). Hallcrest went on to quote projections from the US Bureau of Labor Statistics that between 1980 and 1990 private security employment would continue to increase at a faster rate than public police employment – a 33.3 per cent increase compared to one of 23.4 per cent (Cunningham and Taylor 1985: 108).

The industry in the USA is slightly more competitive than that in Britain. No single company controls as much as 10 per cent of the market, though the top thirty firms (out of 13,500 nationwide) have about 50 per cent of market share (McCrie 1988). Estimates of market size vary. Sales of security equipment and services in the contract sector grew from $511m in 1958 to $2,340m in 1973 (Kakalik and Wildhorn 1977: 55), and by the 1980s the contract sector was generating $5b of business per annum (McCrie 1988). Hallcrest, combining figures from both the contract and in-house sectors, claimed that the total annual expenditure for protective services in 1980 amounted to $21.7b. This total far exceeds the combined total (of $13.8b) for federal, state, and local law- enforcement expenditure. Given projections for a 9.1 per cent per annum increase in private security expenditure (Wildeman 1988), it is clear that growth in the private sector will continue to outstrip that in the public policing sector for the forseeable future.

France: The oldest private security companies in France were established at the end of the Second World War. Ocqueteau (1987) estimates that there are now 96,000 private security guards in France, compared with 110,000 policemen and 90,000 gendarmes. This figure correlates roughly with Tarlet's (1988) estimate that 600 companies employ about 80,000 personnel. In 1987 turnover in the alarm industry was well over 3,000m francs, and that sector is expanding at a rate of 26 per cent per annum (Hazelzet 1988).

Belgium: In Belgium, laws of 1934 and 1936 ban private militias. In order to operate, therefore, private security companies have to obtain a certificate from the Ministry of the Interior exempting them from that legislation. At present, thirteen companies have obtained such exemption. Together, these companies employ 7,000 people, though 90 per cent of them belong to three large enterprises. (Information from Belgian Ministry of the Interior.) The police force in Belgium numbers about 15,000.

Netherlands: A major expansion of the Netherlands security market occurred in the 1970s. As in other European countries, that boom has now steadied, but Holland offers a valuable export market for major producers, there being hardly any indigenous manufacture of security components (Horsthuis 1987). One recent estimate (Slinn 1988) puts the number of security guards in the Netherlands at 8,000. However, this is certainly an under-estimation. In 1979 the Dutch ministry of justice registered 9,000 security guards and by 1987 the number registered had risen to 13,000. In comparison the Dutch police force has a strength of 35,000 (Hoogenboom 1989). Annual sales in the Dutch security market total about Dfl. 2,000m ($1 Billion), 80 per cent of which derives from gatekeeping, surveillance, money-guarding, etc. (Horsthuis 1987). This sector is expected to achieve dramatic expansion in the next few years with government projections indicating that guard numbers could reach 30,000.

Spain: In 1972 'Transportes Blindados', a company for the transportation and guarding of valuables, using secure vehicles, was established. Effectively, this signalled the start of the Spanish private security industry. A law of 1974 made it compulsory for security measures to be used when transporting and depositing funds and, from that time, companies began to develop quickly. Further impetus to expansion was given by a 1984 decree making it obligatory for all banks and credit companies to set up security departments and install protective measures in all of their offices. Having grown from virtually nothing in 1972, the volume of business reached almost 150,000m pesetas (£750m) in 1986 and over the last few years there has been an average growth of between 10–15 per cent per annum (Gomez-Baeza 1988). About 1,000 companies are registered with the Ministry of the Interior and total employment is around 25,000 (60,000 if indirect and related industries are included), though this does not include unregistered firms. Of registered firms 35 per cent operate in Madrid and 25 per cent in Cataluna. Some 350 companies are involved in the installation, sale, and maintenance of security products, about 150 of which are manufacturers. The remainder specialize in legal and technical consultancy and in the transportation and guarding of funds. As industry and commerce rely on contract firms, rather than the recruitment of in-house personnel, considerable possibilities exist for further expansion.

Italy: Here, again, rapid expansion occurred during the 1970s, before which private security hardly existed. A survey of the industry carried about by Reseau Market Research (Milan) showed that out of every 100 companies, 50 per cent were established between the years 1970–5, and the rest after 1976. As in other countries, the alarms sector is increasing more rapidly than others, partly assisted by amalgamations and partnerships (Tura 1985).

Israel: Since 1975 the number of licensed private investigators in Israel has increased by 400 per cent. Private security companies have also mushroomed in the last decade, the number of such companies increasing by between 20 and 30 per cent, and the number of employees by between 200 and 300 per cent. Most companies have about 100 employees, but several have as many as 1,000 (some of them part-time). The number of guard companies has risen by 60 per cent since 1975 and employment in this sector is estimated to be 23,000. Geva (1989) suggests that since there are equivalent numbers employed on an in-house basis, the total of 'about 40,000 employees acting in some kind of security function' is more than twice the number of (17,000) police officers found in Israel. The average security guard in Israel has less than 4 years' experience. There is no legislation concerning age or standards of training for most guards, 20 per cent of whom are over 65, and 48 per cent of whom are aged between 45 and 65. (Information from Geva 1989, and Ministry of Police, Jerusalem.)

Finland: Private organizations carrying out policing functions existed in Finland between the wars. One of these ('Export-Peace') was established by business leaders and had the goal of ensuring production during strikes and defending the property of private enterprises. Its membership was largely identical with that of the Finnish Civil Guard (Suojeluskunta, or SK), a semi-military organization established to oppose the growing revolutionary movements dating back to the period before Finnish Independence (1917). The SK was legitimated in law in 1918 and its volunteer members supported the police and army during periods of instability, finally being abolished in 1944. In that same year a decree was promulgated on private security firms. Firms in Finland are licensed by law. In 1976 there were 144 valid licences for firms, and 2,500 authorized guards. By 1983 there were 160 firms and 2,650 guards. (By comparison, in 1983 there were 9,000 police officers.) Most firms and personnel are found in the south, many of them in and around Helsinki. Turnover is increasing at about 10 per cent per annum (Laitinen 1987).

Suomen Teollisuuden Vartiointi (STV) is the biggest security company in Finland, with a market share of 45–50 per cent. (The second largest company is only about half as big.) The company was established in 1959 to provide static guarding, beat patrols, cash-in-transit services, and special security. Since then it has diversified, now being heavily committed to technological and electronic security (flexi-time control systems, access control systems, CCTV, etc.) and to risk management. The company is divided into three constituent parts: a guarding unit and an alarms unit, which together employ about 1600 people; and a separate security company (STW) established in 1985. STV is a member of the 'Ligue Internationale des Societies de Surveillance' and is closely integrated into the multinational security market. It is, at present, distributing a range of Securitas access control products. The Managing Director of the company (a former assistant professor in electronic engineering) who joined STV in the late 1970s is one of a new, highly qualified breed of security managers. In an interview he informed me that the Finnish security industry enjoyed its greatest expansion between 1975 and 1985, and was now in a steady state. Future opportunities, for growth were probably limited, he suggested. This might be due, in part, to the low Finnish crime rate. Future expansion might, therefore, be directed towards commercial security. In STV considerable emphasis was being placed upon the expansion of the company's risk-management expertise, where new potential was evident.

In comparison with the Swedish private security industry, which dates back to the turn of the century, Finland's is still relatively small. Nevertheless, it is developing within a multi-national context. This internationalization of the industry is precipitated, in part, by the development of sophisticated electronic security technology. A good example of this occurred recently when Wartsila Security (Helsinki), whose subsidiaries have considerable investments in electronic locking systems, decided to expand into the international access-control business. In order to do this it agreed to buy Cardkey Systems Inc from Eyedentify Inc for $40m. (Eyedentify is involved in the marketing of an access-control system which can differentiate between the colours of human irises.) Cardkey's head office is in California, but it has a sales and manufacturing subsidiary (Cardkey Systems Ltd) in Reading, plus a regional office in Manchester, and other offices in the Netherlands and West Germany (reported in *Security and Protection Equipment* October 1989).

Australia: In 1986 the Australian police force (state plus federal) numbered 37,358. In comparison, four major private security companies (Chubb, Wormalds, Mayne Nickless, and Metropolitan Security Services) alone employed 16,000 personnel (Ashby 1982). Ashby also estimated that 100,000 private security patrols/inspections occurred nightly during the early 1980s. Other sources (quoted by Page (1982)), suggest that as many as 50,000 persons are employed in the industry, whilst Rau (1989a) later puts the figure

at between 60,000 and 90,000. In terms of growth rates the annual
turnover in 1977 was $150m compared to $360m in 1982. Currently,
the industry is expanding by 12–14 per cent per annum and private
personnel outnumber police by approximately 2:1 (Rau 1989c).

Though there has been little academic research on private
security in Australia as a whole, Corns (1987) has examined the
position in Victoria. Here, in 1986, there were 8,978 public police
officers of whom 5,655 were constables or senior constables
engaged in operational patrol. Corns collected data on private
security from three sources: (i) Firearms Registry figures showed
that almost 3,000 applications were made for pistol licences in that
year (99 per cent of which came from private security firms). (ii)
The Private Agents Act 1966 (Victoria) requires annual licensing of
guards (companies) and watchmen (personnel). By November 1987
1,059 Guards Licences had been issued to firms, and 7,000
Watchmen's Licences to individuals. (iii) Companies themselves
provided some information. One major firm reported that 4,000
personnel were employed in patrol and guarding functions in
Victoria. None of these figures, of course, includes unlicensed
personnel, store detectives, security advisers, etc. Rau (1989b)
claims that, currently, Victoria has nearly 9,000 registered guards,
watchmen and inquiry agents, unlicensed workers outnumbering
registered ones by two to one.

New Zealand: Though here, as elsewhere, data on the size of the
industry is to be treated with caution, figures on rates of expansion
during the 1980s are more reliable than in many other countries,
since the industry was surveyed by the Department of Statistics in
1980–1 and again in 1986–7. Although demonstrating that the
industry is still small by European standards, these statistics show
that it has undergone a remarkable growth over that 6-year period.
In 1980–1 there were 1,129 persons engaged in full-time employment in the sector. By 1986–7 that number had increased by 85.9 per
cent to 2,099. (Data provided by New Zealand Department of
Statistics.) Interestingly, a later estimate puts the number of
registered guards at something in excess of 5,000 in 1990. (Data
provided by New Zealand Police.) The department of statistics
survey also showed that the number of enterprises had increased:
group enterprises from 47 to 166 (an increase of 253.2 per cent) and
activity units from 75 to 201 (an increase of 168 per cent). What

appears to have happened here is that the security market has expanded with the entry of smaller firms (the average number of personnel per unit having fallen from fifteen to ten). Total income from sales of goods and services stood at more than $75m in 1986–7 an increase of 214.3 per cent over the 6-year period. Net pre-tax profit stood at just over $6m, an increase of 428 per cent. Average wages in the industry in 1986–7 stood at about $16,000. (This compares with an average of $21,424 – before tax and including overtime – for male workers in 1986. This figure is calculated from data provided by the New Zealand High Commission, London.)

New Markets and Future Developments

Finally, there is the question of new markets. Clearly, there is scope for expansion by established companies into less developed markets, something which will be accelerated in Europe after 1992. In Spain, for example, the underdeveloped electronic security sector is an obvious target for foreign penetration (Gomez-Baeza 1986). Equally, there may be potential for expansion into both Middle Eastern (Anon 1985) and African markets (Boyd 1986).

Perhaps more significant are the recent changes in Eastern Europe which have been accompanied by the appearance of private security agencies. In Poland, these new agencies are providing a haven for former state-security personnel whose numbers shrank from 23,000 to 3,000 in 1989–90 (BBC Radio 4 'Eurofile', broadcast 1 April 1990). Recently, it has been reported that Valentin Kosyakov, a KGB officer and former employee of the Ministry of the Interior, has established branches of the 'ALEX Security Agency' in Moscow and Leningrad. Most of his eighty full-time and forty part-time armed agents are recruited from the police and the KGB (Edgington 1990). Kozyakov has also become a member of the Association of British Investigators, a body affiliated to the Internationale Kommission d' Detektiv-Verbrand'. The ABI has also had membership enquiries from investigative agencies in Poland and Hungary, keen to take over business previously handled by the state (Young 1990).

Anyone with remaining doubts about the potential for further expansion of the private security sector should, however, look no further than China. In Beijing three security services have been established in recent years. One of them, the Beijing Electronic

Security Service Company, established in July 1987, has, according to recent reports, enjoyed 'brisk business'. The company, which employs mostly retired policemen and ex-servicemen, dresses its guards in dark-blue uniforms and arms them with cudgels and walkie-talkies. Predictably, it keeps close contact with the Public Security Bureau and assists public security police in maintaining order (Liao Wang 1988).

REGULATION AND CONTROL IN BRITAIN

There is no statutory regulation of private security in Britain, the only legislation directed at the industry being the 1975 Guard Dogs Act. The Northern Ireland (Emergency Provisions) Act 1987 Part 3 ('Regulation of the Provision of Security Services') does, however, regulate the industry there.

Self-regulation is carried out, however, through trade associations. The most prominent, the BSIA, has an annual budget of £1m and a membership of only 124 firms. However, these firms employ 70,000 people and, according to the Association, represent 90 per cent of the industry's turnover. In 1982, the Association established the National Inspectorate of Security Guard, Patrol and Transport Services (the so-called 'Manned Services Inspectorate'). This body regulates guard, patrol, cash-in-transit, and secure parcels services, as well as store detectives. In 1987 a Security Systems Inspectorate was also set up to regulate the electronics sector (CCTV, access control, etc.).

James Hargadon, Inspector General of the Manned Services Inspectorate, has described how the process of self-regulation works (Hargadon 1988). Applicants to join the BSIA have to provide trading records and accounts for a 2-year period. Employment records for all staff are checked back over a 20-year period, and all company operations (control rooms, sites, supervisors, guards, clients, etc.) are scrutinized by a vetting committee of two managing directors from member companies. If satisfied, recommendation for membership can be made to the BSIA Council. Once companies become members they are inspected two or three times a year and, in the event of an adverse report, the company is allowed 3 months to correct defects before reinspection. In cases where companies fail to resolve defects, a disciplinary code can be applied and a disciplinary board (including one lay member) may be convened. In principle, that board can award penalties ranging from a reprimand to fines or expulsion.

Several things may be noted about this process. First, to date 'there is no record of any member being expelled for disciplinary procedures' (Jordan & Sons Ltd 1989: 6). Second, BSIA codes allow 'provisional employment for commercial reasons' (Hargadon's evidence to House of Commons 1990a). What this means is that applicants can be appointed to firms before the 20-year employment check has been made. At present, such a check takes so long that applicants in areas of relatively high employment, if required to await its results, would simply find work elsewhere. In lieu of this, member firms are expected to carry out telephone checks of applicant's employment records for the past 5 years only. Hargadon's evidence also indicated two other points: first, that all inspections of companies are pre-arranged; and second, that out of a total of 40,000 guards covered by the Inspectorate, 'maybe 200' would have their records checked in any one year.

Concern about the inadequacy of self-regulation has been exacerbated by two other factors. The first, is the promise (or threat) that after 1992 the industry will be subjected to European standards of regulation. The second, is the police's changing attitude towards the industry. In 1977 the Home Office asked chief constables whether they had evidence of security companies being used for criminal ends. Their response at that time was that no more crime was being committed in the industry than in other enterprises handling large sums of money (Home Office 1979). In 1988, however, an ACPO questionnaire sent to all chief constables, discovered that no less than 609 firms were giving 'cause for concern'. The report identified 721 specific problems arising with security firms, the majority of which (289) related to alarm installers. In addition to this the report found that in 326 firms, an employer or employee had a criminal record (ACPO 1988). As a result of the survey ACPO threw its full weight behind a campaign for controls to be placed on the industry, either through statutory licensing, or through legislation to establish self-regulation.

Since the ACPO report (1988), there has been a flurry of new initiatives, though essentially they follow the lines of the traditional dispute: either statutory licensing of the industry using the existing BSIA Inspectorates for regulatory purposes (the traditional BSIA position); or statutory licensing with regulation by an independent inspectorate (the view held by critics such as Bruce George). The first of these alternatives (what one might call 'statutory self-regulation') has been proposed both by Sir Stanley Bailey, Chief Constable of Northumbria and Sir John Wheeler, Director General of the BSIA.

Bailey (1988; 1989) proposes the establishment of a Registration and Regulatory Board. This Board would require associations to establish codes of practice and arrange for the provision of inspectorates. It would finance itself from an annual licensing fee of £5–£6 per head. Wheeler's proposals were put forward in another aborted Security Industry Bill (1990), which had proposed the establishment of an inspectorate, formed from and funded by the industry. The Bill proposed that employees be barred from office unless they were in receipt of a certificate, issued by the police, confirming that they held no relevant previous convictions.

The self-regulatory approach is clearly seen by its advocates as similar to the model adopted by established professional bodies. (Wheeler expects, for example, that the BSIA should receive a charter from the Privy Council.) However, as Draper (1978) argues, the fact that the industry has no entry qualifications makes the 'professional' model difficult to sustain. Moreover, Wheeler is decidedly equivocal about the scope of the legislation. The stipulations of the Bill appear to be universal in their application, yet elsewhere he argues that interference with the activities of small security firms is both unwarranted (in the absence of 'some clear evidence of serious public harm' (Wheeler 1989b: 29)) and contrary to Department of Trade policies on deregulation.

In May 1990 Bruce George again moved a Bill to provide for the establishment of a Private Security Registration Council under Home Office control, pointing out that since taxi drivers, betting shops, nursing homes, and consumer-credit agencies were licensed, there seemed little point in making an exception of the private security industry. Again the Bill failed to receive a second reading, though George's proposals have been described by Roy Hattersley, the Shadow Home Secretary, as 'the basis for proper government legislation' (Mason 1991: 24).

Since then there have been two developments. In March 1990, IPSA sponsored the establishment of a national, voluntary, computerized register for the industry (the British Security Registration Board). Though IPSA would prefer statutory registration, it hopes that the Board, run by a non-profit-making body, will give self-regulation some credibility. The scheme will initially be marketed by 421 firms affiliated to IPSA, and officials will issue registration booklets to employees which, it is hoped, may eventually become 'passports' to employment (*The Times* 20 March 1990). At the same time, the Home Office is 'still considering' a report from a working group to see 'whether there is scope for further improvment in self-regulation' (*Hansard* 21 December 1988 col. 384 [w]; 23 March 1990 col. 756 [w]). Amongst the issues to be considered here are whether means can be found to enable companies to submit applicants names to the police for checking on the Police National Computer, and whether companies can be exempted from the provisions of the Rehabilitation of Offenders Act 1974, both of which remain major stumbling blocks to effective vetting.

REGULATION AND CONTROL OUTSIDE BRITAIN

Statutory regulation of the private security industry is common-place in North America. In the USA, although statutory legislation exists in about two-thirds of states, its form and scope vary considerably. Some states, such as Ohio, have very comprehensive policies on the regulation of private agents, laying down mandatory conditions on training (McCormick *et al.* 1983). In other cases, however, there is virtually no regulation at all and it is rare for any minimum level of education, training, or prior experience to be required by the licensing authority. Overall, then, there is 'a lack of uniformity and comprehensiveness' (Kakalik and Wildhorn 1977: 151), and it seems unlikely that this has changed since the Rand survey in the 1970s. In 1984, the *New York Times* was still able to refer to the 'vigorous lobbying efforts' of the industry in resisting increased control over guards in New York State (cited in South 1988: 135).

Future regulation of the industry in Britain is, in fact, more likely to be influenced by European and Commonwealth systems than those of the USA. Events in Europe are already putting pressure on leaders of the industry in Britain. In 1987 the Committee of Ministers of the Council of Europe agreed that governments of member states should 'enact, revise and if necessary complete regulations governing initial authorisation, periodical licensing and regular inspection ... of security and surveillance companies or encourage the profession to adopt its own regulations' (Bailey and Lynn 1989: 35). It has also been noted by several writers (Draper 1978; South 1988) that regulatory systems operating in Australia and New Zealand might provide future models for Britain. This chapter therefore concludes with a short review of these different systems.

Europe: All European Community countries, with the exception of Britain and Eire have legislation in force or in preparation. In some cases this legislation dates back many years. In Holland, for example, a law of 1938 preventing the setting up of private armies, is still the basis of current regulation through the Ministry of Justice.

In France the industry is regulated by an Act of 1983 which amongst other things (i) requires employees to carry identity cards and wear badges and uniforms; (ii) requires employees to have no criminal record; (iii) stipulates that companies may not intervene in industrial conflicts, or engage in racial, political, or religious discrimination (Tarlet 1988).

At present the Belgian industry is regulated by laws of 1934 and 1936 which, like the Dutch legislation, prohibit the setting up of private armies. The system is controlled through the Ministry of the Interior and companies have to gain an exemption from these laws (in the form of a Royal decree) before they can operate. Award of the exemption certificate is for 3 years, subject to companies satisfying certain conditions which include stipulations that: (i) companies shall not present themselves in a way which leads the public to confuse security personnel with public police; (ii) companies shall inform the mayor and local police of their security activities and respond to all requests for information about such activities made by the authorities; (iii) all companies shall submit to inspections undertaken by the Ministry; (iv) all companies shall submit annual reports to the Ministry. This legislation has, however, been replaced by a new law of 10 April 1990, that came into effect on 29 May 1991. That law has wider coverage than the previous legislation, since it applies not just to guarding companies (*enterprises de gardiennage*), but also to alarm companies (*enterprises de securité*) and, indeed, to all security services provided in places to which the public have access (*services internes de gardiennage*).

In Spain the police and the Ministry of the Interior are responsible for controlling security firms. Legislation of 1978 established regulations for the 'Vigilantes Jurados' ('agents of authority') employed by private organizations. Companies apply for the appointment of individuals as agents and appointment involves taking a test and an oath of office before a civil governor. Candidates for employment as bonded guards have to be of legal age, have completed military service (or have promised to do so), and should be without any criminal record. Regulation is, however, only partial since some security services offered by the industry (unarmed and unbonded guards, bodyguards, personal escorts) are not covered by the legislation (Gomez-Baeza 1986; 1988; MacDonald 1985).

Legislation in Scandinavia is well developed. In Sweden an Act of 1974 regulates the industry through local authorities and the police, whilst Danish legislation of 1986 regulates through the Ministry of Justice. In Finland the industry is regulated by the Ministry of the Interior through an Act of 1983. This Act specifies that all operating companies have to be Finnish-owned, all responsible officers being vetted through a private security board. Licences are issued for guards, companies, and for operating areas of companies. Guards must be aged between 18 and 65 and are required to undergo a minimum of 40-hours training. The police are responsible for the issue of guard licences. These are issued for 5 years but the police check criminal records every 2 years to ensure that holders retain an unblemished record. In Helsinki about 7–8 per cent of applicants are initially rejected by the police, a further 1 per cent withdrawing after biennial checks. (Details obtained from an interview with the Helsinki Police.) Guards can be issued with firearms for particular duties, though once a guard ceases to perform that duty the licence is revoked. In Finland all guards wear the same standard-issue uniform, companies being differentiated by a lapel badge bearing the company name or logo. As in Spain, there is some concern that 'receptionists' (bouncers) are used to protect commercial premises without being subject to legislative control.

Australia and New Zealand: There is no national regulatory code for the private security sector in Australia. However, in Victoria, a code existed until November 1989 when the state government implemented a policy of deregulation. The Private Agents Act (1966) required private investigators, security guards and watchmen to be licensed. Those seeking licences had to apply to a magistrates court, be of 'good character', have no convictions for harassment, stealing, fraud, or unlawful entry, provide three character references, and advertise their application in the *Government Gazette* so that members of the public wishing to do so could lodge objections. In 1989 the Law Reform Commission produced a draft bill amending the 1966 legislation in accordance with the principles of deregulation. The Commission's report proposed (i) that licensing of guards and enquiry agents should continue; (ii) that licensing should cease to apply to armed watchmen employed by (licensed) guard agents, and be replaced by self-regulation; (iii) that character references should no longer be required; (iv) that a licence should only be refused or suspended if the applicant had been found guilty of a relevant offence; (v) that guilt by association (e.g. 'mixing with known criminals', not being of 'good character') should cease to apply as a basis for rejecting applicants.

In New Zealand the relevant piece of legislation is the 1974 Private Investigators and Security Guards Act (amended 1978). The object of the Act is to protect the public from incompetence, dishonesty, and excessive zeal by private security personnel. It is also concerned to protect citizens' privacy. (In this regard, the Act prohibits investigators from taking photographs or making recordings without the written consent of the subject.) The legislation is administered by the Justice Department and vetting of applicants is carried out by the police. A barrister or solicitor is appointed by the Justice Department as Registrar of the Act. Included under the jurisdiction of the Act are private investigators, security guards, and those who enter property to install, to sell, to advise on the purchase of, or to monitor alarms, locks, cameras, and other devices. The Act excludes from its jurisdiction persons engaged by a licensee to assist in the maintenance of order on those premises ('bouncers'). (However, in view of concern about increasing violence on licensed premises, the inclusion of bouncers under the Act is one of several amendments under consideration at present.) It also excludes journalists, banks, credit bureaux, and those seeking, obtaining, or supplying information to the Crown, the police, or a local authority. All those covered by the Act are required to hold a licence which is renewed annually. Applications will be refused where the applicant has been convicted of a relevant criminal offence in the 10-year period before the application, and where a licence has been cancelled in the previous 5 years. Similar stipulations are laid down for the granting of certificates of approval to 'responsible employees' of private investigators and guards. The licence, once issued, carries a statement declaring that the holder possesses only the powers of an ordinary citizen. Section 66 of the Act specifically prohibits licence holders from doing anything likely to cause members of the public to believe them to be police officers. This section, in fact, prohibits not only the wearing of misleading uniforms and badges, but also bans any use of the word 'detective' for business purposes.

In the near future it is inevitable that Britain will come into line with other European countries on the issue of licensing, though whether it takes the form of statutory self-regulation or regulation by an independent body remains to be seen. At the international level, however, two issues are likely to dominate. First, given the multinationalization of private security and the 'Europeanization' of economic and political structures, to what extent can common standards of regulation be made to apply across different countries? Second, given the growing diversity of private security functions and the increased interpenetration of private, quasi-private, and public forms of policing, what forms of regulation of the 'mixed economy' of policing will be required in the twenty-first century?

Chapter 5

The private security sector II
Activities

Whereas the previous chapter considered the structure of the private security sector, the present one is concerned with its activities, the range of which is considerable: static guarding, mobile patrol, cash-in-transit, wage processing, undercover surveillance, guarding services, VIP protection, private investigation, risk management, specialized fraud investigation, consultative work related to industrial and domestic security, and so on. Moreover, the list of activities is growing. In the USA police forces have already contracted out a wide range of tasks to the industry: parking enforcement, traffic control, prisoner transfer, court security, non-injury accident investigation, special events policing, prison security, and crime prevention services. Indeed, it seems that there is neither a limit to the types of duties undertaken by private personnel (e.g. Scarborough Council's employment of uniformed guards to deter potential suicides from jumping off the local bridge which has become a suicide blackspot) nor to the industry's capacity to adapt to new situations (e.g. Securicor's 'Community Link' vans, which collect poll tax on behalf of local authorities from willing payees – as opposed to the private bailiffs employed by some local authorities to deal with recalcitrants).

To a considerable extent, of course, many of these security activities have become 'normalized'. Wheel-clamping by private security personnel, far from being a novelty, is now (grudgingly) accepted as another hazard of urban life. Yet, even mundane examples of this sort raise controversial questions about justice, equity, and accountability. Is it fair that there should be no standardization of charges for releasing vehicles from clamps? Is it reasonable for companies, subject to no public regulation or registration, to clamp vehicles on private property widely used by the public, or on property owned by public bodies? (The recent case of a patient who was 'clamped' whilst visiting the Casualty Department of Withington Hospital, Manchester, provides an excellent illustration of the problem.)

In principle, it is possible to provide an account of the activities of the private security sector merely by giving an exhaustive description of what it does. In practice, this is more difficult than it might seem. For one thing, it would be necessary to write a sizeable book in order to cover all of those activities. For another, that approach presupposes a clear definition of the boundaries of private security. In fact, such an absolute definition is difficult to draw. (Indeed, in some countries, it is virtually impossible. In Israel many commercially available security products were first developed by the Ministry of Defence (Slinn 1985) and, here, the boundaries between state security and private security are indistinct.)

For those reasons the approach taken here is a functional one. Rather than attempting to provide an exhaustive description of activities, I shall concentrate on a number of key functions carried out – though not necessarily exclusively – by the private sector. This approach is adopted for two reasons. First, by its very nature it raises the question of whether there are certain essential functions that define private security as an activity. (Much of the literature in police studies has grappled with that same question in respect of the 'essential role' of the public police.) Second, the functional approach provides an appropriate means for considering the changing relationship between public and private policing agencies: what several writers have described as the changing 'police division of labour'. Both of those issues will receive detailed examination in Chapter 9, though they also provide a background to the five areas of activity under consideration here.

AREAS OF ACTIVITY

Guarding and protection

One of the main activities of the private sector involves the guarding and protection of property and persons. Though such duties include the protection of industrial, commercial, and retail premises by uniformed security guards and non-uniformed 'bouncers' (activities which shade over into the preventative functions discussed later), attention is concentrated here on two examples of guarding activity which have become controversial.

The first of these is bodyguarding. As in other areas of the private security industry, bodyguarding tends to have its 'prestigious' and 'cowboy' operators. At one end of the market, there are a number of companies engaged in VIP protection. Here, profits can be considerable. In 1987 Control Risks, a company with offices in London, Melbourne, and Washington had a turnover of £4m and pre-tax profits of £363,000. Many of these companies employ ex-SAS officers, and some estimates suggest that as many as 40 per cent of special force personnel join security companies on leaving the service. One anonymous SAS veteran who runs an ex-special forces recruitment agency to provide personnel to security companies commented: 'We've had certain clients who have suddenly needed twenty men for a week. There is a floating core of ex-SAS guys in Hereford and we bring them in on a daily basis' (Nelson 1988). Ironically, some of these companies now favour statutory regulation the industry because of growing competition from 'cowboy' firms, staffed with nightclub bouncers, who are willing to undercut their prices.

If this first case illustrates the exchange of personnel between public and private security agencies (something to which I shall return later), the second touches directly on the public–private division of policing labour. This example concerns the guarding of military installations by private security companies, an issue which came to public attention after the IRA bombing of Deal Barracks in September 1989. Government policy on the employment of private guards was outlined by Tim Sainsbury MP, in a Parliamentary answer of 5 July 1988: 'It is MOD policy to employ unarmed civilian security guards through private security firms on routine guarding tasks at military establishments to relieve trained service men for other more appropriate duties.' Sainsbury went on to state that the first contract was signed in 1978, such contracts only being placed 'when appropriate security criteria can be satisfied' (Hansard, 5 July 1988). MOD expenditure on private security, in fact, rose ten-fold between 1984–5 (when it stood at £461,000) and 1989–90 (when it totalled £4,418,000). By January 1990 a total of forty-six contracts, covering fifty-six establishments, and employing 500 guards were in operation (House of Commons 1990a).

Considerable controversy has arisen, however, about wage levels. The MOD admitted to the House of Commons Defence Committee that it tended to attract BSIA companies 'of the second rank', due to the wage levels paid to personnel. At Deal, guards received £120.60 for a 56-hour week, and the Chairman of the Guard and Patrol Section of the BSIA stated to the Committee that he would not be prepared to employ guards at the unduly low prices offered by the MOD. (Significantly, after the events at Deal, Reliance Security Services, the company contracted to guard the base, raised wage levels by 25 per cent.)

In a letter to *The Times* (29 May 1990) David Fletcher, Chief Executive of the BSIA, castigated the MOD for 'using price as the major determining factor in its choice of security', suggesting that, as a result, the Ministry would only get what it paid for. According to the findings of the Defence Committee Report, this appears to be the case. The worst example unearthed by the Committee was at a defence depot in North London where nineteen guards were employed at an annual cost of £150,000. For over a year the company received formal warnings from the MOD about its excessive turnover of staff, its failure to have enough staff on duty, and the fact that staff did not always wear the right uniform and were badly briefed. To add insult to injury, on more than one occasion guards were themselves responsible for committing acts of vandalism at the site. In spite of a poor record going back to 1988, however, the company's contract was not terminated until February 1990. Evidence presented to the Committee suggested that examples of this sort were by no means uncommon. Not only had acts of vandalism by guards occurred at other MOD sites. In some cases, guards fell asleep at their posts, were too physically weak to lift security barriers, or were afraid of the dark.

The Committee Report made a number of recommendations: that no new contracts should be issued to private firms until minimum standards are established by statutory legislation; that guards should be more strictly vetted; that existing contracts should be reviewed regularly; and that by May 1992 the MOD should assure Parliament that private guards are only employed at sites carrying no security risk, or where replacement by an MOD guard force has been ruled out. In autumn 1990, however, the Government rejected the Committee's proposal not to issue further contracts until regulatory legislation is pursued. At the same time, the MOD defended its mechanisms for vetting guards, adding that it would continue to use 'competent contract security companies to guard or to assist in the guarding of defence installations in appropriate circumstances' (*Guardian* 8 August 1990).

Critics of the present arrangements might express justifiable doubts about the adequacy of MOD screening mechanisms. In 1990, a member of staff from Office Cleaning Services, who had been employed for only one week and who had not been vetted for security purposes, was found cleaning the Commandant's office at Royal Military College, Sandhurst (*Sunday Correspondent* 17 June 1990). Specific criticisms apart, however, the issue of guarding defence bases has general implications for assessment of the division of policing labour between public and commercial agencies. To date, opinions on this issue tend to be polarized, the MOD view (that private security conforms with the 'value for money' principle) confronting the view of the MOD unions (that only service personnel, MOD police and properly vetted civilian guards should be entrusted with security functions at military bases). In a sense, however, this polarization of attitudes obscures two issues. First, given that guarding is a boring and unskilled task, are we to assume that commercial guards will do it less efficiently than service, police, or civilian personnel, whatever the circumstances – whether they are well paid or badly paid, trained or untrained, screened or unscreened? Second, is there some inherent reason why the security of defence installations should remain only in the hands of state personnel? In the short term there is every indication that these questions will continue to be ducked and, at present, the Government is seeking to find an even cheaper alternative to private security, through civilianization (see Chapter 6). Yet if some future statutory regulation of the industry were to introduce effective modes of public accountability and control over commercial firms, questions about the most appropriate public–private division of labour would be difficult to ignore.

Surveillance, intelligence and undercover work

In August 1990 Lord Chalfont, Deputy Chairman of the Independent Broadcasting Authority, Chairman Designate of the Radio Authority (which will regulate commercial radio) and a member of the new Independent Television Commission (which will award ITV franchises) resigned as general consultant to Hamilton Ingram, a private security company. Hamilton Ingram was engaged in helping existing ITV companies to win back their franchises and, in the course of doing so, sent out a letter offering to gather information for them about potential competitors. The letter indicated that the company specialized in 'gathering information for our clients which may not be available on a day-to-day basis in the course of normal business'. It further indicated that the firm's security division could protect the information of subscribing companies, noting that an increasing number of firms were having their premises 'swept' regularly to ensure that no electronic listening devices were being used against them. The letter added: 'We have every reason to believe that such tactics may be part of the TV franchise bid battles', and concluded by promising to work exclusively for one company (*Guardian* 24 August 1990).

Although Lord Chalfont resigned from Hamilton Ingram, declaring that the events had produced an unacceptable conflict of interests for him, the affair highlights several issues, not least the links between the industry and the political right. Between 1983 and 1986, Lord Chalfont had been a director of Hamilton Ingram's predecessor, Peter Hamilton (Security Consultants) Ltd. This company had grown out of Zeus Security Consultants, also run by Hamilton, one of whose tasks was to carry out covert investigation of anti-nuclear objectors at the Sizewell enquiry. Hamilton, a former military intelligence officer, like Chalfont, served in Malaysia and Cyprus, and both men have had long links with right-wing politics.

Private security companies situated at the respectable end of the market, declare opposition to any involvement in political activity, of course. Clauses in Securicor contracts have long made it clear that the company will not engage in strike-breaking. Nevertheless, it depends what one means by 'political' activity. Even in the 1960s Securicor had a Detective Division, headed by an ex-Metropolitan Police Assistant Commissioner, which advised on the bugging and debugging of conference facilities and the use of surveillance equipment, much to the annoyance of the trade unions (Clayton 1967). The industry would claim, of course, that activity of this sort is 'industrial', rather than 'political' in nature, and to some extent that is borne out in the range of services offered by leading companies. An annual report of the Burns Agency in the USA identified a number of 'managerial problems' which its undercover agents would be willing to investigate: 'inventory loss, pilferage, theft, fraud, falsification of records, forgery, poor employee morale, wilful neglect of machinery, waste of time and materials, theft of tools, unreported absenteeism, supervisory incompetence, [and] inadequate surveillance' (cited in South 1984: 178). Nevertheless, the dividing line between 'industrial' and 'political' activity is a very uncertain one, particularly when leading spokespersons from the industry, including Hamilton himself, have shown a marked willingness to equate trade union activity with industrial 'subversion'.

Direct links between the industry and right-wing politics are, in fact, commonplace. There is a long history of information gathering on workers by employers' trade associations, and several organizations specialize in drawing up blacklists of 'extremists' for industry, sometimes with the help of private enquiry agencies and other bodies engaged in similar work. In Britain the largest and best known of these blacklisting agencies is the Economic League, whose stated aim is that of 'exposing the experiences, the intentions and strategy of subversive organizations and providing positive education to combat misrepresentation by industrial agitators': cited in Bunyan (1977: 248).

Connections between private security and the political right are, if anything, more strongly established in the USA than in the UK. Here, for instance, there is a Society of Former Special Agents of the FBI, a body with almost 7,000 members, many of whom have senior positions in the private security industry, as employees of banks, oil companies, and contract security organizations. The Ford Motor Company has about twenty ex-FBI agents on its payroll, and as O'Toole (1978) indicates, their concern is as much with espionage and counter-espionage, as it is with industrial pilferage. Mention also should be made of the Law Enforcement Intelligence Unit (LEIU). This organization was established in 1956 by the then commander of the Los Angeles Police Department to co-ordinate information and, furthermore, keep it out of FBI hands. In effect, the LEIU is a large, domestic, private intelligence agency. Police forces can apply to join only when sponsored and endorsed by members. No outside bodies have access to LEIU information files, and much of the information gathered is of a directly political nature. As a former chairman of the LEIU told a Senate sub-committee, its function is: 'the gathering, recording, investigating, and exchange of confidential information not available through regular police channels' (cited in Marx 1987: 179). Such information, the spokesman added, is not restricted to that concerning organized crime.

The existence of the LEIU, as well as bodies such as the International Association of Chiefs of Police and the Association of Retired Intelligence Officers, demonstrates that formal and informal connnections exist between public police, private organizations and the state in the USA. LEIU members conduct secret investigations on behalf of corporations and other private bodies, using their status as contract police, to protect them from external scrutiny. In effect, public agents engage in what would be illegal acts if they were carried out in police time. (A typical example is the sharing of intelligence files on private citizens in a manner forbidden by law to public police officers.) This has not, however, prevented the LEIU from receiving state legitimation: first, in the form of generous grants and second, in its involvement in sharing data with the Justice Department (Wildeman 1988). The fact that the LEIU is, like any private firm, exempt from the Freedom of Information Act, means, of course, that the citizen gets the worst of both worlds: 'invasion of privacy and confidentiality, in addition to the impossibility of reviewing the accuracy of his/her intelligence file' (Wildeman 1988: 5).

In America it has been estimated that for every bugging device used by government agents, there are three hundred used by private security personnel, many of them in the hands of active or former police officers employed by private firms (Wildeman 1988). The situation in Britain may be less advanced, but the speed of development of surveillance technology is such that cheap, covert information gathering is now within the reach of any private body willing to invest in it.

Preventative activity

A considerable amount of debate has surrounded the preventative functions of private security. Private policing has increased the emphasis on proactive, rather then mere reactive, modes of intervention, aiming to intervene before crime is committed.

Shearing and Stenning, however, differentiate between two aspects of prevention:

> While the preventative role of the public police is almost universally referred to in terms of 'crime prevention', private security typically refer to their preventative role as one of 'loss prevention', thereby acknowledging that their principal concern is the protection of their clients' assets.
>
> (Shearing and Stenning 1981: 212)

The industry's commitment to loss prevention is well illustrated in the case of risk management. 'Risk management' is concerned with anticipating risks, planning for avoidance of risks whenever possible and, where it is not possible, shifting risks to another location (e.g. to an insurer). A recent commentary on the industry noted that risk management is now, itself, big business, with large accountancy firms and insurance companies offering advice, alongside a new breed of small, independent consultancies. Significantly, Securicor has now set up its own risk-management consultancy (Ashworth 1990). Pomeranz's (1988) list of some of the main elements of risk management ('listing potential causes of loss', 'identifying threats likely to cause loss', 'quantifying estimated loss') demonstrates clearly that the sole concern of the strategy is to prevent loss, rather than to prevent crime. Given this priority, it is clear why security officers in industrial and commercial undertakings are less concerned with applying the principles of public justice, than with invoking the standards of commercial expedience. Hence, those found stealing from employers are as likely as not to avoid referral to the police, receiving instead some version of informal or commercial justice.

Though there is much to be said for the view that private security is concerned primarily with loss prevention, this is by no means its exclusive concern, however. After all, in some cases, it seeks to prevent crime in public places. At the New Jersey Bell Telephone Company in Newark a cordon of private security guards rings the building each night at 5.00 p.m., providing safe passage for commuters wishing to reach railway stations (Tucker 1985). Activity of this sort, whereby private security penetrates public space and engages in activities hitherto the prerogative of public police, would appear to be on the increase. Some of these activities, moreover, seem to be of the traditional 'crime prevention' type (though I shall say more on the 'crime' and 'loss' distinction later).

Take, for instance, the case of residential patrols. Boothroyd's (1989) survey indicated that in Britain there were at least 504 non-police patrols funded by local authorities, businesses or residents. Of these, 239 were contracted by local authorities, 223 by local businesses, and two by residents. Such developments have arisen because of the police's inability to meet the level of public demand for a visible uniformed police presence on the streets. Private patrols are by no means restricted to Britain, however. Corns (1987) describes the situation in Victoria, Australia, where influential groups of tenants, dissatisfied with public police services, lobbied the Ministry of Housing to engage private security companies for residential patrol. Effectively, this exercise of consumer preference enabled tenants to have a right of veto over who should police their neighbourhoods. In Melbourne, one company, benefiting from the growth in fear of crime, has introduced a specialized 'Home Watch' programme. For a fee, groups of home owners can have their street patrolled during the day, or if they require it, their individual homes routinely checked.

Such provision is likely to expand in the future, given finite police resources, growth of crime, growth of fear of crime, and increasing demands from citizens for consumer choice. Simultaneously, there is likely to be a growing tendency for public police forces to withdraw from some traditional areas of preventative activity. In Holland NASEC, a Nijmegen-based private security company, has taken over first response to intruder alarm calls, the police only being notified when someone has actually broken into a building (Slinn 1988). Likewise, the police in New Zealand have now shed their initial response to alarm calls.

In Britain another area into which private security shows signs of expanding is the policing of transport facilities. In the past such facilities have either been policed by public forces or by the 'hybrid' forces discussed in the following chapter. Certainly, there seems to be considerable opportunity for private penetration of such facilities. Recently, Tarmac has been drawing up proposals for the privatization of a 60-mile section of the M40 motorway and, together with three other companies, is putting together bids for the proposed extension of the M62, with the possibility of having 'executive lanes' running alongside the main carriageway (McLean

1989). Plans have also been announced for nine private toll roads and river crossings – including those over the Severn Estuary, the River Tamar, and the River Mersey. In making the announcement, Cecil Parkinson, then Secretary of State for Transport, added that the Government was 'willing to consider proposals for the private financing of any scheme in the roads programme', as well as for toll roads not in the programme (*Independent* 5 April 1990). The question arising here, of course, is who will have responsibility for policing such private facilities?

Already there is some indication that private security companies have expanded into the transport field. At the beginning of 1989 Sealink ended its contract with the British Transport Police, recruiting a private security firm, Protective Security Systems, to police Parkstone Quay in Harwich. Sealink provoked considerable controversy when it arranged for security guards to be sworn in as Special Constables under s. 79 of the Harbours, Docks and Piers Clauses Act 1847, though the security manager at Parkstone claimed that constabulary status was necessary in order for officers to arrest illegal immigrants or act in the prevention of terrorism (Stronach 1989). In fact, Harwich is one of seven ports where security is now in the hands of private companies, though a recent report by the International Maritime Bureau described security at one of these ports as 'utterly appalling' and open to terrorist attack.

The potential for private security to have an expanded role in the prevention of terrorism has also increased with the passing of the Aviation and Maritime Security Act in September 1990. The Act places considerable emphasis on requiring port authorities to search harbour areas, ships, persons and property. Recognizing the impossible strain that this requirement would place on police forces, however, the Act gives powers of search to constables or 'other persons' specified by the Secretary of State. Private security guards have also had the statutory power to search airline passengers and their luggage since 1973. (Those powers were contained in the Protection of Aircraft Act of that year, that legislation being superseded, first by the Aviation Security Act 1982 and then by the legislation of 1990.) Here, again, there would seem to be considerable scope for the industry to extend its preventative activities. In the USA there are more than 6,000 private security personnel engaged in the direct screening of airline pasengers alone (Crenshaw 1988), though the level of effectiveness of such personnel leaves much to be desired. In 1986 the Parliamentary Select Committee on Transport reported training amongst private security employees subcontracted to the British Airports Authority to be virtually non-existent (Smith 1987).

Investigation and detection

Despite the industry's preoccupation with loss prevention and evidence of its expansion into some areas of conventional crime prevention, it cannot be categorized in exclusively preventative terms. In the past, there has also been a tendency to underestimate the extent to which private security agencies engage in investigative and detective functions. To some extent, this is understandable since, if one adopts a long, historical perspective, it is true that there has been 'a glacial drift from a detection to protection speciality' (Morn 1982: ix). Morn's point is that during the twentieth century private security agencies abandoned their earlier crime-detecting function in order to specialize in the protection of property. At the same time, public police forces began to concentrate more and more on the detection of crime, abandoning some of their patrol functions.

Though true as an historical generalization, that view obscures the fact that private security agencies engage, more and more, in specialized investigative activity, often at the expense of public police forces. In part, this is due to the inability of police organizations (and the law itself) to keep up with the sophisticated techniques of those engaged in large-scale fraud. In consequence, there are now a great number of private companies advertising themselves as specialists in the detection and prevention of commercial and computer fraud throughout Europe. In Holland, for example, insurance companies, banks and industrial corporations have been recruiting police detectives to investigate internal insurance and cheque frauds, and the private sector has developed an extensive computerized data bank of commercial fraud, far superior to anything held by the police (Judge 1988: Hoogenboom 1989). In Britain, 'hybrid' bodies, such as the Post Office Investigation Department (see Chapter 6), cognizant of the police's inability to deal with commercial fraud, are also seeking to penetrate the 'cheque book fraud market'.

The other reason for the privatization of fraud investigation, of course, is the fact that it remains private. In 1990 it was reported that four clearing banks and one merchant bank had employed Network Security Management to tackle computer hackers who, having penetrated their security system, were engaged in blackmail. The banks had decided not to notify the police because they felt that exposure of the crime might threaten public confidence in their operations (*Independent on Sunday* 14 October 1990). Sensitivity of this sort is nothing new, of course. In 1984 employees stole a total of $382m dollars from US banks – nine times the amount stolen by bank robbers. More often than not, however, banks choose to operate a private justice system, rather than prosecute offenders (Lipman and McGraw 1988). This 'calculated exercise of discretion against invoking the formal criminal justice process' (Stenning and Shearing 1980: 222) is understandable, given the object of loss prevention. After all, washing one's dirty linen in public is both counterproductive and pointless when deviance is defined 'in instrumental rather than moral terms' (Shearing and Stenning 1983: 503).

Some indication of the factors guiding the exercise of corporate discretion is found in the case of insurance fraud (Clarke 1989). Clarke notes that, in general, there is a reluctance on the part of insurance companies to take 'bold steps' to combat fraud. This attitude is shaped by a number of legal, ethical, organizational, and political considerations: the fact that in law an exaggerated claim does not constitute fraud, even if the intent itself was fraudulent; the fact that actual fraud (e.g. claiming for items which do not exist) is difficult to prove, and that failure to prove it may provoke a civil suit; the fact that companies have a strong service ethic which discourages the denial of claims, thereby exposing the tensions between conflictual and co-operative approaches to the problem; the fact that a policy of resistance to false claims, once communicated to the public, may drive potential clients to seek insurance with competitors; and the fact that publicity on this issue is invariably bad publicity. In consequence, the organization 'manages' the treatment of doubtful and complex claims through loss adjusters (smaller and simpler ones being dealt with by internal claims inspectors). Loss adjusters are contracted to act as intermediaries 'in a private, semi-formal negotiation between insurer and insured, which is intended to protect the insurer's interest in avoiding a public and formal confrontation'. In effect, Clarke suggests that the resources exist to tackle fraud effectively, but 'at root there is a fundamental incompatibility between the profit-oriented objective of the insurance industry ... and vigorous fraud control' (Clarke 1989: 17; 18).

The conclusion that a public policy of fraud control is incompatible with the ethic of profit, seems to be borne out by evidence from the USA where fraud investigation units have sprung up inside the insurance industry. In an analysis of Special Investigation Units (SIUs) set up by the automobile insurance sector, Ghezzi (1983) notes that the investigative process is entirely unregulated, SIUs often collecting information by illegal means. In the USA, as compared to Britain, however, there is far less sensitivity about public image, and SIUs publicize their existence in order to deter fraudulent claimants. The net result of all this is a cost-effective strategy, firms saving more from their reduced pay-outs than the total cost of their outlay on the investigative process. Yet, despite the fact that SIUs exchange information with public police agencies, this hardly amounts to a public policy of fraud control, given that the justice meted out is entirely informal in nature.

In referring to detective and investigative functions, mention should also be made, of course, of the private investigator. Here, reality is distorted by competing media images: the seedy 'gumshoe' versus the slick 'private eye'. Moreover, the abundance of media representations contrasts sharply with the invisibility of the private detective in the real world, there being few reliable estimates of how many people are engaged in detective work. One thing which is certain, however, is that operatives carry out diverse activities: tracing missing persons, process serving, undercover work for industry, vetting prospective employees, executive and diplomatic protection, insurance claims, infringements of patents, investigation for credit-rating agencies, bailiff work, debt collecting, and – to a lesser extent nowadays – matrimonial work. There is also a tendency towards the emergence of corporate and multifunctional agencies, though lone investigators still persist to sustain the media stereotype. In America, for instance, small firms still dominate, the median number of employees being only three (Cunningham and Taylor 1985).

Draper (1978) suggests, contrary to the media image, that

criminal investigation takes up only about 10 per cent of a private detective's time – usually on behalf of the prosecution or defence in a court case. A recent estimate by a representative from one of Britain's largest agencies (in Haselden 1990) concludes that the work divides into four, more or less equal, portions: commercial (e.g. tracing and recovering debt, locating assets such as lost vehicles), legal (e.g. process serving, statement taking), matrimonial (e.g. maintenance violation), and industrial (e.g. fraud, internal theft). Of these, the latter is expanding most quickly, given the police's inability to meet growing demand.

The industry's strong links with the police force is inevitable, given the problem of 'moonlighting' (of which more later) and the fact that private investigation is a normal second career for retired police officers. In the USA, in spite of the Privacy of Information Act, private investigators still get routine access to police data. In Cunningham and Taylor's (1985) study, 58 per cent of firms reported weekly contact with police detectives. Similarly, in Britain there have been well-publicized cases of police officers trading information from the Police National Computer to contacts in the industry. The existence of increasingly detailed data bases is, however, a problem in its own right, given that huge amounts of information are now freely available to private individuals and organizations with the knowledge to extract it. It is developments in this area (and in the area of surveillance technology (Mason 1987)) which are likely to have the greatest impact on private detection in the future.

Containment and control in the criminal justice system

The private security industry is also certain to have an expanded role in the wider criminal justice system. In a speech made in January 1990, David Waddington, then Home Secretary, stated his intention to examine ways in which voluntary and private sectors might play a greater role in supervision programmes, probation work, the provision of bail accommodation, the resettlement of offenders, and work with prisoners. In the case of probation, some indication of official thinking was given in the 1988 Green Paper, *Punishment, Custody and the Community* (Home Office 1988c), where it was suggested that private companies might have a part to play in implementing the new 'supervision and restriction orders'. In

June 1989, the Home Office announced that a plan to place 'punishment in the community' under the control of private sector managers was being considered. Effectively, once implemented, this would introduce market forces into probation. Non-custodial punishment, though still funded by central government, would be run like a business, with six regions under well-paid business managers. Private companies, voluntary bodies and a scaled-down probation service would bid for market shares. Probation officers would continue to supervise court orders and provide social inquiry reports, but the programmes in electronic tagging, day centres, drug and alcohol groups, community service, etc. would be put out to tender. The similarities between these proposals and the introduction of 'internal markets' in the health service should be obvious.

In February 1990 the Government outlined its programme of future legislation in *Crime, Justice and Protecting the Public* (Home Office 1990). One proposal contained in this document was that courts be given the power to confine people to their homes at certain times, through the imposition of curfew orders. Problems relating to the effective enforcement of these orders would be overcome, in most cases, by the electronic tagging of offenders. Since the curfew order could apply in its own right (with or without probation), some offenders subjected to it would not require the supervision of the probation service. In consequence, the Government proposes setting up an agency, separate from the probation service, with responsibility for enforcing curfew orders.

The 'specialist technical expertise' required to advise the agency on tagging, would come from the private sector. Private security companies are, in fact, already aware of the economic potential offered by these policy innovations. The first of three abortive Home Office pilot schemes used a tagging system produced by Marconi (the 'Home Hawk Curfew System'), the operation being supervised by Securicor personnel working from a control room at the Nottingham Crown Court. Despite the inconclusiveness of the pilot schemes (by April 1990 only seven people had completed the experiment, though the total cost amounted to more than £500,000), in September 1990 the Home Office expressed its determination to go ahead with tagging – possibly using a new 'super tag'. (Soon after, this commitment to tagging was confirmed, when the Criminal Justice Act 1990 was published.) Interestingly, officials were examining a new wrist tag designed by Siemens Plessey Defence Systems who, like other defence contractors, are looking to diversify into domestic security technology, given changing relations between eastern and western blocs.

Private security involvement in the control of so-called 'problem' populations is by no means new, of course. Since 1970, the Immigration Detention Centres at Harmondsworth, Heathrow, Gatwick, and Manchester have been managed by private security contractors. Until January 1989, when Group 4 won the Home Office contract, Securicor had been the only company involved in these operations. In 1983 the cost of security was estimated at £250,000 (*Observer* 27 March 1983), though, in fact, the real value of contracts is surrounded by 'a shroud of commercial secrecy' (Green 1989). When Group 4 took over the contract in 1989, its managers negotiated a lower, basic pay rate than Securicor had agreed, with the result that guards now seek to make up the difference by working extra shifts. What is still unclear, however – because the Home Office refuses to say – is whether reduced cost was the sole reason behind Securicor's loss of the contract, or whether (as some have suggested, following a critical report by HM Inspector of Prisons) there was dissatisfaction with their management of the Centres. Apart from the general lack of public knowledge of these operations, there is one other factor worth considering in respect of the recent changes. When Group 4 took over the contract, they purchased new vans and more sophisticated communications systems, as well as employing more guards than Securicor had previously done. Green (1989) suggests that the company is, therefore, unlikely to make much profit from this operation, regarding it rather as a means of establishing its credentials with the Home Office as a potential participant in any future private prison programme.

The issue of private prisons is, of course, now on the political agenda, following the publication of a discussion document, *Private Sector Involvement in the Remand System* (Home Office 1988b), which considered the possibility of private involvement in the building and management of new remand centres, as well as in prisoner escort and court duties. Immediately after the publication of this document, the Home Office appointed a group of management consultants to assess the viability of the proposals, their report appearing in February 1989 (Deloitte *et al.* 1989).

Despite the veneer of participatory involvement engendered by the Green Paper and the semblance of rational assessment of costs and benefits associated with the Deloitte Report, there is good reason to believe that the critical decisions on this matter had already been taken. Nicholas Hopkins, a spokesman for one of the consortia bidding for contracts, put the matter very succinctly when describing the Green Paper as 'a White Paper with Green edges' ('File on Four', BBC Radio 4, 14 November 1988).

The consortia, themselves, are predictable in their composition – a mixture of banks, property developers, private security companies, and private prison corporations. To date, three have been identified; the first consisting of Group 4, the Midland Bank, and Tarmac; the second ('UK Detention Services') made up of Mowlem, McAlpines, and the Corrections Corporation of America – the latter, somewhat bizarrely, a subsidiary of Kentucky Fried Chicken; and the third ('Contract Prisons PLC'), consisting of Rosehaugh, Racal-Chubb, and Pricor.

Justification for the privatization of remand is based largely on the American experience, members of the Home Affairs Committee having earlier visited private prisons operated by the Corrections Corporation. Despite the somewhat uncritical acceptance of the American evidence (House of Commons 1987a; 1987b; Gardner 1989; Ryan and Ward 1988; 1989a), it is increasingly clear that doubt remains as to the economic benefits of privatization. A report written for the US National Institute of Justice, says for example, that privatization can only cut costs without reducing services if 'perfect competition' is achieved in the prison market, or if firms introduce money-saving techniques: 'Right now, however, it is not clear whether, or how, these goals will be met. Corrections . . . is a labour intensive "business". Roughly three-quarters of the budget goes to personnel costs' (Dilulio 1988: 34). As Ryan and Ward say, it is difficult to apply the principle of 'market disciplines' to a case where 'there is only one customer – the state – and where the final consumers of the wares on offer – prisoners – have no part in deciding what to buy' (Ryan and Ward 1989b: 8). In fact, the hesitancy and lack of detail contained in the Deloitte Report confirm the level of uncertainty about costs and benefits: 'contractors felt unable to quantify the expected improvements in cost-effectiveness . . . [private] involvement would offer a reasonable prospect of improvement in cost-effectiveness' (Deloitte et al. 1989:

11, 12). Moreover, if as the report suggests (and the Home Office accepts), effective monitoring is essential for the achievement of public accountability, there are, as Matthews (1989b) indicates, likely to be extra administrative and bureaucratic costs. As Shaw concludes, then, 'no one is really now pretending that privatiz-ation will actually save us any money' (Shaw 1989: 49), though that is not to say, of course, that implementation will not go ahead.

Some of the implications of implementation are clarified in the Home Office discussion paper *Court Escorts, Custody and Security*, published in August 1990. The paper proposes that contracts for the movement of prisoners (currently undertaken by 2,400 police and prison officers) will be put out to tender on a regional basis with between five and ten contracts covering England and Wales. Securicor is one company to have expressed interest in a market estimated to be worth about £80m per annum. One issue of particular significance, however, is the question of what powers are to be held by private security guards employed as Prison Custody Officers and Court Security Officers (Bartle 1990). The Home Office has proposed that private security guards engaged in these activities would have the same powers and rights as police officers. It would, therefore, be an offence to obstruct or assault guards in the execution of their duty, and they would have the authority to search prisoners, stop them escaping, and prevent them committing offences. Clearly, there is a strong likelihood that the same powers would be granted to guards employed in private remand facilities. (For a somewhat equivocal Home Office view on this matter see Fulton 1989.)

As Shaw (1989) has suggested, the debate on private prisons is far from over. The overriding concern of critics, however, has been the issue of accountability. Few would doubt that privatization, under *certain* conditions, *might* produce benefits for a system in chaos. But many are concerned that a new policy-making elite has emerged to 'railroad' the privatization issue through Parliament. (In 1989 a dinner was held at the Carlton Club to discuss the remand proposals. The meeting was chaired by Lord Gardner (ex-Chairman of the Home Affairs Select Committee and Chairman of Contract Prisons PLC) and addressed by Douglas Hogg of the Home Office. Also present were personnel from the building industry, the private security sector, the City, and the legal profession.) Given the speed with which policies are unfolding, despite the lack of serious research, two issues are particularly worrying. First, there is the attempt to mimic the American experience under circumstances where many of the constitutional guarantees enjoyed by American prisoners are absent (Ryan and Ward 1989a). Second, there is the observation in HM Chief Inspector of Prisons Report on the Immigration Centres (Home Office 1989), that duties and standards set out in contracts between the Home Office and private security companies are unlikely to be enforceable in the courts through damages or injunction. If that were the case, the possibility of accountable private prisons would turn out to be a nonsense.

Chapter 6

Hybrid policing

At present, there are approximately 125,000 police officers in the forty-three constabularies in England and Wales. However, even excluding the private security sector from any calculation, this figure represents a gross underestimation of the numbers engaged in formal policing activity, whether they are in possession of constabulary powers or not. A 1977 review of law enforcement by agents other than police officers attached to Home Office forces, calculated that there were about 10,000 persons with full constabulary powers employed by almost forty special police forces in England and Wales. In addition to that, 16,000 prison officers also held the office of constable. When they went on to consider law-enforcement activity carried out by those lacking constabulary powers, the authors estimated that almost 21,000 persons employed by central government departments, plus a further 12,000 employed by local government departments, were engaged in such work. (All figures calculated from Miller and Luke 1977: Appendix D.) On that basis, then, it can be concluded that in the mid-1970s, over 57,000 people – excluding private security personnel and those involved in informal social regulation, which I shall say more about in the next two chapters – were engaged in formal policing activity of one sort or another, alongside Home Office constables. This chapter tries to cast some light on this huge but, as yet, unexplored field of policing.

This field comprises a complex morass of agencies, many of which are 'hybrid' organizations whose formal status and operating territories cut across the public–private divide. Classification of such bodies is difficult because of the wide variations between them. Some are organized, uniformed forces. Others consist merely of agents with the right to exert specific legal powers in given situations. Some employ personnel with full constabulary status. Others do not. In many cases constabulary powers, when held, are limited to a given spatial jurisdiction. But in certain critical circumstances, such limits may not apply. In most cases the powers of hybrid bodies are more circumscribed than those of public police. Yet, in some situations, the legal powers of state bodies and special police forces far exceed those of any sworn public constable.

Lidstone *et al.* (1980) drew a three-fold distinction between 'civil police' (the forty-three forces in England and Wales), 'private police' (uniformed private security guards with citizen powers) and 'other statutory forces' (forces created by statute, such as the British Transport Police or the Ministry of Defence Police). This classification though unambiguous, is rather limited since a number of bodies in government and industry – other than statutory forces – possess law-enforcement powers, either through statute or through administrative practice. This enables them to protect revenue (the Inland Revenue, the Customs and Excise), regulate commerce (the Companies Investigation Branch, the Insurance Division of the Department of Trade), protect populations from hazards (the Health and Safety Executive, Environmental Health Officers), and protect state disbursements (the Department of Social Security's Special Investigators). In addition to that, there are numerous personnel who exercise powers under by-laws relevant to the undertaking which employs them, and who may be described as 'police' or as 'constables' – there being nothing in law to prevent their use of that title.

Essentially, one is talking then, of a mixture of police forces, regulatory bodies, governmental and quasi-governmental agencies, involved in policing and law-enforcement duties of one sort or another. Such bodies may operate in the public sphere, in the private sphere, or across both. In that respect, rigorous classification is probably an impossible task since the functions, practices, jurisdictions, and legal powers of the various bodies overlap in potentially complex ways. For the sake of clarity, however, I shall draw a distinction between five main categories, though it should be said that these are neither exhaustive nor mutually exclusive:

1 Bodies engaged in functions related to state security: Here one can include immigration staff, who possess wide powers of search, detention, and arrest; prison officers; officers of the

Ministry of Defence Police (MODP) and the United Kingdom
Atomic Energy Authority Constabulary (AEAC); and those
attached to the various branches of the military police.

2 Special police forces: public (civil) police officers are sworn in as
constables under a general policing Act (such as the 1964 Police
Act). In the nineteenth century, however, constabulary powers
were frequently granted by specific Acts of Parliament. Usually,
the forces arising from such legislation were attached to the
various (private) transport facilities emerging during the
industrial revolution. 'Special police forces' consisting of
statutory constables (not to be confused with the Special Constabulary), developed to police railways, rivers, canals, tunnels,
and docks. Statutory constables are not, however, restricted to
the transport field. An Act of 1825 granted Proctors of the
universities of Oxford and Cambridge powers to act 'within the
precincts of the University ... and Four Miles of the same
University'. In addition, many municipal authorities have used
local Acts to swear in park keepers as constables (e.g. the
Birkenhead Corporation Act 1923, the Liverpool Corporation
Act 1921). Similarly the Special Constables Act 1923, as well as
granting Yeoman Warders of the Tower of London constabulary status remains the legislative basis for the powers of
AEAC and MODP officers. The latest national force to be
established by Act of Parliament was the MODP in 1987,
though local forces continue to be formed by Local Acts.

3 Departments of state: most departments of state employ
personnel in investigative, regulatory, and law-enforcement
duties (e.g. the Organized Fraud Section of the Department of
Social Security, the Home Office Immigration Service Intelligence and Investigation Unit, the Board of the Inland Revenue
Investigation Office, HM Customs and Excise Investigation
Division). That pattern is by no means peculiar to Britain. In the
Netherlands, where 20,000 people are employed in forty such
bodies, fraud units operate in several departments, including
finance, economic affairs, and social security. Interestingly, a
Dutch commentator notes that these agencies often possess
powers 'more extensive than those of the police' (Hoogenboom
1989: 121), something to which I shall refer later in the British
context.

4 Municipal bodies: local authorities also employ officials in

investigative and regulatory functions (including educational welfare, trading standards, environmental health, and a variety of social work activities) as well as in crime prevention activity.

5 Miscellaneous regulatory and investigative bodies: the existence of such a 'catch-all' category confirms the difficulty of classifying these bodies. Under this heading one can include, amongst other things, agencies attached to both private corporations (the British Telecom Investigation Department) and public corporations (the BBC Investigator's Office); public bodies with agency status (the National Rivers Authority); public bodies undertaking private business (the Post Office Investigation Department); and private bodies ratified by the state (the British Medical Association).

Two central points will be emphasized in this chapter. First, it is clear that a vast area of policing has been excluded from the ambit of 'police studies'. That exclusion is becoming impossible to sustain at a time when issues of transport safety, environmental pollution, nuclear safety, international fraud, and global terrorism (each of them a concern of some hybrid agency) are at the centre of the political agenda. Second, most of the bodies to be discussed here bear a complex relation to the public-private divide in terms of:

(i)   to whom they are accountable (the state, quangos, private bodies, quasi-private bodies . . .).
(ii) the functions they carry out (the protection of public property, private property, or private property deemed to be public for certain purposes).
(iii) the places where functions are carried out (public places, private places, or both).
(iv) their relationship to other policing bodies (Home Office forces, private security, military).
(v)   the impact of the 'privatization mentality' on them.

Since the potential subject matter of this chapter is enormous, I shall examine these issues by considering a small selection of organizations, grouping them under three headings: statutory or 'special' forces, investigative and regulatory bodies, and municipal initiatives.

STATUTORY OR 'SPECIAL' FORCES

The Atomic Energy Authority Constabulary (AEAC)

The AEAC was established by the Atomic Energy Act 1954, Schedule 3. The force was formed in 1955 and consisted of 320 officers, all of whom were initially unarmed. AEAC personnel had constabulary powers both within UKAEA establishments and within a 15-mile radius of them, in respect of offences involving UKAEA property (Lidstone *et al.* 1980). The AEA Act 1971 provided for the transfer of parts of the UKAEA to British Nuclear Fuels Ltd (BNFL, now BNF PLC) and to Radiochemical Centre Ltd. Section 21 (1) of that Act, however, enabled personnel to continue to act as special constables in respect of premises transferred to BNFL. Paragraph 4 of the Schedule to the Act further empowered the Defence Council of the UKAEA to nominate persons for appointment, under Section 3 of the Special Constables Act 1923, at certain specified other companies such as Urenco Ltd.

Legislation also declared UKAEA property to be crown property. Initially, this had been stipulated in Schedule 3 of the 1954 Act, but the AEA (Special Constables) Act 1976 went on to declare the property of specified companies, such as BNFL and Urenco, also to be crown property for the purposes of Section 2 of the Metropolitan Police Act 1860. In effect, this meant that property in the possession of the Authority, but not owned by it, was deemed to be 'Her Majesty's Stores' any constable being empowered to stop, search, and detain any person reasonably suspected of having stolen or unlawfully obtained such property (as well as any associated vessel, boat, or vehicle). This Act also extended the geographical area of jurisdiction of constables undertaking the protection of nuclear matter to any place where it appeared 'expedient' for them to go in order to safeguard that matter.

In sum, then, the 1976 Act extended constabulary powers to the whole of Britain when the officer was escorting nuclear material or dealing with its unlawful removal. It also authorized constables to carry firearms (including sub-machine-guns) for the first time, without the necessity of them obtaining a firearms certificate. Needless to say, it has been noted that such powers 'far exceed those of ordinary constables' (Esler and Woolwich 1983: 2304).

Information about the structure, function, and accountability of

the AEAC is difficult to obtain and until very recently the Chief
Constable's Annual Report was a classified document. At the end
of 1988, Force strength stood at 668, more than twice the total of
thirty-five years ago. In fact, most of that expansion occurred after
the 1976 Act. (In 1975 AEAC strength still stood at only 376.) The
1976 legislation also precipitated a rapid growth in annual
expenditures: from £2m in 1976–7, to £6.2m in 1980–1, to £9m in 1986
(*Atom* June 1981; Cutler and Edwards 1988).

The duties of AEAC constables include maintaining security by
controlling access, preventing and detecting crime, and ensuring
the safety of transported nuclear materials. Constables have the
power to search workers at any time and employees' contracts
specify that they must submit to such searches – though they have
access to a code of conduct specifying their rights. The fact that
officers are employed in high-security installations means, of
course, that they deal with relatively little crime. In 1977 there were
only 348 reported crimes (Lidstone *et al.* 1980: 175). Though a
decade later reported crimes had increased, the total for 1988 was
still only 507 complaints, 46 of which were 'no crimed'. The vast
majority of reported crimes involve theft, either by employees, by
contractors working on the site, or by members of the public.

What we have, then, is a secure environment with little crime
and (with the exception of crime prevention activity) little
conventional police work. This seems to be borne out by evidence
on arrests, detentions and searches. In a Parliamentary answer to
Jeff Rooker MP in February 1981, Norman Lamont stated that since
the implementation of the 1976 Act, thirty-four arrests had been
made on UKAEA or BNFL sites and nine outside. Lamont added
that in none of these cases had constables been armed (*Atom* April
1981). The great majority of these arrests would, of course, involve
in-house theft and between 1976 and 1986 nearly 200 individuals
were charged with 'minor theft and other offences' according to
official figures (Cutler and Edwards 1988). Out of 507 reported
offences in 1988 (UKAEA 1989), over 70 per cent involved theft of
one sort or another, though interestingly, this did not always lead
to prosecution. (Of forty-six reported thefts by employees in 1988,
forty were detected, but only four prosecuted. By contrast, out of
thirty-seven cases of reported criminal damage, fourteen were
detected and forty-six persons prosecuted. How many of these
cases involved non-employees is unknown, though there may be

questions here about the way in which constabulary discretion is exercised in different circumstances and before different audiences.)

The fact that 668 officers were engaged in the policing of only 507 reported crimes during 1988, begs certain obvious questions about the role of AEAC constables. Are they merely expensive security guards? Could the job be done as well, or better, by other personnel: the military? Home Office forces? Private security? Civilian guards?. Significantly, the Constabulary suffered reductions in strength in 1988 and again in 1989, following the Authority's setting up of a senior management working party. That working party seems to have adopted the same 'value for money' criteria as have been applied to Home Office forces, so if history repeats itself, it may not be long before policy makers are putting questions about civilianization and privatization to the AEAC just as they have to Home Office forces.

In the absence of hard evidence about AEAC operational practice, the role of constables remains both mysterious and controversial. This is particularly apparent in relation to the escorting of fissile material. The Chief Constable's Report for 1988, for instance, contains the following enigmatic statement: 'Escorts of nuclear materials have taken place efficiently, with the full cooperation and assistance of other police forces and without incident of any kind' (UKAEA 1989: 17). The issue of escort raises questions both about the accountability of the Constabulary and its relationship with other police forces. In the case of the latter it has been suggested that several chief constables are secretly uneasy about the existence of armed police patrols, dressed in uniforms very similar to those of their own officers, engaging in operations in their force areas. Alan Beith MP, for instance, has argued that 'If an armed guard is required for any purpose, then the local police force should be asked to provide it' (cited in May 1986: 7).

Beith's grounds for arguing this would be that only a force which is publicly accountable should be allowed to police public spaces. Here, the AEAC would make two responses. First, as John Reddington, ex-Chief Constable put it: 'In any major event the local chief constable always has control' (cited in Reed 1988: 49). Reddington's point here is that the operational autonomy of local chief constables over their public jurisdictions, remains sacrosanct. A second response would be that the force is, in any case, an accountable one, in so far as personnel are accountable to the Chief Constable, who is accountable to the AEA Board, which reports to the Secretary of State for Energy, who reports in turn to Parliament.

This view is, of course, at best half-true, for several reasons. First, the Chief Constable's accountability to the Secretary of State is mediated by an unelected quango (the UKAEA). Second, although local chief constables possess operational autonomy, it is difficult to believe that that autonomy would not be politically circum-scribed in the event of any major event involving nuclear material. Third, although the AEAC does have a police committee, it contains no elected members and there is no information on its composition in the Annual Report. Fourth, successive Secretaries of State for Energy have shown a remarkable degree of reticence in answering questions about the Constabulary. Finally, there is the question of the AEAC's ambiguous accountability to both public and private sectors, in the context of an operational brief which bisects public and private spheres in complex ways. For one thing, the AEAC is responsible for protecting public property (and private property deemed by law to be public) in both public and private places. For another, it bears a degree of accountability to both public and private sectors, the ambivalence of which exposes it to (sometimes extreme) criticisms. At least one writer, for instance, has described the AEAC as 'bearing a resemblance to a heavily armed private security firm' (Esler 1983: 5).

Ministry of Defence Police (MODP)

The MODP is a statutory body of civilian police officers under the control of the Defence Council. It is a national force, covering about 150 establishments in the UK, control and administration resting with the Chief Constable. Officers have full police powers within MOD establishments and on board ships. Since 1987 they also have unlimited jurisdiction in respect of crown property, and in regard to persons subject to naval, military, or air force discipline. In some circumstances officers are allowed to carry weapons, and some are deputed by warrant to exercise customs and excise powers at places where no customs officers are present. In 1988 the force had a strength of 4,706 officers (MODP 1989).

The MODP has responsibility for the prevention and detection of crime, the protection of defence establishments, and the security of crown property. The general principle is that offences committed against the MOD by members of the public, or by MOD civilians, are dealt with by the MODP. Offences committed by service personnel are the responsibility of the service police. As a rule, the service police do not deal with civilians in the UK, but the MODP can deal with service personnel where a civil offence is involved (Miller and Luke 1977).

The majority of MOD sites are secure areas, so in effect, 'much of police work is gate control' (Lidstone *et al.* 1980: 172). In garrison towns such as Aldershot or Colchester, however, the force operates more like a general police force, investigating all crimes, except murder and manslaughter, which are always handed over to the local police. The force, like its Home Office counterparts, has experienced an escalation in reported crime. However, the security of sites means that the force deals with much less reported crime than Home Office forces of comparable size. Crime returns for England, Wales, and Northern Ireland show that in 1988 the MODP dealt with 13,208 reported crimes, clearing up almost 50 per cent (MODP 1989). In comparison, Home Office forces of similar size would expect to deal with more than ten times as much, clearing up a rather smaller proportion.

The fact that the force deals with a relatively small amount of crime raises questions about the role of constables. Clearly, the bulk of their activity involves routine, preventive patrol, searching persons and vehicles entering or leaving establishments, and the like. The routine nature of these tasks creates its own difficulties and, predictably, over the years some of the night-watchman tasks previously undertaken by officers, have been shed. Nevertheless, at least one senior MODP officer has referred to 'the boredom which can easily occur when highly trained and enthusiastic young men and women are assigned to posts which, though important, are frequently static by nature' (Chapple 1986: 1345).

Given what is already known about the 'action orientation' inherent in police occupational cultures (Holdaway 1983; Reiner 1985), the problem of static routine is a real one for MODP managers. To some extent, this can be eased by encouraging specialization and creating opportunities for rapid promotion, though the substantial overtime payments officers receive for serving detached duties away from their home stations also help. During the 1980s, of course, the increase in political demonstrations at MOD bases, not only guaranteed plenty of overtime, it also helped to alleviate routine – in much the same way as the 1984–5 miners' strike energized some sections of the general force. The suggestion that the policing of demonstrations may possess latent functions (in this case the relief of routine, mundane activity), is by no means as strange as it might seem. One writer has suggested that the constable's role has a covert political function attached to it:

> One of the MDP's key roles has always been to act as a buffer between the military and civilians. This has become increasingly important with the growth of the anti-nuclear movement. If military personnel were used to hold back the crowds of demonstrators at bases the problem could only escalate. Civilian police are the only appropriate answer.
>
> (Pead 1986: 1189)

The MODP has close contacts with Home Office forces. In 1985, for instance, Wiltshire Constabulary called in the MODP to help remove 'Peace Convoy' members from National Trust land. As with the AEAC, the deployment of non-Home Office constables in public places has raised controversy. Recently, Thames Valley Constabulary expressed concern about armed MODP officers patrolling public roads around an army garrison in Arbfield, Berkshire, and was reported to be taking the matter up with the military authorities (*Police Review* 13 April 1990).

The general issue of accountability has also been a thorny one. Overall control of the force rests with the Defence Council but, in practice, is exercised by the Second Permanent Under-Secretary of State in the MOD, who is Chairman of the Defence Police Committee. That Committee which is responsible for resource allocation, complaints and discipline, is also the locus of MODP policy-making, a fact which raises interesting questions about the operational autonomy of the Chief Constable. Until recently, the force was not subjected to inspection by HMIs, and although employing the same complaints and discipline procedures as Home Office forces, had no police committee. In that sense, it was accountable, in exactly the same way as the Metropolitan Police is accountable, to the relevant Secretary of State.

During the last few years this situation has altered. In 1985, following criticisms contained in the House of Commons Defence Committee Report, the Government pledged to commission 'an independent and wide ranging study of all aspects of the MODP to formulate a long-term strategy for the Force's future role, composition and size' (House of Commons 1984). The Broadbent Report, published in July 1986, made twenty-one recommend-ations, seventeen of which were accepted by the Government, the most significant being (i) that the force should have periodical HMI inspections; (ii) that MODP legal powers should be codified in a single act (the 1987 Ministry of Defence Police Act); (iii) that an MODP committee should be appointed by the Secretary of State to represent the users at top management level, supported by outside professional representation; (iv) that there should be a single, dedicated Inspectorate cell to carry out staff inspections throughout the force.

The decision to centralize the Inspectorate is likely to produce immediate political controversy since its first task is to tackle the problem of constables being used on duties for which they are overqualified. The Broadbent Report said 'At some MOD bases we question the need for 100 per cent manning of the security task by constables. Inspection teams should examine closely the scope for mixed-manning by a combination of constables and watching grades.' In fact, the Committee went on to recommend the intro-duction of 'special constables' (i.e. the Special Constabulary) to provide a reserve against the withdrawal of MODP officers on detachment.

At the time, the Government did not accept this recommend-ation, referring instead to an 'on-going study' whose outcome it would await before making a decision. The contents of that study were outlined in evidence given to the House of Commons Defence Committee (House of Commons 1990a) by Richard Hastie-Smith, Deputy Under-Secretary in charge of Civilian Management at the MOD. The proposals considered the reorganization and strengthening of the civilian guard force which works alongside MODP officers. The aim of strengthening this force was to ease the burden on servicemen and on MODP officers, and to reduce the use of private security companies. Hastie-Smith told the Committee that more unarmed security staff would be recruited to add to the 580 already existing in his Department and in the Property Service Agency. The study suggested that these personnel would be better trained than in the past, and that the eight grades of watchmen, patrolmen, and dog-handlers currently existing, would be combined into a single unit. Hastie-Smith concluded that if such a civilian guard force was established, two benefits would follow. First, the scheme would halve the cost of using MODP officers. Second, it would be cheaper than using private security firms under contract. (MOD spending on private security more than doubled between 1988–9, when it stood at £1.9m and 1989–90, when it stood at £4.4m.) Needless to say, the issue of civilianization is likely to fan the flames of privatization arising in the aftermath of the events at Deal.

British Transport Police (BTP)

The railway boom in the early nineteenth century precipitated the development of private transport forces, railway police originally being sworn in as constables under the act creating a particular railway company (e.g. the London and Birmingham Railway Act 1833). Their jurisdiction was first limited to railway premises or to that part of the line occupying a single county, but in later acts it was usually extended to the whole of the line, plus a distance on either side (Miller and Luke 1977).

In the absence of public policing, private railway forces often helped to keep public order during times of crisis (Gay 1973). Public order functions apart, however, the duties of early railway constables were defined broadly: preserving order on railway premises, patrolling the line, warning of danger, controlling trains by hand signals, advising passengers of arrivals and departures, and assisting in accidents (Sansom 1978)

After the Transport Act 1947 nationalized the railways, a single national force (the British Transport Commission Police) was created, and although the Transport Act 1962 split the British Transport Commission into four public authorities, a national police force was retained, the BTP being established in 1964. BTP constables are sworn in under s.53 of the British Transport Commission Act 1949. The officer has jurisdiction over premises owned, leased, or used by the British Railways Board, Associated British Ports, London Regional Transport, and the British Waterways Board (CIPFA 1989). Section 53 of the Act permits an officer to follow and arrest an offender beyond Board premises, provided that the matter is connected with business of the relevant Board and the offence is one for which the offender could have been arrested if caught on specified premises. Section 54 gives powers in respect of any person in the employ (or employed on the property) of the Board, to stop, search, and take into custody any person who may be reasonably suspected of having stolen (or who may be conveying) property stolen from Board premises. The same power extends to stop, search, and detention of any vessel, car, or carriage on the premises (Miller and Luke 1977). Constables can also work outside their normal territorial jurisdictions in England and Wales, in respect of matters affecting any of the Board's undertakings, without the necessity of an offence having occurred (May 1979). In addition to being a constable, an officer of the BTP is also a servant of the Board and may exercise powers given to an officer or agent of the railway, but not to the police (e.g. a constable may arrest a trespasser who refuses to quit).

The Force deals with the full range of police duties: vandalism, football hooliganism, suicides, fraud, petty theft, public order, and so on. May (1979) notes that, in practice, BTP and Home Office constables frequently penetrate one another's operational territory. For example, on an average Saturday, thousands of football supporters arrive at Euston Station (BTP jurisdiction), pour down the underground (BTP jurisdiction), and spill out on to the streets (Metropolitan Police jurisdiction), reversing the whole process on the return journey and making rigorous demarcation of responsibilities difficult.

In 1989 the BTP dealt with 87,905 reported, indictable crimes (along with a further 105,438 non-indictable offences) of which almost 50,000 involved theft. In that same year the organization was also in the throes of changing from a centrally controlled force, modelled on a county constabulary, to a 'devolved sub-divisional command structure suitable to the national police for the railways' (BTP 1990: 3). This change followed the completion of a management review by Ernst and Whinney in 1988. The changes occurring in the BTP are similar to those being undertaken in Home Office forces, and include the devolution of administration and decision making to divisions and subdivisions, the civilianization of non-operational duties, and the creation of cost centres where superintendents will engage in financial negotiation with railway area managers over budgetary questions. The Force now operates with five divisions, including a separate one for London Underground, and another in Scotland. Force headquarters has a Criminal Intelligence Unit, as well as an Operational Support Department with a Football Liaison Unit and fifteen mobile support units for deployment on public order duties. These units, as well as engaging in multiforce public order exercises, are also responsible for dealing with explosives and suspect packages.

Although the BTP has annual inspections by the HMI, operates with the same entry conditions as Home Office forces, and has personnel attending training courses at Bramshill, Hendon, and elsewhere, officers have never enjoyed the same status as those from general forces. (Smith-Leach (1985), for example, notes that when experienced BTP officers transfer to Home Office forces they begin 'at the bottom'). In fact, the problem of status is merely one of several elements which, together constitute a crisis in Force identity. For one thing, BTP is contracting. On 31 December 1989 Force strength stood at 1,857. During the pre-Beeching era, the BTP had consisted of about 5,500 officers, but in the 1960s numbers fell to about 4,000, and by the mid-1970s the establishment had shrunk to little more than 2,000. It is not merely the reduction in size of the rail network which has caused shrinkage, however, the range of activities undertaken by the BTP has also declined, with successive withdrawals from the policing of canals, waterways, National Carriers, docks, harbours, and ports. In effect, the sole recipients of BTP services are now British Rail and the London Underground Ltd, who provide the bulk of funding. (In 1989 the total budget stood at £63.2m, of which British Rail provided £48.3m and London Underground Ltd £13.6m, the rest coming from British Rail Property Board, Railfreight Distribution, InterCity on-Board Services, and other private sources, together with a top-up Treasury grant.)

A second aspect of this crisis has concerned crime on the London Underground. In 1980 the Home Secretary chaired a conference dealing with violence on public transport which resolved to increase the establishment of the London Underground Division (L Division) from 280 to 500 by 1983. That plan was, however, frozen, after the House of Lords decision on London Transport funding (*Policing London* October/November 1983). By 1988, despite a considerable escalation in reported crime (and £15m of investment following the 1986 Department of Transport Report *Crime on the Underground*), L Division still had only 400 officers. In reponse to the HMI report of that year, the Department of Transport, in an unprecedented move, agreed for the Metropolitan and City of London Forces to second eighty-three officers to L Division on a temporary basis. At the same time, several commentators suggested that a more permanent and cost-effective response to policing the Underground would follow if L Division was simply absorbed into the Metropolitan Police.

Though this suggestion has not been pursued further, it demonstrates that there is uncertainty about the future development of the BTP. For one thing, despite the Force's considerable level of deployment in the public sphere, it still lacks any clear and proper form of public funding (Thomas 1989). Moreover, it has come in for increasing criticism from influential sources. Sir John Wheeler, commenting on Sealink's decision to dispense with BTP services stated 'Sealink is right to sack them. . . . Senior management has become complacent and probably inefficient.' Wheeler went on to propose a change in the law, enabling private citizens to be recruited as special constables for policing the transport system.

This outburst against the BTP is by no means isolated. There have been accusations that officers have 'massaged' crime figures to mask poor detection rates. There have been suggestions that the Force suffers an antiquated management style due to its tendency to recruit retired senior officers from Home Office forces. (One anonymous commentator claimed that 'Headquarters is like an elephant's graveyard' (cited in Leppard 1989).) There was official criticism of Force technology and emergency training following the enquiry on the King's Cross fire. And there is repeated criticism from passenger groups who object to the lack of consumer representation on a police committee, whose membership consists entirely of appointees from the two railway bodies.

Behind all of these criticisms, of course, is the spectre of privatization, for both London Regional Transport and British Rail are prime elements in any future programme. Should such a programme be implemented in the future, the outcome would be very controversial. For not only would it create a very sizeable private force; that force would have a national focus and an operational framework already well-integrated into the existing institutional structure of Home Office forces.

INVESTIGATIVE AND REGULATORY BODIES

Investigative bodies

Here, I want to consider two examples. The first of these, the Post Office Investigation Department (POID) is a good case of a public body engaged in private enterprise. Since the reorganization of the Post Office into separate companies, POID works on a contract basis with Girobank, Royal Mail Letters, Counters Ltd (post offices), and Royal Mail Parcels. It also contracts with the Treasury and the National Savings Bank. Its duties require it to deal with, or assist the police in dealing with, criminal offences against the Post Office and the Department of National Savings, to whom it also provides a crime prevention service (Hyder 1988).

Though POID serves a public function, it now sells its 'spare capacity' to private companies. Its Director, Mike Hoare, an ex-Metropolitan Police commander, has stated, 'we are trying to BUPA-ise the police. We will be doing what the police can or will not do because of their limited resources' (*Observer* 21 August 1988). In offering these services, POID is responding to the growing inability of police forces to commit resources to offences such as cheque book fraud. Though POID is undoubtedly responding to demand in the market place, there remains doubt, however, about the role of such a company. At present, investigators working on Post Office business have access to criminal records, make prison visits, and exchange information with public police forces. If personnel were also engaged in private investigations, there is concern about the ethics of differentiating between their public and private roles.

The Serious Fraud Office (SFO) is an example of a public body whose agents, though lacking constabulary status, nevertheless enjoy powers in excess of the police. Since the passing of the Criminal Justice Act 1987, SFO investigators, like those of the Department of Trade and Industry (DTI), have the right to *require* any individual, believed to have relevant information, to answer questions; to *demand* explanation about business conduct; and to provide relevant documents where necessary, copies of which may be taken.

The SFO is staffed by both permanent and seconded officers, including nineteen accountants, twenty-six lawyers, a number of specialists called in for particular purposes, and various support staff (Wood 1989). Police officers, seconded from the Metropolitan and City of London Fraud Squads, are also housed in the same building, though for constitutional reasons, they remain under the authority of their chief constables. The principal role of civilian staff is to advise and oversee investigations, but they are not precluded from themselves taking a part in investigations. Though the powers of SFO staff do not extend to arrest, detention, search, or seizure, it is they who will be responsible for *initiating* the investigative process. The existence of these initiating powers, coupled with the fact that Fraud Squad officers will be directed by SFO lawyers, suggests that in spite of the decision to leave participating police officers under the control of their chief constables, the UK is gradually moving towards a Continental or American model of prosecutor-direction of enquiries (Levi forthcoming).

Regulatory bodies

Though the study of regulatory bodies has not been integrated into the sociology of policing, the activities they engage in raise issues which are central to that enterprise. Consider two examples. First the public–private division. Regulatory bodies operate across both sectors and the connections between public and private elements can be complex. In Chapter 4, I drew attention to the activities of the BSIA in self-regulation of the private security sector. Here is a private body overseeing private firms, engaged in activities (some of which are, arguably, public functions) across both public and private spheres. Future statutory (public) recognition of the BSIA would add a further level of complexity to that morass of public–private connections. Talk of future statutory recognition also demonstrates that the relations between regulatory bodies and the state are dynamic, since at any time, they may be privatized or subjected to degrees of state control. At present, HM Inspectorate of Pollution is preparing to follow the National Rivers Authority in taking on agency status. This means that, in future, it will gain much of its funding from charging private companies for inspection, advice, and the formal consent to pollute (McCarthy 1990), something which immediately raises questions about the dependence of a public body on private sources of funding – particularly when those sources derive from the population being policed.

Consider next the issue of discretion. Studies of regulatory bodies in areas such as health and safety (Pearce and Tombs 1988) and environmental health (Hutter 1988) show that combinations of 'hard' (legalistic, reactive) and 'soft' (persuasive, preventative, proactive) strategies can be found within and between agencies. The fact that there is empirical variation in regulatory roles indicates that, as in public police organizations, the exercise of discretion is central both to regulatory practice and to the exercise of justice.

In a recent analysis of the Industrial Air Pollution Inspectorate (IAPI), Weait (1989) describes some of the mediating factors shaping the exercise of discretion by inspectors: mitigation (Is the act a deliberate flouting of regulations, or is it pardonable?); persistence (Is it the first offence, or one of many?); visibility (Have influential individuals or groups taken an interest in the situation?); resource factors (Given limited organizational resources should the agency proceed further?); legal factors (Is there evidential weakness or strength?). Moreover, some of these factors expose tendencies within the agency itself. For example, in respect of evidential considerations, field inspectors may be concerned primarily with the substantive merits of a case, whereas officers at headquarters see failed prosecutions as undermining the credibility of the organization.

All in all, Weait (1989) paints a picture of a regulatory body where discretionary activity is widespread, and where decision making over matters of justice occurs before a number of informal audiences (some internal, some external), all of it in a context lacking much public scrutiny. The parallels with public police organizations should be obvious. Nevertheless, it remains to be seen whether the concepts traditionally used to understand discretion in police organizations can be applied to the analysis of regulatory bodies, or whether new forms of theoretical insight are required.

MUNICIPAL POLICING

Although local authorities in England and Wales (other than London) are permitted to swear-in park employees as special constables under the powers contained in the Public Health (Amendment) Act 1907, this Act has not yet been widely used (CIPFA 1989). However, in London, two authorities (Barnet and Wandsworth) have implemented Section 15 of the Ministry of Housing and Local Government Provisional Order Confirmation (Greater London Parks and Open Spaces) Act 1967 which empowers constables to enforce park by-laws and grants them certain powers of detention.

In Wandsworth, a force of thirty-four uniformed officers replaced council park keepers in 1985. The force deals with minor crimes, its jurisdiction extending for one mile beyond park boundaries. In 1988 101 arrests were made and 712 verbal warnings were given. None of the work (except for the processing of prisoners) was transferred to the local Metropolitan Police station and, in consequence, Battersea Division was able to reduce its manpower establishment (McLean 1989). Wandsworth also employs sixty-eight uniformed mobile security officers to patrol council estates. These patrols are equipped with radios and function to deter crime, check council property, and deal with emergencies such as tenants trapped in lifts (Boothroyd 1989b). In an 18-month period, the patrols dealt with no less than 60,000 calls from local residents.

Municipal initiatives of this sort are by no means unusual. In Camden, eighteen plain-clothed council officers patrol estates, libraries, and administrative buildings each night, whilst seventeen officers attached to the Finance Department provide a cash-in-transit service for the authority. In Scotland the Livingston Development Corporation employs forty-two men to provide mobile patrols of council property (Boothroyd 1989b). Many such schemes have received funding through state employment initiatives, such as the Manpower Services Commission, the Community Enterprise Programme, and the Employment Training Scheme. In Birmingham unemployed men were paid to patrol schools, halls, and other council buildings in an attempt to reduce the £2m worth of damage caused each year by vandals. Patrols were uniformed and in radio contact with the police (*Crime Prevention News* 4/1982). A number of councils on Merseyside including Liverpool, Sefton, St Helens, Wirral, and Knowsley have had anti-vandalism patrols since the late 1970s. At its peak the Sefton scheme employed more than 100 people, dressed in bottle-green uniforms with green berets, to provide mobile patrols, whilst Knowsley had over eighty personnel engaged in night patrols under the supervision of an ex-policeman (Boothroyd 1989; Crime Prevention News 2/1982).

Such schemes are by no means peculiar to Britain. The Ministry of Housing in Victoria, Australia, has developed its own security-guard programme employing a number of full-time 'community guardians' who perform a joint welfare-policing function (Corns 1987). These employees are responsible for policing ten inner-Melbourne estates containing 7,300 residential units. They function alongside both the public police and a number of private security companies contracted by the Ministry. As in Britain, some unemployed tenants have assisted in the policing of estates – in this case, through funds provided by the Commonwealth Employment Programme. Interestingly, after undertaking such duties, some of these tenants established their own security company and were awarded a contract by the Ministry, confirming, yet again, the slippage between public, private, and hybrid policing forms.

Another interesting foreign initiative occurred in the Netherlands where an experiment was undertaken to tackle fare dodging, vandalism, and aggression on public transport in three cities (Amsterdam, the Hague, and Rotterdam). An increase in petty crime and fare dodging had arisen as a result of the removal of conductors from buses and trams in the 1960s. In 1984 the three public transport companies operating in the selected cities were authorized to take on approximately 1,200 unemployed young people to act as 'VICs' (roughly translated as 'safety, information, and control' agents) for a period of 3 years. VICs were recruited between 19–28 years of age, 50 per cent of them being unemployed, 30 per cent women, and 25 per cent from ethnic minorities. They received 2–3 months training combining criminal law and ticket-inspection practice. Indications are that fare dodging was reduced, especially in circumstances where VICs were authorized to charge fines, and overall the measures seem to have had an impact in reducing petty crime on the transport system (Van Andel 1989).

All of the examples considered so far concern the policing of municipal public space. However, it should not be assumed that municipal policing is limited to this function. Municipal personnel are engaged in a range of regulatory and investigative functions from trading standards to environmental health, and from educational welfare to the protection of state disbursements. A good example of this last activity is the local authority policing of claimant fraud in the Housing Benefit scheme (Loveland 1989). This scheme was designed by central government (in the Housing Benefit and Social Security Act 1982) but administered by local authorities: a mixture which combined rigid rules at the centre with wide areas of discretion at local levels. As a result of the chaos arising from the implementation of this Act, the Secretary of State ordered a review of procedures. The review team suggested that local authorities should be granted prosecuting powers, thus encouraging them 'to exert greater diligence in fraud prevention, and fostering greater consistency between authorities' responses to abuse' (Loveland 1989: 190). Loveland's account of resulting procedures is striking for its similarity to accounts of the impact of police occupational cultures on the exercise of constabulary discretion. His point is that local authority officers exercise discretion according to the 'administrative culture' of the office in which they work and the political priorities of the council employing them. This means that, at one extreme, those suspected of fraud may be allowed to repay the debt, the payment being categorized as 'overpayment' for accounting purposes; whilst at the other extreme, those defined by the administrative culture as 'criminal' will be pursued with the full force of the law.

Returning to the matter of organized forces, a number of local authorities have taken powers under local acts to have park keepers and other staff sworn in as constables. Such constables do not come under the authority of the local chief constable, though their jurisdiction is limited to parks and open spaces. Amongst those forces currently in operation are the Birmingham Parks Patrol Force and the Brighton Parks Police Force. A more interesting example is the Liverpool City Security Force which was established in 1972. Here, following a review of security operations in the various departments of the authority, it was decided to abolish the Liverpool Parks Police and the Liverpool Airport Police, replacing them with a single, civilian body. This force was given responsibility for protecting all premises belonging to or used by the Council and its Departments (Miller and Luke 1977). Some members of this force retain their constabulary status as a result of being sworn in during previous service with the Parks and Airport Police, or the Birkenhead Parks Police, but it is now no longer the policy of the Security Force to have employees sworn in as constables. The Force, consisting of something in the region of 200 personnel is organized into three territorial divisions. A central, radio communications room directs and monitors all mobile and foot personnel through personal radios, and at one time there were direct telephone links with Merseyside Constabulary. Significantly, in an article written soon after the Toxteth riots, the Chief Officer saw local authority security forces as a suitable second-tier police presence (preferable to the military), able to assist those 'police forces . . . under greatest pressure' (Wright 1981: 109) in towns and cities. Wright suggested that local security forces with full constabulary powers should be encouraged by the Home Office, since they could protect property and deal with minor infractions of the law, leaving serious policing duties to the regular force. Whether this prospect is feasible, or whether private security firms are more likely to take over such functions remains, of course, to be seen. (In the Liverpool case, allegations that the security force had become a 'private army' for ex-Council Leader Derek Hatton, were one factor in its recent substantial reduction in size.) Whatever the future, however, the existence of such schemes has implications for public policing. For one thing, if they were to spread 'local authorities might be tempted to ask for a reduction in their contribution to the police precept' (McLean 1989: 2017).

In fact, there are precedents for the development of a municipal policing tier. In January 1983 the French Government passed legislation allowing for the formation of municipal forces to supplement the services provided by the Police Nationale and the Gendarmeries Nationale (Kania 1989). This development sprang from the decentralization campaign associated with Mitterand's earlier Presidential victory. Such municipal police forces now number about 25,000. Units are small and though employed by cities must comply with national laws. Broadly speaking, officers are meant to have a crime prevention function, though they also have certain powers of arrest. Standards of entry are roughly equivalent to those of the national forces and uniforms are virtually identical to those of the Police Nationale.

Demand for municipal policing in France first appeared in the 1970s as a protest against rising crime and the level of service offered by the *corps urbain* of the Police Nationale. Though the Socialist Party instituted decentralization of various municipal services, including policing, in the early 1980s, it was right-wing mayors who were most attracted to the formation of municipal forces, seeing them as a useful tool in the furtherance of 'law and order' policies. In fact, some of these units have now become 'real cops', engaging in crime-fighting duties which stretch the limits of their legal mandate, and in some cities municipal police are now armed with 9 mm pistols.

Chapter 7

Citizenship and self-policing I
Responsible citizenship

Privatization of policing functions can also be brought about when private citizens take over some of the responsibility for public security from police organizations. Examples of such 'active citizenship' can range from individuals keeping an eye on neighbour's property, to organized collective actions, such as involvement in citizen street patrols. In this chapter and the following one I shall consider two types of 'active citizenship', roughly differentiated according to their degree of autonomy from public police and state agencies.

The first of these forms, 'responsible citizenship', is officially sanctioned and sponsored by the state, and may be located within the broad framework of community crime prevention. Here the object is to construct a partnership between the police, the public, and other relevant social agencies so that a concerted attack can be made on the social basis of crime at the local level. Invariably this means that proponents of the model place considerable emphasis on the alleged virtues of community policing and multi-agency approaches to crime prevention. Amongst the most significant forms of responsible citizenship in Britain today are membership of the Special Constabulary (a body seen by government as having a key role in the implementation of community policing strategies) and participation in neighbourhood watch schemes (a movement regarded by its supporters as already having been effective in the reduction of property crimes, as well as having future potential in reducing crimes of violence). But first, let us consider the role of private enterprise and the media in mobilization of citizens.

RESPONSIBLE CITIZENS AGAINST CRIME

Private enterprise, citizens and the media

In Britain, as in the USA, private companies, encouraged by government, have begun to play a more active role in crime prevention. Often, support takes the form of direct sponsorship of preventative projects. In 1989, for example, Royal Insurance donated £100,000 worth of property-marking kits for use in neighbourhood watch schemes. Another recent initiative, 'Crime Concern', was established in 1988 through financial support from the Home Office and from Woolworth. This organization arose from a pledge in the 1987 Conservative election manifesto to 'build on the support of the public by establishing a national organization to promote the best practices in local crime prevention initiatives'. It is run by an Advisory Board with representatives from the police, local government, business, trade unions, political parties, the voluntary sector, the judiciary, and the Church.

In a statement made shortly after its establishment, 'Crime Concern's' Chairman, Steven Norris, touched on a critical issue about the character of commercially backed initiatives of this sort. One of the main aims of the organization, he said, was 'as far as possible to be financially independent, because with independence comes the ability to be constructively critical from time to time' (Norris 1988: 15). In talking of financial independence, here, Norris is referring, of course, to independence from the Home Office. This is certainly desirable since some of the organization's publications, though presented in the guise of evaluative research, are, as yet, little more than crude reassertions of Home Office thinking (e.g. Bright 1990). Yet, Norris's formulation fails to consider whether the organization's priorities may also be compromised by its dependence on private funding.

This issue has become especially significant with the development of commercially funded media campaigns to encourage citizen involvement in crime prevention activity. One of the most important of these is the 'Crimestoppers' campaign which originated in Albuquerque, New Mexico, in 1976, and was introduced in Britain in 1988. The scheme is supervised here by the Community Action Trust, a registered charity having the support of the Home Office and the Metropolitan Police, as well as financial backing from a wide range of companies including Barclays Bank, Securicor, Racal-Chubb, the Halifax Building Society, Ciba-Geigy, Pleasurama, Whitbread, and the Hawley Group (Painter 1988).

'Crimestoppers' is a co-operative scheme between the media, the business community, the police, and the public. Each week, a target crime (usually a crime of violence) is chosen by the police and publicized by television, radio, and press. A freephone service is provided through which members of the public can transmit information anonymously to the police. If information leads to arrest, the informant can apply for a cash reward, the level of reward being in line with that specified by 'Crimestoppers Incorporated', a multinational organization with a standardized reward scheme across different countries. At present, the Metropolitan Police are considering proposals to establish a 'Central Appeals Response Unit' based on the 'Crimestoppers' programme. This unit would establish a national facility to co-ordinate all information given by members of the public in response to police appeals.

One issue raised by schemes of this sort concerns the ability of corporate bodies to influence crime-prevention agendas. Another programme illustrating this same issue is 'Crimewatch UK' (see Schlesinger *et al.* 1989 for a detailed account) which derives from an earlier West German example dating back 20 years. In the British case, a 40-minute, action-oriented programme aims to mobilize the audience to respond with information about selected crimes. The programme, despite its documentary format, exhibits many of the features of entertainment, playing to large audiences of 11–12 million people. In each programme crime stories are selected from the popular end of the market (murder, armed robbery with violence, sexual crimes, etc.) and illustrated by dramatic reconstructions. Since corporate and political crimes are considered too difficult to visualize, they are excluded from consideration. The programme identifies strongly with the 'fight against crime' and, thus, avoids asking questions about police effectiveness or methods used in gaining results. It also operates with somewhat stereotypical views of police practice. For example, in two of the occasional series of 'Crimewatch Specials' broadcast in 1989 (where details are given of how crimes covered in previous programmes have been solved), it was demonstrated that genetic fingerprinting led to the capture of a multiple rapist and a rapist/murderer. Here, the audience was presented with a classic model of police work as 'detection' (in this case up-dated by 'science') an interesting contrast with what research tells us about the mundanities of everyday police work.

Both of these programmes raise interesting questions about the relationship between the media, crime, and fear of crime. Canadian critics of 'Crimestoppers' claim that it enables a 'deviance defining elite', consisting of the police, the media, and business corporations, to shape public perceptions of, and fears about crime (Carriere and Erikson 1989). In Britain, critics have argued that the narrow concentration of 'Crimewatch' on violent and sexual crime inflates public fear in general and the fear of some groups in particular. Feminists, for example, have alleged that the programme casts women in the role of permanent and passive victims of a crime war.

These examples of commercial and media sponsorship demonstrate that active citizenship is not just about encouraging individuals to give information about crime. It is also about private bodies acting as 'corporate citizens' to shape agendas in the public sphere. This raises the important question of where the discourse of citizenship stands in relation to public and private domains, a question to which I shall return in the final chapter.

Special and volunteer police

A second form of responsible citizenship arises when individuals enrol as special constables or undertake police auxiliary functions on a voluntary basis. Unlike the citizen patrol groups discussed in the next chapter, such 'supplemental groups' (Marx and Archer 1976) have little autonomy, the police exercising complete control over their organization and leadership. Interestingly, in 1989 the Metropolitan Police launched such a supplemental group (the 'Community Volunteers') to counteract the impact of the London chapter of the Guardian Angels. The group, sponsored by Securicor, is trained in self-defence, first aid, law, and crime prevention and provides support to old people, as well as assisting with neighbourhood watch.

Voluntary policing arises in a variety of different social and political contexts. After the 1917 Revolution Soviet citizens augmented the police function, one writer (see Greenberg 1978) suggesting that over 2 per cent of the population were engaged in this activity. Similarly, 'People's Guards', wearing the same red arm bands as their Soviet counterparts, operate in contemporary China, whilst in Cuba the armed miliciano are deployed to carry out guard duties at workplaces. Police auxiliaries are also widely used in capitalist countries. The police reserve in New York numbers 5,000 and originated in 1920, having emerged from the wartime Citizen's Home Defence League, a group of 25,000 volunteers who could be sworn in in the case of emergency. In New York volunteers have no police powers and are unarmed, whereas in other cities, such as St Louis, they carry weapons and have powers of arrest. In the USA, unlike Britain, there is variation in the powers and deployment of police volunteers according to differing political jurisdictions. Nevertheless, commentators on police auxiliaries in the USA have drawn attention to two factors relevant to the British experience: the extent to which regular officers have abandoned the foot-patrol function to volunteers (Greenberg 1978); and the extent to which the profile of volunteer police is typical or untypical of the general profile of volunteers (Sundeen and Siegel 1986).

A further development in the USA which might have an impact on Britain is the emergence of citizen patrol groups acting under police supervision. One such group, 'The Baltimore North West Citizen's Patrol' runs nightly patrols of a dozen men, drawn from a pool of 500 volunteers most of whom are from the Jewish community. Members ride in their own cars, clearly marked with a sign, and carry a torch, a map, and a walkie-talkie. Their function is to act as a form of mobile neighbourhood watch, looking for suspicious incidents and reporting them to the police, direct intervention by members being strictly forbidden. Though some advisors have recommended this scheme to the Home Office, as yet, it is seen as politically unacceptable by the British Government.

In Britain, special constables, the direct descendants of parish constables, are the authentic 'citizens in uniform'. The Special Constabulary Act dates back to 1831, the year of the Reform Bill riots. This Act gave counties and boroughs the right to create special constables where the number of ordinary officers was considered inadequate for local needs. Later Acts of 1914 and 1923 further provided for the recruitment of specials and, nowadays, they are appointed according to the terms of s. 16 of the 1964 Police Act. Essentially, specials have the same powers as regular officers, the only difference being that their jurisdiction is restricted to the force area in which they are appointed. In 1938 the Special Constabulary's strength stood at 118,000. By 1946 it was less than half of that total, and numbers have fallen steadily during the post-war period, current membership standing at less than 16,000.

A report of the Police Advisory Board Working Party (1981) defined the specials' role as that of taking over routine policing in the event of an emergency requiring large numbers of regulars, and providing a reserve in the event of war. Nevertheless, despite assurances that specials should be used in emergencies and 'not to effect economies of management' (Metropolitan Police Policy Statement cited in McCall 1987: 70), some police authorities have used them to avoid making overtime payments to regular officers, and there are suggestions that in some forces specials have worked 8-hour shifts, two or three times a week (Jesperson 1987).

In fact, detailed research by Leon (1989; 1990) suggests that there are wide variations in hours worked. In her survey of specials, 54 per cent claimed to do at least four duties (of 4–8 hours) per month, almost a quarter claimed to do four duties per fortnight, and 6 per cent claimed to do four duties (16–32 hours) a week. On the other hand, 40 per cent said that they only peformed one duty every 2–3 weeks. Of those duties performed, most involved routine patrol, crowd control, and control of traffic. A small amount of time was taken up with training and administration, and a few officers had been used in more specialized work, such as plain-clothes observation. In some forces, an attempt has been made to use specials for community-based work. In the Metropolitan Police, for example, they have given crime-prevention advice and instructed women in self-defence, whilst in West Yorkshire, specials have been involved in work with neighbourhood watch groups (Newton 1987). Interestingly, in the light of governmental desire to use the specials as a community link, however, Leon (1989) found that few were engaged in community activity. More significantly, despite Home Office wishes to expand the Special Constabulary by winning new recruits from neighbourhood watch schemes, only 0.5 per cent of specials' time was spent in work with such schemes.

Clearly, the Home Office is attracted to the idea of expanding the Special Constabulary. For one thing, it believes the office of special constable (the responsible 'citizen in uniform') to have a crucial mediating role in establishing good police–community relations. For another, if achieved, such expansion would provide a cheap means of satisfying public demand for a visible police presence on the streets. Accordingly, as Leon (1989) suggests, it has become clear since the 1987 Home Office Conference on Special Constables that specials are to be seen less as a police reserve, and more as part of the normal mechanism of policing.

However, Leon's (1989) findings would seem to cast doubt on the likely success of these intentions. For one thing, it is unlikely that membership can be increased to the levels the Home Office would like. During the last decade forces have weeded out many of their older, less active members and encouraged younger recruits. This policy has had significant impact, some of it positive, some of it less so. Certainly, more and more recruits come from the young, female, and skilled sections of society. The number of female specials, for instance, now stands in excess of 5,000, twice the number of a decade ago. Currently, one-third of specials are women and, at current rates of wastage, females will outnumber males by 1996. This contrasts markedly with the gender ratio amongst regular officers, in some forces as high as ten men for every one woman. The increase in female specials is obviously a positive development and, significantly, they appear to be deployed in a much wider range of duties than female regulars. However, as Leon (1989) notes, their use in specialized duties, such as interviewing victims of rape and sexual assault, may simply be due to the lack of available women regulars. More disturbingly for the Home Office, the increase in female recruitment has been matched by a corresponding reduction in the recruitment of males, whose numbers now stand at about 11,000, half of what they were a decade ago.

The age and occupational structure of the Special Constabulary is also changing. Gill's (1987) study of Devon & Cornwall Special Constabulary rejected Bunyan's (1977) view that specials had a 'petty bourgeois' social background. In Gill's sample, specials had a similar background to regular officers, differing from other volunteer groups (in probation and victim support) by not being predominantly middle class. Leon's (1989; 1990) research seems to suggest that this may be changing, though that may be due, one assumes, to the changing gender ratio of recruitment. In her sample, 58 per cent of specials were in professional, intermediate, or skilled non-manual employment, and in the case of women, no less than 72 per cent came from these groups. In addition to this, large numbers of recruits now join the specials in their late teens and early twenties. Many have a future police career in mind, and are advised by their local force to gain experience of police work in this way. This development, combined with the pruning of 'dead wood', means that over 90 per cent of specials are now under 45 years of age, almost one-fifth being under 22, and over one-half under 30. This has two negative effects. First, many specials are relatively inexperienced. Second, the professional career orientation of many of them weakens the rationale of using specials as a link between the community and the police organization.

These structural changes have had the effect of producing a disturbingly high turnover in membership, with many specials either leaving to join the regular force, or growing disillusioned and leaving the organization altogether. The effect is that the annual recruitment and wastage figures for most forces cancel each other out, and nil growth is the norm. Even if some means could be found of expanding recruitment, however, it is questionable whether specials could serve as the bridge between police and community envisaged by the Home Office. For one thing, Leon's (1989; 1990) research indicates that many specials absorb the cop culture which surrounds them, resenting the fact that community involvement takes them away from real 'action'. Moreover, Gill (1987) suggests that volunteers who join the specials already have, unlike other volunteer groups, a prior attachment to the cultural values of the police organization, as well as a general commitment to 'law and order'.

In speculating about future developments, Leon (1989; 1990) suggests that the Special Constabulary might, eventually, be split into two sections. One, for young careerists seeking experience of police work, could be deployed at weekends. The other, for older personnel, could replace regular officers on community-liaison duties. Such a development, she argues, would erode the boundaries of the professional force with 'soft' policing tasks becoming the province of specials. When seen alongside the penetration of parks, housing estates, and docks by private and quasi-private police organizations, such a development would justify the formation of a streamlined regular force, whose role would be to concentrate solely on serious crime and violent disorder.

The problem with this scenario is that, as Leon's (1989) own observations indicate, recruitment of sufficient specials to carry out the 'soft' functions might be difficult. One solution might be to offer incentives. (Interestingly, in December 1990, the Home Office announced two experimental schemes in which bounties would be paid to selected specials in order to boost recruitment.) Certainly, there is no legal obstacle to payment, since various acts of Parliament permit local authorities, private companies, and other bodies to grant paid employees Special Constabulary powers. Indeed, it might be the case that unless police forces adopt some version of the 'Profitshire' model described in Chapter 3 (the paid employment of 'civilians for police purposes'), private bodies will do it for them. If that happens, of course, many of the 'soft' policing functions identified by Leon (1989; 1990) will be taken over by the private sector.

As yet, the police have not confronted this dilemma, though at the 1989 Superintendents' Conference, Susan Davies of Dorset Constabulary made proposals which went half-way towards the 'paid civilians for police purposes' model. Here, Davies suggested that, given existing civilianization, plus public demand for a visible police presence on the streets and the police's increasing inability to provide it, a 'two tier' police service might be developed. Davies's essential point is that the bulk of public demand is for police time, rather than police expertise: 'time to stop and have a word. Time to deal with street annoyances, like the litter bug, youngsters with skate boards, or careless pet owners allowing dogs to foul pavements' (Davies 1989: 2277). Such tasks could be performed by uniformed 'street wardens', since many of the duties carried out by patrol officers do not require the exercise of constabulary powers, though they do provide the public with a reassuring police presence. Rather than deploying expensive police personnel for these duties, it is suggested that wardens be made responsible for routine street patrol in much the same way as traffic wardens carry out routine traffic and parking duties. Street wardens, could be identified as part of the police service and, along with traffic wardens and other police civilians, would constitute the first tier of a restructured, two-tier, organization.

A similar proposal has been put forward by Peter Howse,

Deputy Chief Constable of Norfolk Constabulary, who has appointed a project team to investigate whether civilian 'peace officers' can meet public expectations. Both proposals have, of course, to be seen as a response to police fears of 'creeping privatization'. Davies (1989) is adamant that her proposals are preferable to the alternatives of either an expanded private security sector or the growth of council-sponsored security schemes, both of which 'erode the position of the police'. If implemented, the street-warden solution would, she maintains, enable the police to retain control of street patrols and ensure continued access to local intelligence.

Predictably, the response of the police associations has been cool. The Operational Policing Review suggests that the proposal for street wardens 'demonstrates a fundamental lack of appreciation of what constitutes the role of the police officer' (cited in *Police Review* 16 March 1990). Here, it is argued that any uniformed presence on the streets has to have the potential to intervene authoritatively, something which demands both professional skill and the capacity to exercise constabulary powers. The Police Federation response was equally damning, its Vice-Chairman, Richard Coyles, denying that the public would settle for 'second-rate, powerless auxiliaries as a substitute for the real thing' (cited in Tendler 1989). Instead, the Federation proposed the formation of a national police reserve, consisting mainly of retired officers. Such a reserve could take over some of the functions requiring constabulary powers, thus blocking the expansion of private security. Significantly, the Federation saw such a body operating according to 'Profitshire' principles, Chairman Alan Eastwood suggesting that charges for the reserve's use could be levied on commerce, industry, and local authorities (Kirby 1989a).

Neighbourhood Watch

In Britain, the form of responsible citizenship most actively encouraged by government during the last decade has, undoubtedly, been neighbourhood watch. The first British scheme was set up in 1982. By August 1989 the Home Office claimed that a total of 74,000 schemes had been established and John Patten, describing neighbourhood watch as 'an unstoppable movement', announced that new schemes were appearing at the rate of 600 per week. A year later, the official total had risen to 81,000 and a report by 'Crime Concern' claimed that some chief constables were blocking the development of new schemes because of the growing burden placed on police resources. Police hopes that neighbour-hood watch would become more self-sustaining have, in effect, proved false and Home Office expectations that there could be as many as 120,000 schemes by the mid-1990s are causing increased concern in police circles (Cowdry 1990).

Nevertheless, the government remains totally committed to the neighbourhood-watch principle, making – sometimes extravagant – claims that the expansion of schemes has had a direct impact on crime and fear of crime. In 1989, for instance, John Patten, was at pains to stress that the growth in neighbourhood watch, coupled with the reduction in property crime arising in the annual crime statistics, 'must be more than a coincidence'. Patten also went on to articulate a rudimentary theory of neighbourhood watch: 'We have always known that community crime prevention is a force for the good – bringing neighbours together, leading to good relations with the police, and reducing the fear of crime.'

In fact, as Bennett (1987) indicates, there are two theoretical strands to neighbourhood watch. The first of these focuses on the problem of social disorganization arising from the impact of urbanization and industrialization on urban communities. Social disorganization, it is maintained, erodes communal norms and undermines informal processes of social control. This leads, in turn, to increased crime and to greater dependence on formal control mechanisms, such as the police. Here, the message is that informal control mechanisms have to be reconstituted by community programmes if crime is to be tackled. A second strand derives from rational-choice conceptions of human action where crime is seen as a product of individuals exploiting situational opportunities. Here, the conclusion is that crime can be prevented by blocking such opportunities for law-breaking.

Although Patten's statement appears to place emphasis on the first of these theoretical strands, in practice, as Bennett suggests, the implementation of neighbourhood watch in Britain probably relates more to situational theory than to social disorganization theory. Thus, although the rhetoric of neighbourhood watch often identifies with the development of community spirit, the expansion of community participation, and the initiation of increased police–public contact, the mechanisms whereby such lofty ideals might be realized are often unclear. In practice, therefore, schemes have tended to focus on the more limited goal of opportunity reduction, by having participants act as the 'eyes and ears of the police'.

Already, there is the suggestion here that the rhetoric and the reality of neighbourhood watch may not coincide. Moreover, in a context where government has invested so much political capital in the watch principle, it is apparent that objective evaluation of the movement may be undermined by ideological considerations. So what conclusions can be drawn about neighbourhood watch from available empirical studies? Consider first, evidence on participation. In a study of members of schemes in two areas of London, Bennett (1989a) examined the impact of a number of variables on participation. Contrary to claims that watch schemes are narrow in the social base of their recruitment and thereby socially divisive, no significant difference was found in the age, race, educational attainment, employment, or socio-economic status of participants, though home ownership did correlate positively with participation. Victims (measured by total number of property offences and burglaries reported) were no more likely to participate than non-victims. Unlike some American studies, however, where no difference between participants and non-participants in terms of levels of fear of crime was found, London participants were significantly more worried about burglary and robbery than non-participants. In both areas some correlation was found between participation and community involvement (measured by numbers of neighbours considered as friends, numbers of people recognized in the street, etc.), though in neither area was any difference found between a participant's and a non-participant's assessment of the police.

An earlier study by Hope (1988), carried out when only 1 per cent of households were involved in neighbourhood watch, attempted to assess potential support using data from the 1984 British Crime Survey. Here, again, owner-occupiers were more likely to express support than private or council tenants. In this case, however, income had a definite impact on potential participation, households with the lowest incomes being least likely to express support. As in Bennett's study, direct victimization appeared to have no effect on willingness to participate. Hope contends, however, that support is related to potential victimization, though this is mediated in complex ways by people's feelings about their neighbourhood. In fact, he suggests that a 'threshold effect' operates, support increasing with fear of victimization up to a certain point, after which it diminishes: 'A certain level of "fear arousal" may be necessary to stimulate a decision to join neighbourhood watch, but too high a level of fear may paralyse participation, promoting withdrawal behind closed doors' (Hope 1988: 154). One factor shaping this threshold effect is personal satisfaction with the neighbourhood. Hope maintains that for neighbourhood watch to work people need to feel enough at risk from crime and disorder to make the effort of participation worthwhile, and at the same time have sufficient confidence in their community to warrant involvement in self-help activity. This conclusion, he argues, is confirmed by the fact that the greatest support for watch schemes was expressed by those who thought that they would be burglary victims in the next year *and* who believed their community to be socially cohesive. By contrast, where a sense of community is lacking, perceived risk does not seem to affect willingness to participate. On this basis it is hypothesized that support for neighbourhood watch is likely to be strongest in areas where the risk of crime is perceived to be real, but where a sense of community prevails. By contrast, limited support would be likely both where there is little perceived risk coupled with a great sense of community and where there is little sense of community coupled with a great perceived risk.

Hope (1988) maintains that the low levels of support found in agricultural areas (low crime/high community support) and in some urban areas (high crime/low community support) provides empirical confirmation of this hypothesis. Moreover, evidence from American researchers provides some support for the 'threshold' argument (Skogan 1988; Garofalo and McLeod 1988). However, Hope admits that without detailed attitudinal data it is unwise to speculate about collective community sentiments. It also has to be borne in mind that the measure of 'community cohesion' employed in this analysis, as well as in some of the American research, was based upon respondent's answers to a single question. ('In some neighbourhoods people do things together and try to help each other while in other areas people mostly go their own way. In general, what kind of neighbourhood would you say you live in?') One has to have serious reservations about a model of community action based upon a subjective response to a single question. After all communities are constituted, not merely through subjective sentiments, but by a variety of social and organizational conditions. Confirmation of this is found in Fowler and Mangione's (1986) account of the Hartford crime prevention experiment. In this case, community action to improve the neighbourhood and to prevent crime was dependent upon the prior existence of certain social conditions. One of these was the establishment of communal (neighbourhood) space, a condition only met when planners were given the task of restricting vehicular access to communal territory. In this case community, far from being the mere expression of a sentiment, was a product of the establishment of definite – albeit mundane – spatial and social conditions.

Empirical studies of participation, though interesting, remain somewhat inconclusive. For one thing, analysis of community action is notoriously difficult to operationalize. For another, as Bennett (1989a) admits, it is naive to seek simple explanations of participation, since patterns of community action will vary substantially from time to time and place to place. This fact alone should, of course, rule out the possibility of any simple 'neighbourhood watch effect'. The problem is, however, that those with an investment in neighbourhood watch are more than ready to invoke precisely such an effect. In that sense, empirical analysis has tended to be undermined by exaggeration and rhetoric.

This is most evident in claims made about the alleged impact of neighbourhood watch on crime rates. There is considerable evidence that police evaluations of the impact of watch schemes in both Britain and the USA have been highly optimistic. Some of these studies have had serious methodological shortcomings, being based upon very small areas with lower-than-average crime rates. An evaluation in Northumbria, for example, reported a 22 per cent fall in burglary as the result of a reduction from 18 to 14 offences, whilst in Cheshire a 90 per cent fall arose when a mere 19 offences were reduced to 2 (Bennett 1987).

Governmental claims about the efficacy of neighbourhood watch have been no less problematical. John Patten was by no means the only Conservative politician to draw attention to the 'coincidence' of neighbourhood watch's expansion and the dramatic fall in recorded property crime between 1987 and 1988. Yet, a more guarded assessment might have noted that that reduction followed a substantial rise in recorded burglaries between 1985 and 1986, and that 'booms' and 'slumps' in the burglary rate are, in any case, relatively commonplace. Evidence from the British Crime Survey of 1988 (Mayhew *et al*. 1989) suggests that the relationship between neighbourhood watch and burglary rates is uncertain. The real rate of burglary with loss increased more slowly between 1972–87 than police statistics suggest, the rate being inflated by an increase in reporting by victims and in recording by the police. In 1972, about 45 per cent of reported burglary was recorded. By 1987 this figure had risen to 73 per cent, a trend caused by the combination of greater home insurance (on propensity to report) and increased police manpower (on propensity to record). Though the number of burglaries recorded in official statistics fell after 1986, it is likely that some of this reduction was the result of a fall in the number of reported offences, rather than any simple reduction in crime. Such a reduction in reporting may arise for several reasons. Victims may have the (justified) perception that the police's small chances of solving the crime make reporting redundant. Alternately, some may be deterred by police policy itself. In some forces policies of 'crime screening' (where offences are 'screened in' or 'screened out' on a points system, according to potential solvability) mean that the bulk of burglaries will not be investigated at all. (Interestingly, a Metropolitan Police investigation of 'crime screening' pointed to the danger that public awareness of the system might have discouraged people from reporting crime – especially when calculations indicated that crime 'screened in' was unlikely to exceed 15 per cent of all allegations.)

The inference is, then, that part of the initial rise in the burglary rate was due to greater reporting, whilst part of the recent fall has been due to a reduction in reporting. Changes in the burglary rate need, therefore, to be treated with caution. This casts doubt upon the evangelical zeal with which the Government and the police have marketed the neighbourhood watch idea as a panacea for crime. Overall the British Crime Survey is more suggestive of agnosticism than evangelism. Probably the only certain conclusion to be drawn is that, at present, it is impossible to say whether neighbourhood watch schemes have any effect on the crime rate at all.

In fact, the most detailed empirical study of neighbourhood watch in Britain (Bennett 1989b; 1990) also draws a highly qualified conclusion about the system's efficacy: 'The most important general conclusion is that the NW programme had no measured impact (either favourable or unfavourable) on the crime rate in either of the two NW areas' (Bennett 1990: 167). Bennett's study identified two experimental areas in Wimbledon and Acton which were about to implement neighbourhood watch, comparing then with one adjacent non-watch area in Wimbledon (a displacement area) and one non-watch area in Redbridge (the control area). Using the method of quasi-experimental design, the procedure was repeated after the implementation process had been given time to take effect. In both watch areas the changes shown were 'less promising than might have been hoped' (Bennett 1989b: 8), the incidence of household and personal victimizations increasing after the implementation of the schemes. In the displacement area the rate for both remained constant, whilst in the control area the rate went down for household offences and up for offences against the person. The results relating to public attitudes and behaviour were more encouraging. In Acton there was significant improvement in fear of household crime, area satisfaction, and sense of social cohesion, whilst in Wimbledon improvements in area satisfaction and home-protection behaviour were reported. In neither area, however, was there any reduction in fear of personal crime or in the perceived probability of household or personal victimization. In Acton there was improvement in public evaluation of police performance, though in both locations there was a significant decrease in police–public contact, measured both by telephone and street contact.

Bennett considers two types of explanation for the absence of any clear neighbourhood watch effect. The first of these is simply that the theory is wrong. In his view, this is a premature conclusion, though he accepts that there are some difficulties with the theory. For example, suburban households are unoccupied for long periods during the working day. In some areas there is high residential turnover. In others the presence of large numbers of legitimate outsiders makes identification of 'non-legitimates' difficult for watchers. (For an outline of American findings on theoretical shortcomings, see Rosenbaum 1988.) Bennett's own preferred explanation is implementation failure, the programmes implemented being, in his view, somewhat 'weak' versions of the theory, which failed to activate the appropriate mechanisms. Here, for example, he notes that little information was distributed to divisional commanders in the Metropolitan Police, and despite the dependence of the scheme on the Seattle programme, key elements of that programme (such as ensuring 'signs of occupancy' in houses) were not incorporated. Instead, there is the strong suggestion that the police, caught up in the politically generated public enthusiasm for watch schemes, opted for quantity, rather than quality, of implementation.

In one sense, the end of neighbourhood watch's 'honeymoon period' was signalled by the publication of the crime figures for the first quarter of 1990. These indicated the sharpest increase in recorded crime since records began in 1857 with thefts rising by 16 per cent, criminal damage by 12 per cent, and burglary by 18 per cent. These figures confirmed what many commentators had always predicted – that the improved crime figures for 1988 were an aberration in an otherwise steady post-war trend of annual increases in recorded crime of around 5 per pent per annum. Yet, John Patten was not to be deterred by the encroachment of reality. In 1988 he had announced that the falling crime figures were a positive result of neighbourhood watch's coverage of no less than 3.5 million households. In 1990 he declared that the disturbing rise in recorded property crime was a result of the benefits of neighbourhood watch being restricted by its limited coverage to, as yet, 'only (sic) 4 million households'. Here is confirmation, then, that neighbourhood watch, as part of a general governmental commitment to the virtues of responsible citizenship, cannot be seen to fail.

CO-PRODUCTION AND COMMUNITY

Analysis of community-based approaches, such as neighbourhood watch, can be aided by an examination of social change in localities. Some writers maintain that, nowadays, most of the informal networks necessary to effect social control have disappeared (Hope 1988). Clarke (1987), for example, argues that social control has passed through three stages. Before the new police emerged communities managed crime themselves. Then the public police took over responsibility for crime control, though a considerable amount of informal control was still exerted in working-class communities. During the last 50 years, however, this situation has altered in two ways. First, working-class communities were destroyed by redevelopment policies. Second, the expansion of citizenship led people, newly informed of their rights, to demand the exercise of formal 'due process'. According to Clarke the combination of these developments destroyed the basis of informal social control. Thus, contemporary community solutions, rather than managing crime, merely create an illusory 'sense of control over crime and disorder' (Clarke 1987: 397).

The argument that informal social control has simply disappeared, like the periodic hysteria about 'family breakdown' and 'community decline', owes more to moral pessimism than sociological analysis. Certainly, communities have been affected by social and political development, but the changes which have occurred in informal behaviour have been both complex and diverse. For one thing, the thesis that informalism has simply been eradicated fits uneasily with sociology's recent 'rediscovery' of the 'informal economy' and of continued informal activity in a variety of social institutions. For another, in the context of debates on social control, there is increasing empirical evidence that people continue to engage in various forms of 'self-policing' and 'self-regulation'.

Here, it is interesting to contrast Clarke's thesis with Shapland and Vagg's (1987; 1988) study of 'self-policing' in urban and rural localities. In this study a considerable amount of informal activity (watching, noticing, informing the police, informing property holders, direct action) was seen to occur, 'members of the public . . . engaging in a great deal of "policing" work' (Shapland and Vagg 1987: 54). The authors make two observations about this activity. First, though 'remarkably prevalent' in both urban and rural locations, it was less evident in the former than the latter. This suggests that urban renewal may have had some negative impact on informalism. However, the suggestion that it eradicated informal social control (or, indeed, as Cohen (1972) maintains, that it 'privatized' working-class communal space, thereby disrupting class-conscious solidarity) is too simplistic. Such an interpretation invokes a model of working-class solidarity which is dubious (see Cronin 1984; Johnston 1986; Pahl and Wallace 1988 for three different forms of criticism of that model). It also exaggerates the privatized element in contemporary neighbourhood relations (Proctor 1990). In fact, neither the 'solidaristic' past, nor the 'privatized' present allow for the complexity of local social relations. Redevelopment is one of several variables (including environmental design, housing type and tenure, age structure, population density, quality of local political organization, quantity and quality of existing police provision) which will affect the character of informal social control in any locality. This means that there is likely to be considerable diversity in the ways in which, and the extent to which such control is exerted in particular places. Indeed, Shapland and Vagg's second observation confirms that diversity, since they note that people's problems, nuisances and crimes are, themselves, highly localized: 'The precise manifestation of a particular problem . . . was very localised; to one street, or even part of a street' (Shapland and Vagg 1987: 55). Accordingly, informal responses to such problems were, themselves, also highly localized and particular.

Evidence of this sort confirms that citizens, far from being passive consumers of police services, engage in various forms of productive activity. These may range from individual/household activities undertaken with police co-operation (property marking, volunteer policing) to those without such co-operation (buying a guard dog, staying indoors); and from group activities supported by the police (liaison groups, police-sponsored patrols) to those lacking such support (citizen patrol groups: see Percy 1979). Once citizens are perceived as producers, rather than as passive clients, it becomes important for policy makers to understand the factors affecting self-policing in any locality. In Britain there has been very little attempt to explore the extent to which citizens engage in such productive activity (for exceptions see Hough and Mayhew 1985: 47-9; Smith 1986: Chapter 7; Jones et al. 1986: 24-7), though in the USA the debate on the 'co-production' of public security has begun to explore the relationship between public police provision and informal mechanisms. Here, it is emphasized that public bodies need information on the determinants of co-productive activity in order to plan successfully: 'If planners were aware of what characteristics are related to what form of co-production, policies could be developed to mesh the actions of service bureaucracies with communities with these characteristics' (Rosentraub and Harlow 1983: 451).

Certainly, the American research raises penetrating questions in the present climate. Should higher-income areas with greater potential for private self-protection enjoy the same level of public police provision as poor areas? Given finite resources and varying patterns of co-production, should police services be allocated unevenly in order to maximize equity between different categories of co-producers? But the research is also limited in two respects. First, there are conceptual and methodological problems. Some of this research (Warren *et al.* 1982) has tried to distinguish mere 'parallel' production (actions undertaken without any contact with public police agencies – such as buying a guard dog) from genuine co-production (actions 'which are intended to augment ... the actions of public agencies and involve conjoint behaviour' (Warren *et al.* 1982: 43). The object here is to demarcate private productive activity (parallel production) from public co-production, on the grounds that policy makers need to be able to assess the public–private balance in production. The problem is, however, that the different categories are not mutually exclusive, individuals and groups engaging in complex combinations of public and private forms. It is not merely that one can simultaneously own a guard dog *and* participate in neighbourhood watch. One can also be a member of neighbourhood watch group *and* engage in those citizens patrol activities (see Chapter 8) of which the police so thoroughly disapprove. Analysis of this complex interweaving of public and private productive forms may be possible, though it requires the gathering of qualitative data, rather than the quantitative aggregates found in existing co-production research – most of which, in the USA at least, has come from crudely executed telephone surveys.

A second problem is that co-production research has adopted an excessively 'administrative' focus. Often, the assumption is that the crime problem can be solved as soon as policy makers activate the newly discovered tripartite structure of co-production (public police, private security, and responsible citizens). As Henderson puts it 'law enforcement, given these new developments, is best understood as a problem of public administration' which can examine 'the possible benefits from various possible permutations of public agency/private sector relationships' (Henderson 1987: 49, 55).

The problem is that this administrative focus lacks any politics.

As such, it fails to explore the political, ethical, and legal factors which will determine whether a given co-productive practice is either desirable or feasible. It cannot be assumed, for example, that co-production invariably generates positive relations between citizens and the police. In fact, Pennell's comparison of citizens taking private and collective measures of protection with those engaging in no self-protective activity at all, concludes that more contact with the police, far from leading to better public evaluation of police services, may produce the opposite effect: 'the more frequent pattern appears to be that membership in community organizations is associated with a higher frequency of negative contacts with the police' (Pennell 1978: 71). Pennell's point, like my earlier comments about the unforeseen consequences of consumerism on modes of public evaluation of police services (see Chapter 3), is that greater citizen participation may, in certain circumstances, result in higher levels of alienation from the police.

In that sense, community approaches in general, and co-production in particular, may be double-edged in their impact. Take, for example, the following scenario. A public, repeatedly encouraged by government to support the police through engaging in responsible citizenship, perceives (rightly or wrongly) police services to be inadequate to local needs. As a result, a number of vigilante-style citizen-patrol groups emerge to supplement police services. This scenario, far from being exaggerated is borne out by evidence from the USA, which indicates that community organization against crime more often arises as a result of police failure to protect citizens, than as a consequence of neighbourhood watch theory (Skogan 1988). In the following chapter I shall consider the implications of autonomous versions of such spontaneous citizen action in detail.

Finally, let us return to the general question of informal social control. Earlier, I commented on the fact that informalism was both localized and diverse. This observation raises a number of problems for police policy. First, if social control is localized and variable, 'the street being too large a unit for people to watch' (Shapland and Vagg 1987: 56), uniform policies of crime prevention such as neighbourhood watch – itself instigated by central government – may be misdirected. (For a discussion of this point see Shapland and Vagg 1988: 8–9.) Likewise, the structures of consultation and communication which accompany these initiatives, such as police liaison committees – another product of central state influence – might be misdirected. Existing community-based policies may, in other words, be spatially flawed. Shapland (1988), for one, has commented on the discrepancy between localized concerns and 'the areas subsumed by operational command in the police force and in local authorities' where 'divisions' 'district councils' and 'subdivisions' are too large to have much bearing on people's concerns about crime.

What may be required for the effective implementation of community solutions, then, are specific forms of police–public partnership, tailored to the characteristics of informalism in local areas. However, such localized policing will inevitably expose issues of local justice. As Shapland and Vagg observe 'informal social control carries within itself the seeds of a very local justice and the potential for constantly varying standards of expected conduct' (Shapland and Vagg 1988: 178). In one sense, of course, this is hardly a novel observation. After all, informal justice has always been exercised in communities, not just by individual citizens, but by corporate actors as well. (Business enterprises have always acted according to their own private standards of commercial justice, refusing to report crime, or doing so only for insurance purposes.) The difference here, however, is that a genuinely localized policing would politicize the issue of informal justice, and that is certainly something that neither police nor government would wish to encourage. For that reason, there is every likelihood that formal police agencies will seek to restrain informalism by supplemental strategies. At the same time, it has to be recognized that that policy remains both unstable and inherently contradictory.

Last, there is the question of citizenship itself. Clarke (1987) sees citizenship as incompatible with informalism because people demand their rights and insist that the police exercise 'due process'. For him, citizenship is concerned with individual rights to the exclusion of social values. It is, in effect, another manifestation of privatized social relations, active citizenship being an exclusively individualistic act. Here, Clarke's analysis raises an important issue. Can citizenship have a social content? The autonomous forms of self-policing to be discussed in the following chapter would suggest an affirmative answer to this question, though one which raises considerable controversy.

Chapter 8

Citizenship and self-policing II
Autonomous citizenship

Some reactions to crime and disorder, or to fear of crime and disorder, involve citizens in autonomous forms of self-policing: those which are undertaken, in the main, without the co-operation or involvement of public police organizations. The first section of this chapter considers some examples of such autonomous activity, and the varied circumstances in which it may arise. In the second section some of the empirical evidence relating to one form of autonomous self-policing is reviewed – the citizen street or subway patrol. The final section makes a political and theoretical assessment of autonomous self-policing.

VIGILANTIST SELF-POLICING

In Britain, the issue of citizen participation in the control of street crime and disorder has become increasingly topical. It is apparent, however, that 'active citizenship' can mean different things to different people. After all, citizens can be active in many different ways and for many different purposes – from acts of individual vengeance, carried out in response to some perceived injustice, to the relatively inactive participation in state-sponsored, crime-prevention initiatives described in Chapter 7.

The existence of such activity raises a number of theoretical issues. For example, vigilantism has been a continuous theme in the history of social control and policing in America. In Britain, organized vigilantism (though not informal self-policing within communities) has been comparatively rare since the emergence of public policing in the last century. The question of how vigilantism is to be located in any conceptualization of policing as a social function is, therefore, likely to be a more contentious one in this country than in the USA. Yet, academics who have analysed the phenomenon of vigilantism are by no means agreed as to its nature and characteristics. There is, for instance, disagreement about whether or not it is essentially violent, conservative, extra-legal, or directed only towards crime; whether it can be undertaken by state agents (such as the police) as well as by private citizens; whether it is a movement or a mere reaction (Burrows 1976: Rosenbaum and Sedeberg 1976: Abrahams 1987).

Leaving aside such conceptual and theoretical ambiguity for the moment, and using the term in an ethically neutral sense, it may be said that 'vigilantist self-policing' is prevalent in many different social and political contexts. Within the recent past, vigilante groups are reported to have operated in places as varied as Haiti ('vigilance brigades' lynching four men who tried to destabilize the presidential elections), the Phillipines (civilian vigilante groups co-operating with the police to defeat the spread of communism), Brazil (police allegedly being involved in 'death squads' organized to drive young, homeless people from the streets), and China (the police publicly praising a group of more than twenty people who clubbed a mugger to death in Shaanxi Province). Jepsen (1989) reports a case from the Danish provincial town of Herning, where local people formed a squad to defend foreign refugees from a fascist youth group. In France there is a 'Legitimate Self-Defence Association' which advises its members how to set traps for prospective thieves and vandals without contravening the law. In one celebrated case (described in the *Independent* 31 August 1988), a garage owner, Lionel Legras, whose cottage had been burgled a dozen times, rigged up a transistor radio with batteries and explosives, left the device on his kitchen table, and nailed a sign to the cottage: 'Keep Out. Danger of Death'. That night, two men broke down the front door, one of them being killed in the subsequent explosion. Legras was found guilty of manslaughter, but that verdict was subsequently reversed in an assize court.

Vigilantism is, in fact, prevalent in a variety of social systems. Its occurrence in African societies is well documented by anthropologists. In Tanzania, for example, a village-vigilante movement ('Sungusungu') began as a defence against armed cattle theft and highway robbery:

> Every man ... had to be equipped with bow and arrows and with a gourd-stem whistle which was blown in emergencies. If

a theft was committed, a hue and cry was raised and the thieves were to be followed by the young men of the village. The whistles would alert the members of neighbouring villages who would in turn forewarn others in the same way.

(Abrahams 1987: 181–2)

Sungusungu, like other vigilante movements, signals a loss of public faith in the state's system of law enforcement. In Tanzania this raises serious political questions about the capacity of a new state system to retain authority over its subject populations. In a discussion of vigilante groups in the Bugisu district of Uganda, Heald (1986) also relates their development to the wider political context. Here, the situation is equated with that described in Hobsbawm's (1959) account of the Sicilian Mafia, whose emergence is traced to a power vacuum arising from the abolition of feudalism, the impact of capitalism, and the ineffectiveness of a foreign state. In this power vacuum, the mafia 'grew out of the needs of all rural classes, and served the purpose of all in varying degrees' (Hobsbawm 1959: 41) to the extent that 'central government, the landlords, and the peasants arranged and rearranged themselves in conflict and accommodation' (Blok 1974: 10–11).

From the early 1960s a similar power vacuum pertained in Bugisu. After Ugandan independence in 1962, districts lost their previous autonomy, as political leaders tried to achieve a unitary state. The authority of local chiefs was undermined and replaced by an alien formal–legal authority. The effect of this was to create a mood of disorder:

Fear of witchcraft, theft and violence flourished, while self-help appeared as the only remedy. . . . The problem of what to do about a neighbour when he flouted all his obligations towards you came to the fore in the face of a distant police force, an alien judicial system and a chief whose powers had been curtailed. . . . Lukoosi, 'order' was seen to have broken down and, with it, self-respect.

(Heald 1986: 450)

In practice, Bugisu vigilantism tended to be directed at the deviant and the disreputable and, like many vigilante movements, it became a form of social control exerted by the 'haves' (the respectable and landed) upon the 'have nots' (the disreputable and landless).

All of the examples described so far confirm that it is far from unusual for policing functions to be undertaken by private individuals and groups in a variety of different social contexts. There are, moreover, societies where the formal distinction between public police functionaries and citizens is defined much more loosely than is customary in the west. This is particularly so in certain socialist systems. In Nicaragua, the principal mechanism of social control is the Sandinista Defence Committee (CDS). These committees have a membership of more than half a million people organized in 10,000 block committees. The function of the CDS is 'revolutionary vigilance' and, like the Cuban Committees for the Defence of the Revolution, there is a general concern to control criminal and deviant behaviour (Adam 1988).

Probably the most developed form of popular involvement in policing is found in China, where no professional police presence is found below the district level of organization. Here, policing has an organic relationship to a highly politicized grass-roots communal organization. Contrary to the British experience, where public debate on policing has been dominated by the various attempts to draw 'correct' boundaries between 'the community', 'politics', and 'policing', such conceptual distinctions are meaningless in the Chinese context. Instead, 'law enforcement is part of a macro-control system that relies on citizen participation in watching ... public security being integrated within the informal controls of the neighbourhood' (Johnson 1983–4: 8–9: see also Alderson 1981; Brewer *et al.* 1988).

In Britain, by contrast, debate on vigilantism and self-policing has centred around the emergence of citizen patrol groups (Boothroyd 1989a). Those patrols which have emerged display a wide diversity of personnel and objectives. A group mobilized in Grimethorpe, South Yorkshire deployed between sixty and eighty volunteers every night of the week on all-night patrol of residential streets. Here, the main object was to deter property crimes (Boothroyd 1989b). A similar group in Gosforth, Newcastle upon Tyne, operated on a nightly basis with over 100 men, half of whom were retired, and included former police officers, a former lieutenant-colonel and a major. Some groups, by contrast, seek to protect commercial property. In the Anfield area of Liverpool, one shopkeeper set up a group after his premises were broken into forty-eight times (Craig 1989).

The emergence of such groups, together with the growth of private-security street patrols and municipally organized patrols of public spaces has had an impact in police circles. John Dellow, the Metropolitan Deputy Commissioner has publicly supported the idea of civic patrols, and the Metropolitan Police has now launched its own force of civic volunteers – the so-called 'Blue Angels'. Although such proposals are intended to ensure that active citizenship should, by coming under police jurisdiction, transform itself into responsible citizenship, the Police Federation continues to reject the very idea of citizen patrol. At the Federation's Annual Conference in 1989 it was proposed, instead, that a reserve force, consisting mainly of retired police officers, should be developed. Such a force, it was said, could patrol shopping malls and housing estates, particularly those with large elderly populations, remaining at the same time, accountable for its actions (Kirby 1989a).

Not surprisingly, the police response to citizen patrol has been to assume that once groups come under police jurisdiction it will be possible to eradicate what are perceived to be isolated and pathological outbreaks of vigilantism. Such a view is questionable for two reasons. In the first place, it is likely that such activity is neither isolated nor abnormal. It is almost certainly more prevalent than we assume and, probably, has always been so. Second, as can be seen from the previous examples, vigilantist activity may arise as a normal consequence of communal uncertainty, instability, or disorder. This can be illustrated by a number of instances from communities in the United Kingdom.

An extreme example of self-policing is found in Northern Ireland's punishment squads. Recently, there has been an escalation of punishment shootings directed at anti-social behaviour (burglary, mugging, assault, etc.) by both Republican and Loyalist paramilitaries. Typically, these shootings have occurred in hardline areas where police patrol is difficult, and it has been suggested that the remarkable rise in 'kneecappings' in Loyalist areas has arisen because of the community's loss of faith in the effectiveness of the Royal Ulster Constabulary. Interestingly, a recent article suggests that there appear to be informal rules of punishment which are recognized by everybody, including offenders: a verbal warning is usually given before a beating or a shooting; if a victim is too young, then the father will be beaten up in lieu of the offender; victims have to accept that, on occasions, punishment will occur in public, and so on. In addition, the author suggests that despite the savagery of the punishments, its practitioners enjoy widespread support from sections of the community: 'Paramilitaries on both sides of the sectarian gulf are plainly acting on the demands of the people in their communities. .... People tell you that their only criticism of the punishment squads is that they are too lenient' (Thomson 1988).

The Northern Ireland example is one of sectarian self-policing under exceptional political circumstances. There are, however, other examples of communities policing themselves in order to retain cultural identity and cohesion when they are perceived to be under threat. Factor and Stenson (1987) describe how the adult Jewish community in London has sought to exert social control over Jewish youth in the 1980s. Since 1983, affluent Jewish youths have congregated around a North London underground station in large numbers, a situation which has created a potential for conflict with local non-Jewish youths. Significantly, this phenomenon has coincided with a moral panic in the Jewish community about its young people being a target for drug pushers, muggers, and right-wing skinheads. In the Jewish press, young people are seen as the deviant and ill-disciplined product of overindulgent parents. This moral panic is, however, part of a much wider concern in the community about the character and conditions of existence of Jewish social identity.

In response to this perception of deviance amongst Jewish youth, the community instituted a partial form of self-policing: 'the Jewish Board of deputies negotiated with the local police to use its own trained representatives, known as "Bozos" to the kids, to co-operate with the police in a softly-softly approach to maintaining order' (Factor and Stenson 1987: 19). The function of these individuals was to defuse situations of potential conflict, provide protection for Jewish youth, and maintain order on the streets and in residential and commercial areas: functions having a remarkable similarity to classical definitions of the (public) police mandate.

Whereas the previous two examples demonstrate that self-policing may arise as a response to internal disequilibrium in a community, the remaining examples concern communal response to different types of external threat. A 'Brass Tacks' television programme broadcast in 1986 drew attention to two vigilante groups – one operating in North Mosely, Birmingham, the other in Waltham Forest, London. The 'North Mosely Residents Association Direct Action Committee' was formed to respond to the problem posed by the growing number of prostitutes and kerb-crawlers in the suburb. Its membership was middle class, consisting of barristers, housewives, and local business people, both white and Asian. The committee set up street patrols on six nights a week, with between twelve and twenty members participating, in order to discourage prostitutes, pimps, and their clients from frequenting the streets. In Waltham Forest, by contrast, a vigilante group grew out of the local Pakistani Welfare Society when members of the community were faced with a spate of racial attacks in the early 1980s. Here, at weekends, groups of members toured the streets of the borough to check on the homes of those subjected to racial threats and harassment. Since the number of racial attacks has now decreased, the group has, since 1987, been demobilized, though it remains in reserve should it need to be deployed again (Pakistani Welfare Society of Waltham Forest 1989).

Though occupying different locations, responding to different problems and having different memberships, these groups have two important things in common. First, they arose out of a belief that the police were unable or unwilling to respond to their problems. Second, as the programme's presenter, David Henshaw put it, 'they are the police's natural constituency. They believe in law and order, have always supported the police, and only as a last resort have they taken to the streets' (*Listener* 23 January 1986).

This last point is an interesting one. Many of the groups to have emerged in Britain in recent years can be said to be part of the police's 'natural constituency', but this is by no means always the case. On Merseyside, spasmodic acts of violent vigilantism (physical assaults, burning down of houses) have been directed at heroin dealers who have infiltrated the Toxteth area, at a time when police-community relations are, to say the least, strained. Delroy Burris, a prominent member of the black community, remarked on the serious problem of heroin dealing on the streets:

> Last week it was like the city centre in Granby street, there were so many junkies here. They come here because they know there are less police and they are less likely to get done.... But we don't want them here so we move them on, we take their money

until they get fed up and move off . . . the community gives them a good hiding. . . . Effectively we police it ourselves.

(*Independent* 15 October 1988)

The last three cases suggest that vigilantism can arise when the public regards the police response to community problems as inadequate. To what extent, then, can citizen groups, once mobilized, do any better? The next section addresses this and other issues through an examination of evidence from the USA.

CITIZEN PATROL ACTIVITY

During the 1960s there was a proliferation of citizens' vigilante groups in the USA. These took a variety of forms: black self-protection groups (such as the 'Oakland Black Panthers' or the 'Deacons for Defence and Justice', which organized armed patrols against the Ku-Klux-Klan): white residents, mobilized against the perceived threat of black rioters (such as Anthony Imperiale's 'North Ward Citizen Committee' in Newark, New Jersey): and groups organized against crime (such as the 'Maccabees', a group of Hasidic Jews from Crown Heights, Brooklyn, threatened by an escalation of muggings and robberies). Since that time, there has been a steady stream of citizen activity in the USA. Some of this has involved individuals in isolated acts, the most famous being the shooting of four black youths by Bernhard Goetz in 1984. But most recent controversy has surrounded the deployment of organized citizen patrols on subways and streets by the Guardian Angels.

In conjunction with this resurgence of vigilantism, a body of empirical research has begun to appear in the USA, assessing the activity of such bodies and their relations with police and public. In a study of twenty-eight self-defence groups carried out in the Boston area in the early 1970s (Marx and Archer 1973; 1976), 55 per cent of the white population and 69 per cent of the black population supported the idea of citizen patrols. In this study seventeen of the twenty-eight groups were black, the preponderance of such groups reflecting the controversy surrounding the policing of black neighbourhoods. Desire for mobilization was strongest amongst males, the young, the less well educated, and blacks, with black males expressing the greatest willingness to mobilize. With increase in age and education, willingness to mobilize decreased, leading the authors to suggest that middle-class persons were less likely to favour street patrols than lower-class persons, preferring instead more traditional political action.

In the study, a distinction was drawn between supplemental groups (those seeing themselves as ancillary to and supportive of the police) and adversarial groups (those seeing their function as one of defending their communities against alleged police excesses). Though the former groups often developed into police auxiliaries or became part of municipal projects, such as housing patrols, the relationship of both groups to the police was complex. Police support for supplemental groups was not always prevalent. Often the police opposed such groups because of their encroachment on the professional territory of law-enforcement personnel. Equally, police opposition to adversarial groups was by no means universal. At times of intense social disorder the emergence of such groups could fill a vacuum between a hostile community and the public authorities. After such groups had provided that buffer, they usually encountered hostility from the police and frequently disappeared.

By and large, however, only supplemental groups were likely to survive for any significant length of time, since they were subjected to less police harassment and could draw financial help and legitimacy from local government. However, this also created a dilemma. In order to survive, supplemental groups had to accommodate to the local power structure. But such accommodation threatened to compromise them in the eyes of their constituency of support in the community. On the other hand, the problem faced by adversarial groups exposed contradictions within the community itself. Though adversarial groups emerged because of the conflict between some sections of the community and the police, community leaders often withheld support from such groups, believing that the community needed better public police provision, not a citizen substitute.

By 1977, research commissioned by the US Department of Justice (Yin *et al.* 1977) indicated that there were approximately 900 residential patrols in operation, many arising in response to a sudden spurt in local crime. The average duration of groups was between 4 and $5\frac{1}{2}$ years, though more than half ceased to operate within 4 years, and less than 15 per cent survived more than 10 years. The study revealed a variety of citizen activities including foot patrols, automobile patrols, watchmen, gatekeepers, and stationary or mobile building patrols. In addition, some of these patrols had social service functions, such as civil defence, sanitation or youth employment. All in all, neighbourhood patrols (those covering a given residential area) comprised 27 per cent of the total, the remainder being divided equally between building and social service patrols. Patrol members consisted mainly of volunteers (63 per cent), though about one-fifth employed private guards, and a small number paid residents for undertaking patrol activity. Those with paid residents or private guards usually had less than ten members, and always under twenty. Volunteer patrols, by contrast had memberships ranging, more or less evenly, from below twenty-five to more than seventy-five.

The report made specific comments about two categories of patrol activity. First, it suggested that building patrols could succeed in reducing crime and increasing residents' sense of security: 'The small enclosed areas protected by building patrols may facilitate the effective screening and identification of intruders or potential troublemakers' (Yin *et al.* 1977: 19). This view was qualified, however, in respect of some public housing projects. Here, in contrast to wealthier areas, crime was, at least in part, an internal problem, requiring additional measures above and beyond patrol.

As for neighbourhood patrols, the report was more guarded. Here, effective surveillance was a greater problem because of the lack of clear territorial boundaries. 'Strangers' are more difficult to identify in residential streets than in housing complexes. This means that neighbourhood patrols are restricted to 'observing' behaviour, rather than 'challenging' behaviour. It also means that they are more likely to make mistakes and generate conflict when they do intervene.

These operational difficulties cast doubt upon the impact of street patrol on crime levels and on fear of crime. Recent research on the best-known citizen patrol group to have emerged in the last decade, the Guardian Angels, addresses precisely these issues. A study carried out in New York in the early 1980s (Ostrowe and DiBiase 1983) compared the attitudes of civilian subway passengers, transit police, and the New York Police Department (NYPD) officers towards the group. Civilians were more favourably disposed towards the Angels than were either of the two police groups: 61 per cent of civilians (13 per cent transit police; 12 per cent NYPD) wishing there were more Angels, and 67 per cent (27 per cent transit; 28 per cent NYPD) believing that their presence made the subways safer. A mere 4 per cent of civilians (43 per cent transit; 52 per cent NYPD) opposed the actions of the Angels and only 25 per cent of them (83 per cent transit; 74 per cent NYPD) believed that only the police should fight crime. The authors of the article suggest, however, that there is public concern about the unaccountable nature of the group, one comment repeated by several civilians being especially pertinent: 'I'd rather see more police, but if we can't have them I'll take anything that will help.'

A recent study carried out under the auspices of the US National Institute of Justice (Pennell *et al*. 1985) drew comparisons between Angels chapters in twenty-one cities and fifteen other citizen groups. Angels chapters had an average of twenty members each (forty-five in other citizen groups): 66 per cent of Angels were aged 20 or under (66 per cent aged 50 or over in citizen groups): 32 per cent were white (94 per cent in citizen groups): 59 per cent were educated below high-school level (43 per cent of citizen group members having 4 or more years of college): 84 per cent of Angels were male (53 per cent in citizen groups).

The average number of patrols per week ranged from one to twelve across the twenty-one cities. In eight cities considered 'primary sites', where patrol activity was logged, six of the chapters patrolled less than three times per week, on average. The researchers suggest, however, that data may not be reliable and observation suggested that some chapters with fewer members had problems undertaking scheduled patrols. National guidelines suggest that patrols should consist of eight or more members, but although this figure was met in eastern cities in the sample, the average number in western cities was four.

The research team saw many incidents on patrol where Angels assisted citizens (escorting, carrying bags, etc.), but only 6 per cent of patrols involved helping in a crime incident. In 672 patrols studied during a 6-month period, only two citizen's arrests were documented and only ten crime-related incidents resulted in the Angels contacting the police. The researchers note (Pennell *et al*. 1985: 22) that this seems to be inconsistent with group claims that almost 600 citizen's arrests have been made in a 6-year period, though, in part, this may be due to confusion as to what constitutes a citizen's arrest. There are cases where Angels detain suspects for the police, but do not make an arrest, though these may be counted as such by Angels.

In one of the study sites, San Diego, an assessment was made of the impact of Angel street patrols on crimes of violence and property crimes over a 3-year period. The research compared changes in levels of reported crime in an experimental area (where the Angels patrolled) with those in a control area (with no patrol). Findings suggested that 'the Angels did not have an impact on violent crime in San Diego', despite violent crimes (assault, battery, robbery, rape, etc.) being the primary target offences for preventative patrol activity. Although violent crime dropped by 22 per cent in the patrol area during the period of research, it fell by no less than 42 per cent in the control area, suggesting that factors other than patrol explained the reduction.

Property offences did, however, decline at a greater rate in the patrol area (25 per cent) than in the control area (15 per cent). This suggested that 'Angels may have contributed to the greater reduction in property crime in the areas patrolled'. However, even this finding is not conclusive as the San Diego Police Department initiated a foot patrol in the experimental area during the period of research which could have affected crime levels. The report therefore, concludes only that 'patrols may have had a short-term effect on property crimes when their visibility was at peak levels'.

Public reaction to the Angels was, however, easier to assess. Over 60 per cent of respondents said that they felt safer as a result of Angels' patrols, female and older citizens in particular saying that the Angels had most impact on feelings of safety. Citizens rated the effectiveness of the Angels in reducing crime higher than did police or city government officials. Most police administrators and city officials saw Angel patrols as beneficial and nearly half wanted them to continue. But most were unwilling to describe their official position as supportive of the Angels.

The report makes a number of other points which are worthy of note. First, it is suggested that Angel patrols offer potential for generating informal social control, thereby preventing crime and reducing fear of crime. This view is in accordance with both the 'Wilson–Kelling' thesis (the view that order maintenance is a precondition of crime control) and with empirical evidence on police foot patrol (showing that it reduces fear of crime rather than crime itself). Indeed, the reports' assessment of Angel patrols (good at reducing fear of crime, bad at reducing crime levels) is more or less the same conclusion that researchers have reached when examining the effectiveness of police foot patrol. Second, it is argued that the Angels offer an alternative approach to citizen involvement in crime prevention which provides positive role models for youth, bridges the gap between older citizens and adolescents, and reduces the fear of crime for certain sections of the community. In particular, it is emphasized that the most significant feature of the Guardian Angels may be that they represent 'a group of young people generally recognized as contributing to the crime problem'. Third, the authors comment on the 'relative longevity' of the Angels compared to other citizen groups. In part this seems to be due to the leader's awareness of the danger of establishing too close ties with public bodies, thereby compromising community support. Finally, the researchers raise an interesting question about the impact of different forms of patrol activity undertaken by the Angels:

> The transit systems [subways] are more or less neutral territory compared to communities in which feelings of loyalty, pride and ownership are more evident. Guardian Angel patrols may be more acceptable on the subways than in residential neighbourhoods where Angel patrols have *not* been specifically requested.
>
> (Pennell *et al.* 1985: 22–3)

This raises an important question about spatial and territorial aspects of citizen patrol activity to which I shall return in the next section.

The most detailed piece of research on the Angels (Kenny 1986) used a quasi-experimental design technique to examine their impact on crime and fear of crime on the New York subway – a particularly important topic, given their recent deployment on the London Underground. Kenny argues that people's fear of subway crime is, in fact, not as great as the media would have us believe. When asked about fear of subway crime at night, 21 per cent of respondents did declare themselves 'very worried' and 26 per cent 'somewhat worried'. But 27 per cent said they were 'only a litle worried' and no less than 25 per cent said that they were 'not at all worried'. Having said that, Kenny's study demonstrated that women's fear was significantly higher than men's, and there were also differences between racial groups in degrees of fear, Hispanics being more fearful than blacks and blacks more fearful than whites. In effect, this means that although the 'average' citizen experienced moderate levels of fear, some groups exhibited acute fear of crime (e.g. 80 per cent of Hispanic women and almost 60 per cent of white women came into the 'very/somewhat fearful' category). Interestingly, there was no evidence of greater fear of crime amongst the elderly than amongst adults or teenagers and, contrary to expectations, the elderly rated 'teenage crime', 'assault' and 'robbery/mugging' as less of a problem than did teenagers.

The majority of respondents (66 per cent) believed that the Angels could reduce crime. Furthermore, most people, including the majority of transit police, approved of the Angels and their methods. When asked whether the Angels reduced fear of crime, most answered in the affirmative, though again, differences in response according to age, sex, and race could be identified. The actual, rather than expected impact of the Angels was, however, both questionable and difficult to assess with any degree of accuracy. In the first place, most people (54 per cent) reported 'seldom' or 'never' having seen an Angel subway patrol in operation – despite the fact that the group claimed more than 1,000 members. But, in any case, Kenny (1986) found that whether patrols were present or absent, they had little impact on people's overall and long-range levels of fear of crime, or on their estimation of the likelihood of victimization. Nor did the presence of Angel patrols appear to increase people's propensity to intervene as active citizens, when faced with incidents of crime and disorder.

The most controversial aspect of the study, however, concerned the impact of Angel patrols on rates of crime and incivility. Kenny (1986) had selected a number of subway locations with reputations for high levels of crime, with the intention of assessing the effect of patrols on crime levels (using both official statistics and victimization evidence). However, despite the moral panic about New York subway crime, he found that such crime was difficult to find, an analysis of reported incidents during the project's 3 months offering support for the conclusion that the system was, 'in reality, quite safe' (Kenny 1986: 168, 91). In effect, this meant that the number of crimes and incivilities occurring in each of the project areas was so small as to make meaningful conclusions about the impact of patrol impossible. Kenny's point is not that patrol cannot reduce crime: merely that in this case, there is very little crime to be reduced. The crime problem on the subway, which gives the Angels their legitimacy, does not, in his view, appear to exist.

This observation led him to identify two serious problems. First, although the presence of the Angels may make some passengers feel temporarily safer, they must accept responsibility for fuelling public apprehension about the problem of crime. Even worse, because their patrol activity is sporadic, and their capacity to reduce fear correspondingly patchy, they may be exacerbating the overall problem of fear. Second, he suggests that the absence of a genuine crime problem has serious implications for the future direction of the organization. For one thing, it may be difficult to retain members. This, in turn, may encourage less-rigorous vetting procedures in the selection of members – procedures which are, in any case, already weak. Finally, the organization may 'become more involved in social control activities and less selective in the methods it employs' (Kenny 1986: v). This latter course of action is, in Kenny's view, implicit in Lisa Sliwa's claim that: 'The Angels don't need crime to stay in business.'

SELF-POLICING: AN ASSESSMENT

What conclusions can be drawn, then, from available evidence on autonomous self-policing, and what implications do they have for the future of such activity in Britain? Classic vigilantism of the sort found in the USA during the last century occurred where there was no developed criminal justice system. Modern vigilantism, by contrast, often arises when two circumstances occur. First, communities believe (rightly or wrongly) that public tranquillity is under threat from escalating crime and social disorder. Second, they believe that the criminal justice system is failing to deal with the perceived crisis: either because of a lack of resources, or because of inefficiency and misplaced priorities. One American commentator on contemporary vigilantism puts it thus: 'If there is a widespread feeling that the state is no longer holding up its end of the bargain, then people will start "taking the law into their own hands" – which is where it was in the first place' (Tucker 1985: 27). It is hardly surprising, then, given high levels of fear of crime, that members of the public in the USA (and the same is likely to be true in Britain) express consistently high levels of support for the principle of citizen self-policing. Nor is it surprising that this support is often highest amongst those most in fear of victimization (women, the elderly).

Evidence discussed in the last section, however, suggests that there are a number of problems associated with self-policing. First, there is the question of its impact on crime and disorder. Both Kenny (1986) and Pennel *et al.* (1985) comment on the relative infrequency of Guardian Angel patrols. This infrequency is hardly surprising, in view of the fact that public police forces, with vastly greater resources of personnel, find it difficult to provide adequate foot-patrol coverage. But, notwithstanding the quantity of patrols, there remains serious doubt that patrol activity, whether carried out by citizens or by public police officers, has any significant impact on crime levels (Clarke and Hough 1984; Kelling 1983). Given that doubt, it is entirely predictable that Angel patrols had little impact on crime in San Diego and New York.

A more controversial matter concerns whether self-policing has a positive effect on people's fear of crime, on their willingness to involve themselves in helping others and, most important of all, on the generation and regeneration of mechanisms of informal social control in communities. Probably, the answer to this is that 'it depends', amongst other things, on the location being policed. Kenny's (1986) observation that the experience of patrol fails to generate such informal mechanisms on the anonymous terrain of the New York subway is, after all, hardly surprising. Yet, Pennell *et al.* (1985) clearly see more potential for such developments in locations with greater spatial and social coherence.

The relationship between spatial and social factors in any assessment of autonomous self-policing is both complicated and controversial. It is clear, for example, that spatial factors will have an impact on the effectiveness of patrol. As Yin *et al.* (1977) point out, neighbourhoods have less definite spatial boundaries than public housing projects. This makes effective surveillance of neighbourhoods relatively more difficult and increases the likelihood of conflicts arising when mistakes are made, thus confirming that the operational success of patrol groups is affected by varying spatial conditions. Equally, however, success is likely to be affected by different social conditions. As Pennell *et al.* (1985)

suggest, there may be less social controversy about subway patrol than about street patrol. Subways, after all, are socially 'neutral' territories whilst streets are often claimed as the social property ('turf') of one or other group within a community. The problem is that any trade-off between social and spatial conditions may be detrimental to operational effectiveness. The spatial neutrality of the subway may offer a climate which is conducive to minimum social controversy, but that same neutrality may, as I have suggested above, be inimical to the generation of active citizenship amongst those being policed.

This suggests that those involved in self-policing may be required to resolve certain contradictions: in this case, how to balance a desire for operational effectiveness with a desire for conflict avoidance. But this is, by no means the only trade-off that may require resolution, a point which is well demonstrated in a recent publication of the Adam Smith Institute (Elliott 1989), also concerned with the impact of spatial and social factors on the operational success of citizen initiatives.

Drawing upon the experience of certain cities in the USA, Elliott proposes that government should delegate much of the responsibility for crime prevention and public security to residents' and homeowners' associations. One of his reasons for arguing this, concerns the need to establish residential control over 'undefined space'. The concept of undefined space is associated with a number of writers, including Oscar Newman (1973), Jane Jacobs (1984), and Alice Coleman (1985). Jacobs, for instance, argues that public peace is kept, not by the police, but by an intricate network of voluntary controls which are enforced by people themselves. These controls are only effective if certain spatial criteria are met, however. Both Jacobs and Coleman insist that voluntary social control is impossible to achieve where there is confusion or ambiguity about the division between public and private space. For under such circumstances, surveillance over 'outsiders' becomes impossible.

On the basis of these arguments, Elliott proposes that Britain should follow the example of some American cities, where areas of undefined space are placed under the control of residents' and homeowners' associations:

> The association should then be free to fence the area in, making it the clear property of the residents. Where, as was found in St Louis, the openness of the street was found to hinder security,

the option of street closure should be available. Where requested by the residents association, the local authority should allow them to close off their street.

(Elliott 1989: 26)

Contrary to current government thinking, Elliott sees no reason why residents' groups should not undertake neighbourhood patrols. His point is, merely, that without the elimination of 'undefined space', they are likely to be ineffective. Street closure, by contrast, will serve as a way of 'marking out ownership' thereby 'organising residents into defending their own property' more effectively.

Elliott's suggestions offer a practical response to some of the difficulties of neighbourhood street patrols remarked on by Yin *et al.* (1977). In particular, he recognizes that effective patrol may require modification of spatial and territorial boundaries. The problem is, however, that such proposals raise serious ethical and political questions. Elliott proposes that six pilot schemes be established in British cities 'where crime and urban decay are localized, and where there is a large measure of civic pride among a stable population elsewhere' (Elliott 1989: 27). Essentially, this seems to involve residents of 'stable and well-maintained areas', exerting a 'stabilizing' influence on the rest of the city by exerting social control over shifting and 'footloose' populations: in other words, a strategy of 'containment' of problem populations.

Such a policy may be desirable or not, depending on one's political persuasions, but in the context of historical vigilantism and self-policing, it raises two interesting issues. First, there is the age-old question of whether vigilantism is an inherently conservative force. Probably the answer to this is in the affirmative, though there is more than one sense in which 'conservatism' can apply here. The example of self-policing in a London Jewish community shows us vigilantism being employed in an attempt to reconstitute a threatened Jewish social identity. This, like the Northern Ireland example, is a form of cultural or sectarian conservatism, activated by an establishment, though not necessarily by an elite (Rosenbaum and Sedeberg 1976). The image offered to us by Elliott's proposals is, however, rather more akin to that found in Bugisu vigilantism: a vigilantism of the elite ('haves') against the non-elite ('have nots'). And in the context of a society with tangible material inequalities, this has obvious social and political dangers.

A second issue concerns the character of self-policing as a mechanism of social control. The policy of 'containment' proposed here, though ostensibly about the control of criminality in urban communities, is just as much about the regulation of 'problem populations' by 'stable' ones. Such social control is, thereby, justified as a legitimate response, not just to criminality, but to any form of behaviour deemed abnormal or threatening by groups of active residents. The American conservative criminologist, Wilson, has presented similar arguments in the past (Wilson and Kelling 1982), but it is another American conservative, Tucker, who gets to the crux of the matter, when he demands a 'vigilantism of the majority'. Such a vigilantism involves 'rediscovering a certain unwillingness to tolerate bizarre, dangerous, or irresponsible behaviour, and redeveloping a taste for public order' (Tucker 1985: 224).

In circumstances where self-policing is subject to a degree of democratic regulation, the dangers implicit in such a development might be avoidable. But the whole purpose of Elliott's proposal is to remove responsibility for public security from political bodies and delegate it to groups of local residents. The problem is, that historical studies of vigilantism are full of examples of movements which got out of hand. Many of these began with the express purpose of confronting criminality in communities, only to diversify into the regulation of other, ever wider, realms of deviance. Invariably, when classic vigilantes ('Regulators') went too far, other vigilantes ('Moderators') intervened to exert constraint. Without some degree of public regulation of self-policing, the same anarchic situation could be repeated.

Interestingly, despite its professed commitment to the virtues of self-help, active citizenship, voluntarism, and market forces, the Conservative Government has been somewhat hesitant about how to deal with the issue of self-policing. Partly, this is due to recognition of the need to forestall criticism from the police unions. But, there is a genuine tension within the Party as to how far active citizenship should be encouraged with respect to law and order. Grass-roots sections (including the Young Conservatives, who passed a motion in favour of the Guardian Angels whilst they were in Britain) are positive in their support. Official policy, however, is concerned to play down the issue as much as possible. In the context of what was discussed in Chapter 2, it would seem that the

Party's neo-liberal commitment to private initiatives is outweighed by its traditional Tory commitment to the state, as monopolistic provider of the conditions of social order.

In policy terms, the result has been an uncertain compromise. At present, the Home Office is committed to a second phase of neighbourhood watch, directed at the problem of street crime. One aim of this will be to enlarge the Special Constabulary by recruiting members (especially young people) through the mechanism of local watch schemes. The rationale of this is to 'keep the lid' on active citizenship by rendering it 'responsible', John Patten, the Home Office Minister, having declared his personal opposition to all autonomous patrol groups. Indeed, this opposition goes as far as to discourage members of Neighbourhood Watch schemes, who have not become Special Constables, from patrolling their own communities. The message is that citizens can help to tackle street crime by becoming the 'eyes and ears of the police'. But unless they are prepared to join the Special Constabulary, they should watch and listen from indoors. The problem with this, of course, is that is certain to be even less effective as a strategy directed towards street crime than existing schemes are towards property crime.

The Government's dilemma over active citizenship – having extolled its virtues, how to control it – is, in part, understandable; for it does raise issues which are difficult to resolve. Despite the aborted attempt to establish the Guardian Angels in Britain, these issues are unlikely to go away. Some years ago, Laurie Taylor (1976) wrote an article in which he considered the prospects for, and the desirability of, vigilantism in Britain. Taylor's assessment of vigi-lantism was partly negative: it is uncontrolled, arbitrary in its effects, unaccountable; its members are inexperienced, unscreened, untrained, and may break the law; it may be hijacked by extreme political interest groups, and so on. But, for all that, he refused to see vigilantism in entirely negative terms. After all, he asks, is not self-help likely to be the best available response to many people (especially the poor) when faced with crime? And does not vigilantism have certain democratic and participatory resonances attached to it, in contrast to a criminal justice system which is, all too often, experienced as bureaucratic, insensitive, unresponsive, and inefficient?

Taylor's ambivalence about vigilantism is entirely justified. It is reasonable that people should (and inevitable that they will) participate in the provision of their own security. But such participation has to be regulated by some responsible public body. In short, active citizenship, in both its responsible and autonomous forms, needs to be given a social dimension. Moreover, discussion of it, in the context of law and order, cannot be divorced from problems of citizenship in general. It is all very well to invoke civic values, but some of the most likely recruits for citizen patrol in Britain will be, as in the USA, young, male, lower-class blacks: precisely those groups which are most alienated from civil institutions and organizations which are supposed to represent their interests (Ben Tovim *et al.* 1986: Lea and Young 1984). The issue of citizenship is, in short, inseparable from questions of social justice.

Part III

Theoretical conclusions

New directions in the sociology of policing

Anyone compiling a bibliography of major works on contemporary British policing in 1970 would have been hard-pressed to find more than a handful of texts written by researchers, other than those employed by the Home Office. (The books by Banton (1964), Whitaker (1964), Marshall (1965), and Lambert (1970), immediately spring to mind, but after that the list tails off rapidly.) Since the early 1970s, however, that situation has changed dramatically and, today, there is a huge and ever-expanding literature on the sociology of British policing.

Obviously, that literature is variable in form, content, and quality, making any attempt at generalization difficult. Nevertheless, in this chapter I propose to draw attention to certain general preoccupations – and related problems – which can be identified in much of this work. The chapter is divided into three sections. In the first I identify the general features of the sociology of policing in Britain. In the next two sections I describe the shortcomings of that sociology in respect of its analysis of the 'functional' and 'structural' dimensions of policing. In the course of the third section I suggest that the adoption of some new approaches to the sociology of policing enable those existing theoretical shortcomings to be rectified.

THE SOCIOLOGY OF BRITISH POLICING

In Britain (as in North America) the sociology of policing has been shaped by a variety of disciplinary approaches, including criminology, socio-legal studies, psychology, and the sociology of work and organizations. Despite the range of influences, however, the focus of research is often disappointingly narrow. This narrowness is due, in part, to the influence of several dominant emphases which, whatever their merits (and there are, undeniably, some) have distorted the subject's development. For present purposes these emphases will be examined across three dimensions: a sectoral dimension, a spatial dimension, and a structural dimension. (The relationship between the three is a crucial issue to which I shall return in the final section of the chapter.)

At the *sectoral* level two emphases are apparent. The first of these is an obsessive preoccupation with the study of public police personnel. As most of this book has been directed towards rejecting the equation of 'policing' and (public) 'police', I need say no more on this for the moment. The second is what one might call an overformalistic approach. In part, this arises because of the prior emphasis on policing as a public function. Since that function is associated with the structure of the formal state apparatus, there is an inevitable concentration on formal aspects. That formalism is further accentuated by certain disciplinary influences. Criminology invariably defines policing in the context of the formal criminal justice system. Law defines police behaviour in terms of a formal legal–constitutional discourse. Of course, formalism, in itself, may be no bad thing. There is obviously a need to understand how public police forces are located within the structure of state apparatuses. Equally, it is impossible to understand the nature of police behaviour without first understanding the legal powers contained within the office of constable. The problem is, however, that once formalism becomes a preoccupation, certain areas of study are automatically excluded from consideration. Consider, for example, my earlier suggestion that policing research has been influenced by the sociology of work and organizations. Though this is undoubtedly true – not least in discussions of police bureaucracy and police occupational cultures – it is significant that the most important area of work-related research to have developed in the last decade (that relating to informal economic and social activity) has had no influence at all on the sociology of policing. Although there are lengthy debates about the discrepancy between formal rules and informal practices in police organizations, informalism in this case, remains imprisoned within the formal problematic of the police organization. What is singularly absent from discussion is any attempt to recognize informalism as a distinct organizing principle in its own right. Yet, the examples of self-policing and co-productive activity referred to in earlier chapters demonstrate that, just as people engage in autonomous 'self-provisioning' in the informal economy (Pahl 1985), so they engage in the production of personal security through 'autonomous' or 'responsible' citizenship.

A second problem concerns the limited *spatial* focus of police research. This has two aspects. First, there is a tendency to concentrate on local or national, rather than international dimensions of policing. Second, the bulk of empirical research has focused on the activities of front-line personnel, something which is confirmed by the abundance of North American and British studies devoted to the examination of the patrol function.

In respect of the latter, one is reminded of a cruel, yet devastating, critique of so-called 'bourgeois sociology', made during the heyday of student radicalism: 'the eyes of sociologists, with few but honourable ... exceptions, have been turned downwards, and their palms upwards' (Nicolaus 1968). Though Nicolaus's comment reflects the politics of a different age and, in fact, concerns an entirely different issue (sociology's obsession with studying the working class), taken literally, it provides a remarkably accurate resumé of the empirical sociology of police work – a publicly funded enterprise whose gaze has been turned almost exclusively on those found at the bottom of the pile, in a single organizational form (i.e. front-line personnel in public police organizations).

Now I am not intending to dismiss a body of research which often gives important insights into police behaviour. Nor could one dispute that the analysis of front-line behaviour is a necessary precondition of any adequate theory of police work. But Nicolaus's comment raises important questions about research priorities. Why is it that there are only a handful of studies whose spatial gaze is directed towards the pinnacle of the organization e.g. Grimshaw and Jefferson (1987) on police policy; Reiner (1989a; 1989b; forthcoming) on chief constables? Why is it that there are so few studies of international policing? Why are there so few genuinely comparative studies of policing systems? Partly, of course, the answers are obvious. For one thing, those in charge of large bureaucracies do not always welcome external scrutiny. For another, lower-level functions undertaken in public places near to home, are more easy to observe than operational decisions made behind the doors of smoke-filled rooms. One cannot help feeling, however, that 'eyes-down', empirical police research addresses a field with a limited spatial range and, in consequence, generates more and more data with less and less scope. The effect is to construct a sociology which, although producing an encyclopaedic knowledge of the ins and outs of the patrol function, excludes other key areas of policing activity from serious consideration. In short, we come to know more and more about less and less.

Sociology's preoccupation with front-line police behaviour also has implications for the *structural* dimension of policing research. At the structural level, the dominant concern, as in other areas of sociological study, has been to assess the extent to which (police) behaviour is shaped by structural factors – such as law, rules, and organizational hierarchies. Broadly speaking, there are two approaches to this issue. The 'structuralist' position maintains that police behaviour is, to a large extent, shaped by legal and organizational factors. An alternative approach maintains that rank-and-file police behaviour is more or less autonomous, such autonomy arising from the relative invisibility of patrol activity, the incapacity of managers to exert effective supervision over officers, and the unprecedented amount of discretion given to officers by their occupation of the office of constable. Within this second approach, one can find a range of different emphases. At one extreme, for example, there are those who adopt a phenomenological viewpoint, seeing control of police behaviour (whether through internal management supervision or through external political control), as inherently problematical (Manning 1979). An excellent example of this approach may be found in Fielding's (1988) account of 'the minutiae of routine policing', where police work is seen as an entirely 'situational' activity. Far from being determined by rules, the constable's discretion is exercised in accordance with his or her perception of the exigencies of any particular situation. Given the diversity of situations, there can be no rules for policing, since it is an activity without structure.

Such an extreme methodological individualism is, however, difficult for some advocates of the relative autonomy of police action to swallow. An alternative approach reintroduces a 'soft' version of structure into the proceedings, in the form of 'occupational cultures'. Advocates of this approach, though still recognizing that structural control of behaviour is problematical, nevertheless see policing as more than merely 'situational' in form. Here, police behaviour is conceptualized in cultural rather than individualistic terms, proponents identifying distinct occupational cultures within police organizations (e.g. Ianni and Ianni 1983 on 'street cops' and 'management cops'; Holdaway (1983) on 'canteen culture'). According to this version, control of police behaviour may be possible, though it requires structural reforms which eradicate or defuse the negative aspects of 'cop culture'.

Though the phenomenological and cultural approaches are distinct, the key point is that their concentration on 'the lowliest but most significant policemen' (Brown 1981: 3) gives them a common microsociological research methodology. The problem with this methodological approach however, is that even where structure is recognized, it is defined in a peculiarly reductive manner. 'Structure', it seems, refers exclusively to the interplay between 'laws', 'rules', and 'culture'. The possibility that alternative structural conditions might have an impact on policing is ruled out of court by the very 'taken-for-grantedness' of the microsociological enterprise, its rank-and-file subject matter, and the structure/culture dialectic contained within it.

All in all, then, once one assesses the sociology of policing in terms of its dominant emphases across these various dimensions, it becomes apparent that reductive assumptions about 'sector', 'space', and 'structure' operate at each level, effectively excluding certain issues from consideration, and foreclosing analysis at key points. In the final section of this chapter I shall suggest ways in which that analysis might be broadened. For the moment, however, I shall draw attention to a further key problematic in the sociology of policing, the question of the policing function.

THE FUNCTIONAL DIMENSION OF POLICING

The preoccupation of police researchers with the examination of rank-and-file behaviour undoubtedly gives valuable insight into street-level policing. The volume and detail of that research is, however, both a strength and a weakness. Researchers now have considerable knowledge of the dynamics of front-line policing, yet, in some respects, there is a danger that the product of that research – the cumulation of multiple observations of rank-and-file behaviour – appears as a form of 'abstracted empiricism' (Mills 1959). In that respect, there is an understandable tendency for researchers to try and impose some conceptual structure on this mass of empirical observations. As I have suggested previously, one way of producing order from apparent chaos is to employ 'culture' (or 'subculture') as a means of endowing police behaviour with some degree of structure and continuity. Another approach focuses on conceptualizing the essential core of the 'police function'.

In the past, debate on the police function has gone in two directions. First, there has been prolonged debate about whether that function should be defined in terms of law enforcement (Kinsey *et al.* 1986), social service functions (Punch and Naylor 1973), or order maintenance (Wilson 1968). Second, there has been debate about the form which that function should take: whether police intervention should be maximal/proactive (Alderson 1979) or minimal/reactive (Kinsey *et al.* 1986). Despite the sophistication of some of this work, subsequent debate has tended to be polarized between what are, ultimately, rather crude models of policing: the police being seen either as a reactive force (the 'fire-brigade' model), a proactive service (the community-policing model) or as some, usually pathological, combination of the two (what one might call the 'velvet glove and iron fist' model – see, for example, Gordon (1984)).

To a certain extent these discussions have gone around in circles. Reiner notes, for example, that one 'perennial chestnut' (Reiner 1985: 111) of this debate – the question of whether the police are best regarded as a force or a service – rests upon a false dichotomy, since the two functions are interdependent. In his view, some police work involves law enforcement, some involves social service activity, but most of it consists of order maintenance 'the settlement of conflicts by means other than formal law enforcement' (Reiner 1985: 114). Here, Reiner follows Bittner's (1980) view that although the police function may involve 'dealing with all sorts of problems', its essence consists in having the legitimate capacity to exercise force in resolving them – where such force is required.

The idea that policing consists of 'dealing with all sorts of problems' whilst in possession of a capacity for the legitimate exercise of force, provides a solid foundation for theorizing the police function. Its strengths are obvious. For one thing, it is sufficiently all-embracing to be able to incorporate not only the multifarious duties that public police officers carry out today, but also those 'moral' and 'administrative' tasks that they may have carried out in the past (see Chapter 1), as well as any additional activities which they may undertake in the future. In some senses, then, this is an excellent solution to the problem of the police function. Perhaps its greatest strength is that, unlike some other approaches, it refuses to define policing in terms of some esssential body of tasks. Echoing the old political adage that 'socialism is what Labour Governments do', 'policing' would thus be defined as what agents with police powers 'do' at any particular time.

The problem is, however, that the formalism contained in this argument – the view that a necessary precondition for 'doing policing' is the possession of a capacity to exercise legitimate coercion – draws a rigid barrier between those activities carried out by police and comparable activities carried out by private agents. In certain respects, of course, it *is* necessary to demarcate between the actions of sworn police officers and those of private individuals. There are clearly important differences between actions carried out with the legal authority of the state and those carried out without such authority – especially when coercion is involved. But the question remains whether a sociology of policing should not develop some conceptual means for dealing with the multifarious activities we call 'policing' without isolating those carried out by police from those carried out by others. As it stands, the legal–formal criterion has the effect of barring most of the private and quasi-private agencies discussed in previous chapters from inclusion in the mainstream sociology of policing, despite the fact that many of the activities carried out by these bodies are similar (and sometimes identical) in form to those undertaken by police officers.

This demarcation seems both pedantic and unsatisfactory when one considers the sorts of contradictions which arise from following through the logic of formalism. For example, it is obvious that public police coerce with the state's authority behind them. But it is equally clear from evidence on police corruption (e.g. Punch 1985) and police vigilantism (e.g. Bowden 1978; Rosenbaum and Sedeberg 1976) that police also coerce without the state's authority. To exclude such acts from police research would be absurd. Yet to include them only because deviant police officers retain a legal capacity which, in this case, has little bearing on their conduct, carries nit-picking to extremes. Likewise, if such acts are not be excluded, there is no more reason to exclude acts of coercion carried out by private security guards lacking the legal authority of the state: and even less for excluding those cases where private personnel exercise limited coercive powers, after being granted the authority to do so by the state.

What these examples show is that policing consists of a complex of connections between formal and substantive powers, and between private and public activities, which the sociology of policing has, by and large, failed to address. Though these issues require careful consideration in any revised sociology of policing, one thing which seems apparent from the outset, is that policing can be defined neither in terms of some essential legal capacity, nor in terms of some essential set of functions. This last point can be pursued further by examining debates about the private security function and the place of that function in the so-called 'policing division of labour'.

Researchers on private security, like those on the public police, have also been preoccupied with functional questions. Here, attention has been concentrated on two issues: the essential function of private security and the relationship between private security and public police in the overall 'policing division of labour'. Stenning and Shearing provide what is probably the most widely accepted answer to the first of these questions. Though they see private security as encapsulating a preventative philosophy which has also taken over public policing ('a conscious move towards preventive, rather than curative, policing' (Stenning and Shearing 1980: 231)), they insist that a distinction has to be made between different types of preventative activity. Thus, whilst public police engage in crime prevention (as well as other activities, such as apprehension and detection), private security engages in the prevention of loss. This commercial imperative should not be lost sight of, they insist, in circumstances where private security is invading the public sphere, the most significant sign of this invasion being the extent to which foot patrol, once the mainstay of the public police, has (at least in North America) become the almost exclusive preserve of private security. The private sector's monopoly of this role leads Shearing and Stenning to argue that Sir Robert Peel's 'dream' of providing an 'unremitting watch' by foot patrol officers, is now being realized – though by private rather than public means (Shearing and Stenning 1981).

South (1985), for one, expresses justified reservations about the excessive neatness of this position, noting that, in reality, both private security firms and the public police provide a combination of mobile and foot-patrol services. However, whether empirically justified or not, the argument is central to a second aspect of Shearing and Stenning's position: the suggestion that the essence of the private security function is one of surveillance. Here, their thesis consists of three propositions: first, that private security is essentially about (loss) prevention; second, that the industry has selected foot patrol as the principal means of effecting such prevention; third, that 'the feature uniting the diverse activities undertaken by private security under the heading of prevention is surveillance' (Shearing and Stenning 1981: 213).

Now, clearly, there is a case for saying that surveillance is a key element of private policing, and the examples given by Shearing and Stenning (watching, patrolling, locking doors, controlling access, checking for fire hazards, screening employees, etc.) involve various degrees of it. However, this view of the core function of private security, is no less problematical than essentialist definitions of the police role. Chapter 5 demonstrated that private security engages in a multiplicity of activities including, patrolling, guarding, order maintenance, arrest, search, detention, prosecution, interrogation, protection, detection, observation, inspection, regulation, registration, state security, control of traffic, parking enforcement, crowd control, risk management, the transportation of cash, and the collection of taxes. In short, private security does anything that public police (or other state officials with special powers) do, and rather more besides. Any attempt to differentiate the private security function from the police function through the concept of 'surveillance' is, therefore, less than helpful. Certainly, many of the activities listed here involve surveillance in some form or other. But then, so do many of the activities of public police, social workers, journalists, and teachers

Attempts have also been made to locate private security in the so-called 'policing division of labour'. In order to understand this, it is necessary to identify some of the links which exist between public police organizations and the private security sector. Such links can be divided into six types:

1 *Interpersonal links.* These take two forms. First, there is the industry's recruitment of senior police officers, army and intelligence personnel, something which is commonplace in both Britain (Bunyan 1977) and North America (Marx 1987; Shearing and Stenning 1981). Second, there is 'moonlighting' by public police officers engaged in private security work. In the USA about 50 per cent of police (Reiss 1988) and 80 per cent of departments (Cunningham and Taylor 1985) are engaged in such activity, and the police unions act as job brokers for the industry. Though forbidden in Britain, it does occur occasionally (see Thomson (1989) for a recent example), and Hoogenboom (1989), discussing its occurrence in Holland raises the interesting question of whether a common police culture is emerging which crosses the public–private divide.

2 *Joint operations.* Marx (1987) outlines the growing number of cases where private companies and public police forces undertake shared operations in the USA. In Britain there is little evidence of major developments along these lines, though there are isolated examples. At Stonehenge, in 1989, a joint operation of sorts occurred, involving Wiltshire Constabulary, the Ministry of Defence Police, and private security guards who operated behind police lines.

3 *Exchange of services.* This can take a variety of forms, though the exchange of information is probably the most important one. Though in Britain private security firms are not granted access to criminal records, in the USA 65 per cent of respondents in Cunningham and Taylor's (1985) study had access to conviction information on at least a monthly basis. Indeed, the FBI accepts fingerprint applications from non-criminal justice agencies at a charge of $12 per card.

4 *Granting of special powers.* I have already mentioned proposals for granting police powers to private guards responsible for court security and prisoner escort in Britain. In the USA 'special police officer' (SPO) status is granted to private agents in locations as varied as New York department stores (Stewart 1985) and Las Vegas casinos (O'Toole 1978).

5 *Public bodies hiring private personnel.* Cunningham and Taylor (1985) estimate that in the USA, 36,000 of the nation's 1 million private security personnel work for the government in some capacity (guarding military bases, public buildings, nuclear

facilities, etc.). Though no estimates are available for Britain, private agents are widely employed in guarding the property of departments of state (including the Home Office and the MOD), as well as in protecting police premises and municipal property.

6 *New organizational forms.* Marx (1987) draws attention to the emergence of new patterns of organization which blur the public–private divide. This might involve, for example, private bodies engaging in joint activities with the state to the extent that the organization begins to take on a quasi-public status. A good example of this can be seen in the development of the LEIU in the USA.

The existence of these institutional links, together with seepage of policing functions across the public–private divide inevitably leads to speculation about how one should theorize the division of labour between public and private sectors. Broadly speaking, one can identify two interpretations of these links. First, there is what one might call the 'complementarity' or 'junior partner' model. According to one version of this model (see Cunningham and Taylor 1985), the industry's preventative activity supplements the police's law-enforcement function. Since the police cannot cope with increased public demand for preventative policing, the industry 'fills the vacuum' by taking over more and more non-law-enforcement duties. The implication of this view is that the police adopt a more narrowly defined crime-fighting role, dispensing not only with prevention but, in some versions of the argument, with traditional social service functions as well (Albanese 1986). Though the industry obviously favours such a 'junior partner' role, the police, whilst recognizing many of the benefits partnership can offer, have reservations about aspects of the division of labour proposed. In particular, there is a fear that police forces might be left with the sole function of maintaining public order through 'fire-brigade' methods. A second interpretation is what one might call the 'disciplinary society' or 'one big police force' model. Flavel, for instance, suggests that the growth of systematic links between public and private sectors demonstrates that 'an increasingly coherent security ideology is being expressed' (Flavel 1973: 15). This idea of 'one big security ideology' is reflected in Shearing and Stenning's view that the extent of co-operation between public and private sectors justifies seeing the result – in the words of one of their respondents – as 'one big police force' (Shearing and

Stenning 1983: 503). Their only disagreement with advocates of the 'complementarity' theory is that, as these links develop, the private sector becomes less and less the 'junior partner' in that relationship.

Though neither of these models should be dismissed out of hand, they are both guilty of simplifying the relationship between public and private sectors. For despite the growth of links, it is clear that relations between the sectors are, as often as not, based on mutual suspicion and avoidance. Even in the USA, where links are more highly developed than elsewhere, the Hallcrest survey found that two-thirds of public law-enforcement managers did not even maintain a list of private security managers in their areas. And despite the constant exchange of personnel between the sectors, relations were still characterized by lack of mutual respect, poor communication and little co-operation (Cunningham and Taylor 1985). This sort of evidence sits uncomfortably with the idea of the private sector as 'junior member' in a cohesive public–private partnership, and it does little to confirm the claim that that partnership comprises 'one big police force'. If there is to be a restructuring of social control in the direction of a 'disciplinary society', the nature of that change will be far more chequered, complex, and messy than existing predictions allow for.

Part of the problem with these predictions arises from the concept of the 'policing division of labour'. Policing is a multi-functional activity whose content and form are variable. The 'labour' contained in the 'policing division of labour' is neither static nor finite in character. In different historical periods it contains different components. The form in which that labour is provided involves different combinations of public and private agents at different times. The links between these agents may be co-operative and complementary, or conflictual and hostile: and, as likely as not, they will exhibit conflict and co-operation simultaneously.

The concept of a 'policing division of labour' is a legitimate one if it enables such complex functional and institutional connections to be taken into account. In some cases, however, the term invites the reduction of those complex connections to a simple 'parcelling out' of functions, themselves perceived in relatively static form. In these cases, the idea of a division of *functions* between different policing agents (itself a perfectly legitimate one) deteriorates into a *functionalist* model in which policing is seen as the guarantor of social cohesion ('the junior partner' model) or of social discipline ('the one big police force'). Though some writers who have used the concept are careful to avoid such functionalist implications, there is a sense, again, in which an influential line of argument forecloses consideration of important issues.

RETHINKING THE STRUCTURAL DIMENSION: THE ROLE OF SPATIAL AND SECTORAL FACTORS

Social researchers have adopted narrow conceptions of the spatial and sectoral aspects of policing. The full significance of those dimensions can best be considered if we visualize them across two parallel continua (see Figure 9.1).

According to this model, 'policing' consists of different forms and combinations of forms (from public to private) located at different levels and combinations of levels (from local to supra-national). It also involves the relations within and between those forms and levels. Such relations are of two types:

1   *Interactions* occur (horizontally) across each continuum. At the sectoral level, for example, interactions take place between private security companies and hybrid police forces, between groups engaged in self-policing and the police, between the police and private security companies, and so on. Policing also involves interactions at the spatial level. The local rank-and-

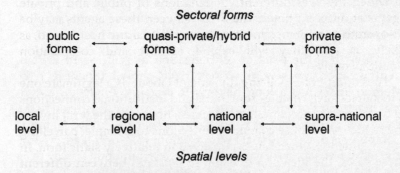

Figure 9.1 Sectoral and spatial continua.

file police officer has ready access to a national database through the Police National Computer. The operational autonomy of local chief constables is increasingly circumscribed by influences from the centre. The expansion of CCTV systems at local levels has to be related to changes in the electronics, security, and defence industries at the international level.

2   *Intersections* occur (vertically) between continua. In essence, this is simply to state that policing (in its various forms) always occupies some, more-or-less complex, spatial location. This point may seem obvious – though it is usually ignored. But, its very 'obviousness' requires us to acknowledge that policing is not a unitary form occupying a single, spatial plane – and once this is admitted, there is no reason to assume that it can be subjected to singular forms of theoretical interpretation.

The idea that sectoral and spatial dimensions might constitute important elements in the analysis of policing structure and behaviour, conflicts with a sociology of policing, dominated at the theoretical level, by the problematic of street-level interactions and the narrow conception of structure (law + rules + culture) associated with it. Continued failure to take account of these dimensions will, however, become increasingly difficult, since it is precisely at the sectoral and spatial levels that future changes in the structure of policing are likely to be determined. Since most of this book has sought to demonstrate the impact of sectoral change, the remainder of the chapter will consider some of the implications of changes in the spatial dimension, by looking at two examples from the public policing sphere.

Centralization

Consider first, the issue of centralization of policing in Britain. Centralization, as several writers have shown (Spencer 1985; Morgan 1987) has a long history. It remains, however, a contentious topic. For one thing, the police are highly sensitized to the semantics of the issue. It is no accident that the Police National Computer is not a 'National Police Computer'. Nor is it surprising, given the accusations of national policy determination arising from the 1984–5 miners' strike, that the National Reporting Centre was renamed the 'Mutual Aid Coordination Committee'.

Evidence of growing centralization and co-ordination of policing has been apparent throughout most of the post-war period: the emergence of Regional Crime Squads in the 1960s; the refinement of mutual-aid policies in the 1970s; the expanded role of the Home Office and the Inspectorate over matters of policy in the 1980s. These tendencies have remained in evidence to the present, with the formation of a National Football Intelligence Unit and proposals for the establishment of a National Police Air Service (presumably to be retitled the 'Police National Air Service'). To that list must be added, of course, Sir Peter Imbert's recent prediction that by the year 2000 plans for the creation of a national police force will be under serious discussion (*The Times* 18 July 1990). An earlier proposal from Imbert that a British FBI might be established to compensate for the inadequacies of the existing system of Regional Crime Squads, has already borne fruit. Under ACPO's influence this idea has evolved into a new National Criminal Intelligence Unit, under whose umbrella will be gathered the existing National Drugs Intelligence Unit, the National Football Intelligence Unit, existing Regional Crime Squad databases, national indexes on animal rights activists, etc. In fact, this initiative provides the basis for a national intelligence databank without the legislation which would be required to bring about a wholescale nationalization of the police.

Despite the fact that these changes at the spatial level of policing raise complex social, political, ethical, and operational issues, they have been relatively unexplored by academic researchers. Confirmation of this fact can be found by considering one example. For much of the last decade there has been an ongoing debate about police accountability in Britain. In part, this debate was sparked off by concern about some of the centralizing tendencies described here, and in that sense, the definition of centralization as a 'problem', gave the discussion a distinct spatial focus – defining the issue as one of local democratic accountability versus authoritarian centralism. Now two things can be said about this formulation. First, the problem of centralization was rarely defined with any degree of rigour by proponents of local accountability. The assumption seemed to be that a centralized (or nationalized) police force was undesirable because, by its very nature, it would be less accountable than one subjected to local democratic control. Yet, such was the singularity of focus that no attempt was made to differentiate between forms and degrees of centralization, their associated costs, and possible benefits (cf. Waddington 1989). A second problem concerned the assumption that localism provided a solution to the 'pathology' of centralization. Here, the difficulty was that proponents of localism tended to make *a priori* assumptions about the superiority of local democracy over central democracy. Apart from raising complex questions about whether local control of policing was feasible or desirable, however, there were no obvious grounds for accepting this assumption. After all, it would have been equally plausible to argue that an effective form of democratic accountability at central state level would be more effective in limiting central power than any localist strategy.

The debate on local accountability generated a considerable amount of heat, though depressingly little light. What was, perhaps, most disappointing about it (given that many of the issues it raised were legitimate ones) was its lack of political realism. Thus, demands for local control of policing policy were easily outflanked by a centralizing government determined to concede only local consultation through police liaison committees. More disturbing than this, however, was the fact that Labour advocates of local democratic control seemed unaware of the implications of other aspects of Party policy which were in train. In particular, current proposals for regional assemblies in England and Wales are certain to increase the chances of regional police forces emerging should a Labour Government be elected. That development may not be incompatible with the principles of local accountability, but it raises many questions about the mechanisms through which such control is to be achieved.

Demands for local control of police 'policies, priorities and methods' are now dead and buried. (The Labour Party (1986) committed itself to this objective prior to the last election, but the demand was mysteriously absent from the 1987 manifesto, since which time the Party has been silent on the issue). The significant point, however, is that while activists in the debate continued to invoke local solutions to the ill-defined spectre of centralization, the real debate about nationalization of policing went on behind their backs. Here, one contribution was especially significant. The Home Affairs Committee Report on *Higher Police Training and the Police Staff College* (House of Commons 1989) had floated the possibility of merging the forty-three local forces in England and

Wales, into a small number of regional bodies. Sir John Wheeler, Chairman of the Committee, pressed strongly for this solution, arguing that it would require removal of the anachronistic system of 'tripartite' accountability (between the Home Secretary, the Chief Constable, and the local police authority) which dominates police governance in England and Wales. Instead, Wheeler proposed that each regional force 'would have a Board of Directors appointed by the Home Secretary'. This would include the Chief Constable and Deputy Chief Constable of the Force, as well as 'non-police officers with a knowledge of finance and of the local community, including a representative of the consultative committees' (Wheeler 1989a: 15). In response to those who saw this as eliminating local accountability, Wheeler added that such accountability (whose embodiment in police authorities was, in his view, 'mythological') would best be achieved through local consultative committees.

Government response to these deliberations was mixed. In April 1989 the, then, Home Secretary, Douglas Hurd, dismissed plans for regional restructuring and expressed commitment to tripartism. Hurd also called, however, for ACPO to be 'bolstered', so as to give 'stronger support at the centre', thereby suggesting that central-ization might be attained by other means. Such 'other means' do not, of course, preclude the application of market principles. Cozens's (1989) suggestion that the agency model provides the best basis for facilitating the national co-ordination of police services, whilst still retaining a form of local governance (see p. 61 above), demonstrates two critical facts. First, it is possible to achieve cen-tralization without de jure nationalization. Indeed, as Waddington (1989) insists, we already have a national force 'where and when it matters'. Second, if anyone was in any doubt, there really are situations where the principles of privatization and national-ization are perfectly compatible.

Internationalization

Should further evidence be required of the impact of sectoral and spatial change on the structure of policing, one needs look no further than Europe. By signing the Single European Act, member states are committed to 'progressively establishing the internal market over a period expiring on 31 December 1992'. Article 13 of the Act states that the internal market shall comprise 'an area without internal frontiers within which the free movement of goods, persons, services and capital is ensured'. Predictably, there has been considerable speculation in police circles about the likely impact of 1992 on operations and policy. Birch (1988) sees the restructuring of the British Police along regional lines as a probable consequence of developments in Europe. Some such development is inevitable, he says, when one considers the operational impact of 1992. The development of a common traffic policy, for instance, inevitably implies the standardization of safety-belt laws, laws on alcohol levels, speed limits, and construction standards for vehicles. Such standardized practices, Birch suggests, cannot be co-ordinated through the existing structure of forty-three forces, nor can it be funded through the existing local authorities. Van Reenen (1989) makes much the same point in respect of public-order policing. Here, already, there is evidence that problems are spreading across borders in mainland Europe, and it is not difficult to envisage a future where common protests (e.g. against EC agricultural policy) might be co-ordinated across different countries.

Debates about the prospects for a European Police Force ('Europol') have gone on since the 1970s, and there has been formal co-operation at the governmental levels through the Trevi Conferences, instigated in 1976 to counter the threat of terrorism. In 1985 Trevi broadened its brief to cover questions of international crime and, in so doing, put the 'Europol' issue back on the political agenda. Some advocates of a 'Europol' envisage a 'Pan-European' policing body with member states seconding officers to a central office in Brussels (Alderson 1988). Others (Baker 1988), conceive of a system of branch offices, with member states seconding officers to a central national unit. The goal of European police integration seems to have been enhanced by the signing of the Schengen Agreement in June 1990 by Germany, Belgium, Luxemburg, the Netherlands, and France. According to the terms of that agreement, police checks at the frontiers of signatories are abolished, hot pursuit across borders is permitted and the co-ordination and sharing of computer information between participants is encouraged.

Realistically, however, there remain severe obstacles to the 'Europol' ideal. For one thing, lengthy experience of border co-operation amongst the Benelux countries, where differences in national police organization create obstacles to effective co-ordination, leave room for scepticism (Fijnaut forthcoming). For another, the mere fact of trying to co-ordinate countries with different laws on firearms, extradition, data protection, and the like, creates serious problems. In consequence, even advocates of the 'Europol' ideal recognize that integration of police systems will involve a mixture of mechanisms (Alderson 1988). Though, at some point, there may be moves towards the formation of a federal organization to deal with multinational crime, it is more likely that internationalization will proceed through the formation of specialized supranational units for dealing with particular problems (see the recent proposals to set up a European Drugs Intelligence Unit (*The Times* 4 May 1990)) and through the furtherance of existing informal arrangements (phone calls, telexes, faxes, exchange of information on databases, etc.). Indeed, in the short term, it is likely that informalism will be the main mechanism of integration (Fijnaut forthcoming; see also Wilkinson 1985).

Van Reenen (1989) provides a useful outline of the different dimensions of future internationalization of policing in Europe. Developments, he suggests, are likely to proceed in four directions:

1 *Co-operation*: at this level, the nature and powers of national police systems are not required to change, co-operation occurring between self-standing forces. Examples of co-operation include both the informal exchange of information described above, and the recent proposal from the British staff associations to establish a 'European Police Unit', in which representatives from the member states (without executive powers) would meet to improve communication and co-operation.

2 *Horizontal integration*: this arises when officers obtain authority to operate in another country, or where government officials from one country get authority over the police (or parts of the police) in another country. An example of horizontal integration would be the right of hot pursuit across borders.

3 *Vertical integration*: this exists when a police organization is created which can operate within the area of the EC as a whole. Vertical integration requires such a force to possess a supranational authority which, in turn, presupposes a central political power at EC level. This form of integration, van Reenen

suggests, is a distant prospect in the context of 'mainstream' policing. Significantly, he notes, however, that within the area of 'administrative policing' (that concerned with the enforcement of EC regulations on health and safety, the environment, the nuclear industry, etc. (cf. Chapter 6 above) such developments are much more likely.

4 *Competition*: the internationalization of policing in Europe presents itself, more and more, as a market in which different policing systems trade their products. It is not difficult to envisage a situation where (say) police training becomes an international commodity and where buyers calculate the relative costs of different national suppliers. ('Does the Belgian product offer better value for money than the Italian'?) Competition is accentuated, of course, when commercial companies are involved in the provision of services and facilities to police forces (e.g. supplying computer systems, computer hardware and software, communications systems, security equipment; sponsoring conferences and exhibitions). At this level, the processes of internationalization and privatization intersect and, with the intervention of defence companies into the private security market, a situation develops akin to the 'military–industrial complex'.

CONCLUDING COMMENTS

The examples considered in the previous section, though merely illustrative, demonstrate that an understanding of spatial factors is fundamental to the analysis of policing structures. Moreover, Van Reenen's comment about competition shows that the intersections between (international) spatial levels and (private) sectoral forms are likely to be an important determinant of future patterns of European policing. In principle, further analysis of the connections between spatial and sectoral dimensions should enable the analysis of policing structures to be developed beyond its present, rather narrow (and, in the case of Britain, somewhat parochial) confines. Since this is not the place to develop that analysis, however, I shall conclude by identifying two areas which might benefit from subjection to a more refined structural approach .

The first of these concerns the question of agency. When the sociology of policing bothers to address the question of agency at all, it tends to do so from the 'rank-and-file' perspective. In other words, it is assumed that, ultimately, those functions we call 'policing' are enacted by individual agents, occupying the office of constable. Now apart from the obvious fact that policing is carried out by individuals who are not constables, it also has to be recognized that a variety of supra-individual agents engage in policing as well: private organizations and public organizations; national bodies and supranational bodies. There is no necessary reason to reduce the action of these supra-individual agents to the actions of their constituent individuals. In other words, there are good sociological reasons for regarding organizations as irreducible agents of action. (I have argued this point at length, elsewhere, though in a different context: Johnston 1986.) Yet, even if one rejects this view, it has to be admitted that actors (even essential individual ones) operating in different spatial and sectoral contexts will be subjected to different conditions of action. To try and reduce those conditions to a narrowly defined conception of structure is facile, since that action will be affected by different conditions: whether the agent is in a commercial or non-commercial organization; whether the agent is operating at a local or national level. It is, therefore, reasonable to assume that decisions and actions will be constituted differently at different sectoral and spatial intersections.

If the analysis of agency is one area which can benefit from a wider conception of structure, the issue of accountability is another. In Britain, the debate on accountability has been remarkably narrow. The material discussed here shows that the issue can no longer be confined to its present spatial and sectoral context. (A debate about local versus central democracy in the public police system in one country.) If nothing else, the fact that British policing may, eventually, be centralized through agencies and markets, rather than through Parliament, and the likelihood that a new military–industrial complex might have a significant impact on the restructuring of European policing, suggests that developing intersections between sectoral and spatial dimensions will place new questions of accountability on the political agenda.

Chapter 10

Privatization and social control

In this concluding chapter I want to consider the relationship between public and private spheres in the context of debates about social control. In 1983, Stan Cohen, noting the state's displacement by the private sector in areas such as mental health, argued that displacement was impossible in the case of policing: 'For the state to give up here would be to undercut its very claim to legitimacy' (Cohen 1983: 117). In contrast to Cohen, Shearing and Stenning (1983) have suggested that such a displacement is already occurring. At present, they say, we are experiencing a 'new feudalism' in which huge tracts of public space are controlled and policed by private corporations. This calls into question the view that the state is becoming more dominant in capitalist societies. Instead, they suggest, it indicates that sovereignty may be shifting from the state to private corporations and opens up the possibility of direct control by capital over important aspects of social order.

Clearly, these contrasting positions indicate that the resurgence of private policing and its complex relationship to the public sphere may be interpreted in different ways. In the course of this chapter I shall consider a number of these interpretations. The chapter falls into four sections. First, I make a few preliminary comments about the problem of drawing precise conceptual distinctions between 'public' and 'private' domains. Next, I consider different interpretations of the changing historical balance between public and private sectors in the policing sphere. The third section examines the significance of contemporary changes in the public–private policing balance, for wider issues of social and political theory. The fourth section outlines some topics for further consideration, paying particular attention to the concept of social control and to the status of the public–private dichotomy.

THE PUBLIC–PRIVATE DICHOTOMY: AMBIGUITIES AND FUZZY EDGES

From what has been said already it is clear that public and private domains relate to each other in complex, dynamic, contradictory, and sometimes ambiguous ways. Indeed, there are occasions where the relationship between them seems little short of bizarre. Take, for instance, the case of Parkhurst Wanderers Football Club whose pre-season photograph appeared recently in a magazine. The Wanderers (sic), all of whose matches are played inside the prison walls, were shown posing in a new strip, bearing the logo of the security firm (Chubb) responsible for supplying the locks which assured their continued incarceration (*Police* September 1990). Perhaps one should avoid the temptation to view this picture as a metaphor for social control in the twenty-first century. But, at the very least, it provides us with graphic evidence of the interpenetration of public and private spheres in criminal justice.

Having said that, of course, the concepts of 'public' and 'private' are by no means unambiguous. For one thing, notions of 'publicness' and 'privateness' are subject to considerable cultural variation. This point is well illustrated in Haviland and Haviland's (1983) account of life in a Mexican village. Whereas most anthropological studies have drawn attention to the 'publicness' of face-to-face interaction in small-scale societies (compared to the privatized anonymity of modern societies), Zinacanton is a small community where social life is, in fact, 'extraordinarily private'. Here, strict rules limit the physical intrusion of others' private space. Zinacanteco houses have no windows, thereby preventing people from being watched. Zinacanteco language (Tzotzil), far from facilitating communication, serves to preclude others from sharing information and confidences: 'A Tzotzil greeting constitutes a metaphorical shutting down of interaction and communication. A greeting is formally, a farewell and not a hello' (Haviland and Haviland 1983: 349–50).

Nor is the legal distinction between public and private domains an unambiguous one. Historically, public and private places were defined, almost exclusively, in terms of the concept of ownership. Private places were those which were privately owned and where private peace prevailed. Public places, by contrast, were not subject to private ownership and here, the King's (public) peace prevailed. However, there was never an absolute congruence between private ownership and private space. It was, for example, recognized that taverns (private places) had to be subjected to public law, if the King's peace was to be maintained. Though privately owned, such places were, then, recognized as coming under public jurisdiction (Stenning and Shearing 1980).

A certain amount of legal ambiguity about the distinction between public and private places remains to the present day. In Britain, for example, private shopping malls retain their status as private property, and all activities take place with the consent of the owner, even though the public enjoy free access (Emmott 1989). Significantly, Anglo-American criminal codes tend to define public places as those to which the public has access, as of right, or by invitation – though, at the same time, owners of such public–private places retain the right to exclude persons from entry. In Britain, moreover, areas such as malls may be subject to 'walkway agreements', made under s.35 of the Highways Act 1980. This permits walkways to be designated through such developments by agreement with the owner. When this happens all public areas become, effectively, highways for pedestrians and, as such, can be subjected to public by-laws. Examples like this illustrate the ambiguity which can arise with respect to order maintenance on 'mass private property' (i.e. on privately owned public places): 'More and more public places are located on private property and are under the effective control of persons who are exercising not only public law enforcement powers but also powers derived from the rights of private property ownership' (Stenning and Shearing 1980: 240).

There is further ambiguity in respect of the jurisdiction of public police officers over areas of private space, something which is illustrated in a recent legal judgement (McConnell v Chief Constable of Greater Manchester, heard at the Court of Appeal on 6 November 1988). Here, the plaintiff, McConnell, had been escorted from a commercial premises by PC Smith after refusing to leave. When he tried to re-enter, he was arrested on suspicion that a breach of the peace was likely to occur. The Court found against the plaintiff's claim for damages for false imprisonment on the grounds that events occurring on private premises, where no member of the public is affected, may, nevertheless, constitute a breach of the peace. This case demonstrates the complexity of the public police mandate, since here, again (as in the medieval tavern) the public jurisdiction of the constable extends into the private commercial sphere. Whether or not that legitimate right of intervention is exercised, of course, depends on the application of constabulary discretion. Police willingness to intervene in the private domestic sphere has been conspicuous by its absence, as feminist writers on domestic violence have noted. (For a feminist critique of the public–private dichotomy in social and political theory see Pateman 1983).

I shall discuss the question of the public–private divide in policing (as well as its wider implications for social and political theory) in more detail later. To begin with, however, it is necessary to locate that dichotomy in the context of arguments about historical change. Accordingly, the next section examines debates on the history of policing and social control.

HISTORIES OF POLICING AND SOCIAL CONTROL

Histories of policing are dominated by what might be called the 'Anglo-American model'. Though this model has both conservative–orthodox and radical–revisionist strands, in essence, it sees the emergence of modern policing (here equated with the emergence of public police forces) as a response to the problems of crime and disorder arising from capitalist industrialization and urbanization.

The orthodox version of British police history, represented in the works of Reith (1952), Critchley (1978), and Ascoli (1979), explains the emergence of the new police in terms of the inability of a corrupt and inefficient system of justice to cope with the growing crime and public order problems attendant upon urbanization and industrialization. Upon their formation, the public police, it is maintained, introduced standards of efficiency, integrity, rational organization, and co-ordination, previously absent; though without introducing a degree of centralization likely to undermine civil liberties. By virtue of this unique, non-ideological compromise, the police were able to win substantial legitimation from most sections of the public within a relatively short period of time. In the English case, as Reiner puts it, 'the irresistable force of industrialization and its control problems, meeting the immovable object of stubborn English commitment to liberty, could result in only one outcome – the British bobby' (Reiner 1985: 19).

Orthodoxy deploys a functional and teleological model of police history. The 'police solution' emerges, to provide a rational response to the order maintenance needs of an industrial society. Revisionism, represented most clearly in the work of Storch (1975; 1976) also deploys functional and teleological arguments, though producing very different substantive conclusions. Here, it is argued that it is less a fear of crime than the need for a disciplined working class, which precipitates the police solution in Britain. Capitalism, having subjected the workforce to factory discipline, and having replaced all social ties by the cash nexus, generates inevitable social tensions. The system of parish constables is unable to deal with these tensions; not because of any inherent inefficiency in that office, but because of the danger that civilian constables might show more loyalty to the local community than to the state. The solution is the formation of a professional, bureaucratic police organization which guarantees consistent standards of policing under state jurisdiction: 'Intermittent, spasmodic law enforcement dependent on private initiative was replaced by continuous policing financed by the public purse' (Reiner 1985: 27). The police officer becomes a 'domestic missionary', subjecting the leisure and cultural pursuits of the working classes to the same level of discipline as they experience in the factory. This is functional for industrial capitalism, but generates a significant degree of street-level resistance to the police, a resistance which persists until the present day. Police legitimacy, far from being assured, is both brittle and fragile.

Though this account of the orthodox–revisionist debate has referred to British evidence, a similar debate exists about the development of public policing in America. For example, some American writers have pointed to the fear of riot and disorder in precipitating police development (Silver 1967); some have pointed to the criminogenic effects of immigration and urbanization (Lane 1967; Richardson 1970); some have drawn attention to the role of rational bureaucratic administration in municipal affairs (Monkkonen 1981); and some have concentrated on the structural contradictions of industrial capitalism (Spitzer and Scull 1977b). To that extent, the orthodox–revisionist debate can be located across a broad Anglo-American model of police history; a model which, none the less, has a number of shortcomings. Two of these are especially pertinent to the present discussion. (Readers wanting a more detailed analysis of the orthodox–revisionist debate should consult Reiner 1985: Chapter 1).

The first problem concerns the empirical adequacy of the model. Here, it is increasingly evident that local studies of police history show a degree of variation which the dominant model is unable to explain. Two brief examples confirm this point. Swift (1988) suggests that nineteenth-century English police history is distorted by concentration on London. When other urban localities are considered (in this case, Wolverhampton, York, and Exeter), a diversity of police forms are exposed. In Wolverhampton, the new police emerged to deal with the problem of escalating crime. Organized on paramilitary lines (with a chief constable recruited from the Royal Irish Constabulary), they cracked down on street crime and penetrated working-class cultural and leisure activities. By contrast, in York (where there was relatively little crime, though some concern about the adequacy of policing) and Exeter ('an anachronism in an age of progress; an ordered, deferential and conservative city' (Swift 1988: 215)), there was no attempt to discipline the working class in a systematic way. Swift's point is that we need to concentrate on local aspects of policing during the period, in order to understand historical change. Thus, instead of focusing on the police function *vis-à-vis* the capitalist state, local political considerations are a crucial mediating factor in development: 'the character of urban policing needs to be placed within the existing structure of local government, since it was local rather than national considerations which underlay the organisation, role and modus operandi of the new police' (Swift 1988: 236)

This point is confirmed in Davey's (1983) analysis of policing in a single locality, Horncastle in Lincolnshire, between 1838 and 1857. In nineteenth-century Horncastle, it was the problem of general disorder – what Davey calls 'public morality offences' – rather than fear of crime, which concerned most people. In response to this, a police force was established in Horncastle, under the auspices of the 1833 Lighting and Watching Act. It was financed from local rates, and controlled directly by the municipal authority. Contrary to the dominant model (of provincial police inefficiency leading to the inevitable adoption of the 1856 Act), the Horncastle officers proved highly efficient in controlling 'lawless and immoral' behaviour. Moreover, Davey suggests that the force enjoyed considerable public support by virtue of its direct municipal control, something that was lost after the implementation of the 1856 legislation. Here, then, we have a case of a variant police form (direct municipal funding and control) arising from local political conditions, a direct confirmation of Swift's point. Much the same point has been made about the American experience by one writer who, in criticizing the functionalism of social historians, points to their tendency to explain the development of urban institutions, such as the police, by treating the political realm as merely 'dependent' and 'epiphenomenal' (Ethington 1987).

The second problem (confirmation of which can be found in Chapter 1) concerns the fact that the Anglo-American model has segregated 'police history' from 'the history of policing'. This is indicated by what Brogden (1987) sees as the narrow and ethnocentric character of that model: the fact that it fails to consider a variety of alternative policing forms which have appeared throughout history. In this respect, not only does the model ignore highly politicized forms, such as the 'high policing' of Fouché's France and the colonial police structures exported from Ireland to the British Empire; it also ignores the 'administrative', 'moral', 'vigilantist', and 'commercialized' policing forms discussed earlier, the persistence of which cannot easily be accounted for in the reductive terms of orthodoxy versus revisionism.

These two areas of criticism suggest that what is required is a model of history which is neither teleological nor functionalist, but which can take into account the 'uneven development' of policing. Such a model would place less emphasis on the supposedly rigid break between old and new police, giving greater recognition to the variable forms of provision occurring during that transition period and beyond. This would suggest both a need to take into account the impact of various cross-cutting relations on varieties of policing provision (such as the local/national and formal/informal dimensions referred to earlier); and a need to consider the interpenetration of private and public policing forms from the nineteenth century to the present day.

The production of such a historical model would have immediate benefit for the analysis and understanding of some current policing issues. For example, there is much talk nowadays of the problems associated with the exponential growth of the police role. Yet, the expansion of that role in *some* directions, has to be located in a historical context where *other* policing functions have been usurped by, or hived off to, other agencies: the various municipal bodies, special forces, organizations with special powers, private companies, and groups of active citizens discussed in previous chapters. In that sense, the 'growth' of the police role has been both an uneven and an inconsistent one, though that unevenness and inconsistency is obscured by the dominant historical model.

Despite the fact that histories of private security (virtually all of which are written from a revisionist standpoint) are few in number compared to histories of (public) policing, they tend to exhibit similar shortcomings to those described above. Consider two typical examples. Spitzer and Scull (1977a) provide a three-stage account of the emerging police division of labour. First, capitalist development erodes the basis for traditional forms of private control. Next, the established capitalist state begins to share in the (policing) costs of social reproduction since, for individual capitalists, public law enforcement is 'more attractive than private arrangements from the point of view of both *legitimacy* and *costs*' (Spitzer and Scull 1977a: 23). Finally, the fiscal crisis of the state, arising under corporate capitalism, produces a 'recrudescence of policing for profit' (Spitzer and Scull 1977a: 27). Like Spitzer and Scull, Shearing and Stenning (1981; 1983) also attempt to trace the history of private security to changes in capitalist property relations, arguing that the key feature of the contemporary period is the emergence of mass private property. Whereas small individual landholdings appear to be associated with public policing initiatives, '[w]henever one finds a shift in property relations toward ... large geographically connected holdings of mass private property, one also finds a shift toward private policing initiatives' (Shearing and Stenning 1981: 229).

Now these positions offer some useful insights into historical change, but like histories of public policing, are prone to the same teleological and functional modes of interpretation. Though there is certainly justification for Shearing and Stenning's claim that 'more and more public life now takes place in property which is privately owned' (Shearing and Stenning 1983: 496), the thesis does invite simplistic conclusions. It is not unusual for commentators to construct a scenario in which the progressive movement towards privatized space heralds in a process of order maintenance which lacks any recourse to principles of public justice. The problem is, of course, that this image of the future is far too crude, assuming both a unitary movement from public to private property holding, and a crude corresponce between the eventual property form and the available mechanisms of order maintenance. In reality, future mechanisms (like past ones), are likely to reflect neither unitary historical forces, nor crude principles of correspondence between property ('base') and policing forms ('superstucture)'. As I have suggested in the last chapter, the totality of relations which we call 'policing', is the product of complex social and spatial interrelations.

A good example of the tendency of revisionists to ride rough-shod over the empirically complex and the socially specific is found in Scull's analysis of decarceration. In the original version of this work (Scull 1977), Scull maintained that the fiscal crisis of the state was precipitating a process of decarceration in the fields of mental health and community corrections. In a revised edition of the study Scull (1984) was forced, however, to recognize that although the thesis stood up in respect of mental health, the same could not be said for community corrections. For, contrary to his predictions about the expansion of (private) punishment in the community, it was (public) prison populations in the USA (and to a lesser extent in Britain), which grew substantially during the period. This process reflected the impact of right-wing ideology, the capacity of professionals to subvert moves towards deinstitutionalization, and the presence of implementation problems in the penal system. In short, the impact of politics and policy on the process of decarceration obliged Scull to accept that prisons and asylums could not be analysed as a unitary phenomena, subject to common trajectories.

The tendency of revisionist writers to deny the specificity of empirical forms is sometimes coupled with their engagement in functionalist modes of analysis. This is particularly evident when they come to assess the impact of private security on politics and social order. South (1984), for example, rightly argues that despite the 'private' nature of private security, companies still function within the legal ambit of the state. (Even illegal acts make reference to legal codes.) Less convincingly, he concludes that private security is, thereby, located within the 'unity' of economic and political relations that comprise the capitalist state (South 1984: 189). Far from indicating a decline in state sovereignty (as argued by Shearing and Stenning 1983), the expansion of private security involves 'a commercial compromise between the sovereignty of the state ... and those sections of society whose commercial interests are most benefited by the maintenance of the status quo' (South 1984: 190). In effect, he says, this amounts to another instance of capital's assertion of its relative autonomy from the state.

Now this conception of the capitalist state (the state as a unified, functioning, totality of elements welded together by a principle of 'relative autonomy') has been subjected to sustained criticism during the last decade and, nowadays, even many Marxists writers have dispensed with it. (Significantly, South's more recent analysis of state–private security relations allows both for greater complexity and, for a healthy degree of ambiguity: see especially the excellent discussion in South 1989.) The important point here, however, is that the adoption of the notion of state as 'unity' invariably generates a functionalist conception of the police division of labour: private security functions to keep mass private property in order; the public police concentrate on dealing with public order and political challenge. Or, as South (*circa* 1984) puts it: 'The relationship between the state and private security is, at its simplest, one in which a "buffer" function is performed' (South 1984: 191).

Historical analyses of policing and private security are, of course, invariably linked to some wider conception of change in the structure of social control. In recent years, a number of revisionist writers have begun to accept criticisms of the type outlined above – though, oddly, most have been concerned with the history of prisons and asylums, rather than with the history of policing. To conclude this section, it is useful to list some of the 'self-criticisms' made by these authors, since they summarize much of what has been said in this section and also raise important questions about the public–private dichotomy, which will be discussed later. (Cohen (1989) provides by far the most detailed 'auto-critique' of the revisionist model of social control, whilst Ignatieff (1981) offers a lucid account of several key theoretical shortcomings of revisionism. The following list of areas of self-criticism draws, selectively, upon both of these authors. Readers wanting a fuller account should consult Cohen 1989).

The main elements of the revisionist self-critique consist of the following points:

1 The model adopts essentialist principles. Though it is recognized that social control occurs in a variety of specific contexts and cultures, there is a tendency to see particular cases as manifestations of some common 'essence'. Usually, essentialism is accompanied by a teleological mode of analysis which overrides the analysis of specific empirical forms, something which is illustrated in the earlier discussion of histories of public policing.

2 The model presumes that social control is inevitably malignant, sinister and negative, rather than benign or neutral. (Orthodox histories of policing are equally problematical, of course, because they assume the opposite.)

3 The model presumes that there is some logical or rational trajectory to changing patterns of control, determined by some dominating agency (capital, the state, societal needs, or whatever).

4 The model assumes that there is an overriding tendency towards 'more' social control (e.g. in the proposition that 'destructuring' tendencies, such as community corrections, paradoxically give rise to 'net-widening').

5 The model operates with a functionalist view of the connections between public and private sectors, seeing the amalgam of state–private forms as essential to the reproduction of capitalist social relations. (The orthodox model, by contrast, operates with a consensual version of functionalism, whereby the state fulfils certain common social needs.)

6 The model grants a privileged role to the state (the public–formal realm) and relegates informal mechanisms (family, peer group, community, religion) to the sidelines. Correspondingly, all social relations tend to be reduced to relations of power and domination and alternative bases for moral authority and order are ignored.

THE PUBLIC–PRIVATE DICHOTOMY: WIDER THEORETICAL CONCERNS

At this point, it is useful to ask how the resurgence of privatization in policing and criminal justice, fits into the debate on changing patterns of social control. In fact, as Matthews (1989a) suggests, privatization does not sit comfortably with the theme of 'destructuring' (decarceration, community care, de-institutionalization, etc.) which has come to dominate the social control debate. Far from being a destructuring movement which took off in the 1960s and subsequently failed, it is a complex and differentiated development which has been implemented in many different ways. Nor are other dominant aspects of the social control model, such as 'net-widening', easy to apply to privatization.

For these reasons there has been considerable confusion about how best to respond to the process. Some critics have simply adopted an 'about-turn': the attacks once directed at the 'sinister state', now being directed at the 'sinister market' (Matthews 1989a). Others have slowly, and sometimes grudgingly, begun to consider the possibility that under certain circumstances, privatization might produce benefits. But, by and large, critical analysis has been slow to get off the ground. The main reason for this is that there is considerable conceptual confusion about the public–private dichotomy. Invariably, these are taken as natural and self-evident distinctions. But in fact, the extent of their overlap makes simple opposition between them (and related oppositions between the state and the market, the formal and the informal) impossible to sustain. Furthermore, conceptions regularly deployed in the social control literature, such as 'blurring of the boundaries', do little more than confuse the issue, since they tacitly assume the existence of definable boundaries which can at some point be subjected to 'blurring'.

In drawing attention to these issues, one is, in fact, touching upon a long-standing, yet unresolved, problem in social and political theory about the nature of the public–private divide. Most mainstream political theory (at least, for most of the time) takes the public–private distinction for granted. There may be a grudging admission that the concepts leave something to be desired, but by and large, 'theorizing' is permitted to go on 'as if' the distinctions were clear and relatively unproblematical. Periodically, however, someone 'pulls the rug away' and exposes the fragility of the public–private distinction. At that point the problem surfaces in political discourse.

Consider two examples of this periodic surfacing, one from the Marxist left, the other from mainstream political science. Half a century ago, Gramsci produced concepts ('integral state', 'extended state') whose purpose was to come to terms with the complexities of the distinction between state and civil society. For Gramsci, traditional Marxian distinctions between the public and the private, the state and the market, the economic and the political, were flawed and, in particular, he rejected all attempts to explain the relationships between them in terms of crude 'base' versus 'superstructure' models of causality. In fact, for Gramsci, economic, political, and ideological relations are superimposed upon each other in complex ways. Consequently, he dispenses with the traditional Marxist schema whereby economic, political, and ideological elements occupy distinct and mutually exclusive theoretical locations and maintains instead that social institutions may occupy more than one theoretical space at a time. This means that parts of the state apparatus such as the police (traditionally defined as part of the public sphere), or institutions such as the Church (normally seen as part of civil society/the private sphere) may breach their traditional boundaries, displaying characteristics which locate them in political and civil society simultaneously. In effect then, for Gramsci, the distinction between public–private and political–civil is a methodological distinction, rather than one with any natural or inherent content (Togliatti 1979; Showstack Sassoon 1980). Unfortunately, as I have suggested elsewhere (Johnston 1986), Gramsci having dismantled the base–superstructure distinction that sanctions the crude public–private (state–civil society) dichotomy, then reconstructs it, in a revised form, through the concept of hegemony. Nevertheless, though failing to achieve its initial promise, Gramsci's work comprises a sophisticated attempt to recognize the complexities of the public–private divide. Moreover, the fact that it was written half a century ago confirms that the problem is by no means a new one.

More recently, political scientists have used the concept of corporatism to examine the complex connections between public and private sectors. Though corporatism is an ill-defined concept, the term usually refers to a process of interest intermediation involving the negotiation of policy between state agencies and private interest groups, policy agreements arising from this process being 'implemented through the collaboration of interest organisations and their willingness and ability to secure the compliance of their members' (Grant 1985: 3–4). Schmitter (1974) suggests that relations between the state and corporate interest groups consist of many possible 'modalities': official state recognition, government subsidy, devolved responsibility, informal connections, joint public–private operations, and so on. Furthermore, he argues that an 'osmotic process' has arisen between state and private interests which has the effect of dissolving the public–private boundary.

Corporatist writers are keen, then, to emphasize that conventional distinctions between 'state' and 'non-state' are difficult to sustain, because the state shares its powers with (or, in some versions of the theory, loses its sovereignty to) other institutions. Though there is much to be said for this argument, caution needs to be exercised on two fronts. First, as Held (1987) points out, arguments about the demise of state (or, in some cases, parliamentary) sovereignty can be exaggerated, since the public sphere has never had autonomous sovereignty over policy in the past. Second, it is often implied, quite wrongly, that the corporatist process is something new. Yet, if one considers a major arena of public policy such as the National Health Service, it is clear that corporatist modes of policy making and implementation have been evident since inception (Klein 1977).

Despite these problems – and the fact that the concept of corporatism is used in too loose a fashion by many writers – the corporatist debate is important for two reasons. First, it recognizes that public policy is not the exclusive prerogative of the state. Second, it confirms that the state is neither a sovereign body, nor a unitary entity operating in accordance with some inner rationale. Instead, corporatism concentrates on the fragmented nature of policy making and implementation: 'Corporatism means, in effect, the fragmentation of state power and involves a centrifugal dynamic' (Cawson 1982: 41). Or, as Schmitter puts it, the corporatist process leaves us with 'an amorphous complex of agencies with very ill defined boundaries, performing a great variety of not very distinctive functions' (Schmitter 1985: 33).

Both of the examples considered here, the first from 50 years ago, the second from the contemporary period, emphasize the fragility and ambiguity of the public–private divide. The extent of this fragility can be confirmed if we return again to the question of policing. In the previous chapter I denied that policing could be defined in terms of a legitimate capacity for coercion and discussed the implications of that argument for the sociology of policing. But what are its implications for our understanding of the state and political theory?

Consider, again, the issue of privatization and, in particular, the possibility of private security personnel being granted constabulary powers when undertaking duties in court rooms and prisons. Many commentators on privatization, if asked 'What can be privatized in respect of policing?' will answer 'Anything except those things requiring a capacity to exercise legitimate force.' Now, two things can be said about this statement. First, it is an ethical declamation ('certain things *should* not be privatized') rather than an analytical statement (about what *could* be privatized). Ethically, the declamation may or may not be justified, but that is an issue which need not concern us here. Second, the statement is based on tautologous foundations. If one were to reconstruct the reasoning upon which the statement rests it would take, roughly, the following form: (i)   the state is defined (after Weber) as an apparatus possessing a monopoly of legitimate coercion in society; (ii)   since the essence of police work consists of the possession of a legitimate capacity for exercising coercion, policing is, necessarily, a public (state) function; (iii)   *ipso facto* any agent possessing constabulary powers is a public functionary. This includes private security guards, occupying the office of constable, whilst engaged in prison or court security duties.

The solution, then, is simple. A sworn constable is a sworn constable. Whether the occupant of the office wears the badge of Sussex Constabulary or Securicor, he or she is firmly located in the public (state) sphere. Thus, the existence of private agents with constabulary powers raises no particular problems for the coherence of the public–private divide. Such a conclusion is justified, however, only if we accept tautological reasoning and adopt the discourse of logic-chopping. The problem is, of course, that once private agents in the employ of commercial companies are granted constabulary powers, it is no longer possible to define the public (state) sphere in terms of its monopoly of legitimate force and the commercial (market) sector as something else. Instead, one has a hybrid form of public–commercial coercion, and the conventional state–market distinction upon which so much political theory rests, is undermined. The example confirms, then, the fragility of the public–private dichotomy. More importantly, it exposes the inadequacy of conceptions of the state which have been accepted, without question, for generations.

Examples of this sort wreak havoc on mainstream political

theory, calling into question many 'taken-for-granted' assumptions about power, legitimation, and authority in modern societies. Though some writers have begun to address the issue, it has ramifications which, as yet, remain unrealized. Commentators on policing and social control, for instance, often recognize the substantive impact of privatization, yet struggle to come to terms with its theoretical significance. Wildeman's (1988), otherwise excellent, account of contract security in the USA illustrates the problem very well. Here, the approach is a conventional one, in so far as it addresses the question 'of whether the privatization of the social control function ... represents ... an increase or a decrease in the power of the state' (Wildeman 1988: 12). Wildeman's contention is that private policing (paradoxically) increases state control by reducing citizens' civil rights and liberties. Now the problem here is not so much in the substance of the argument – it is, undoubtedly, true that some aspects of private policing threaten civil liberties – but in the initial formulation of the question: and, in particular, with the way that the public–private dichotomy is *articulated*. That articulation rests upon a conventional Marxist (though it could, just as easily, be Weberian) conception of public–private relations. Essentially, this amounts to a zero-sum conception of power. Since 'public' and 'private' are seen as contradictory forces, each gains power at the other's expense. Either private security dilutes state power, or it complements state power. This position, if followed through to its logical conclusion, of course, can only produce two alternatives: either the struggle between competing forces produces an anarcho-capitalistic free market in security; or it produces totalitarianism. Wildeman opts for the latter, seeing the development of private security in China as a corollary of developments in the USA: 'Whether it be in communist China or in Capitalist America, what we see happening is the same phenomenon ... contract policing reinforcing and extending the social control powers of the centralized state' (Wildeman 1988: 11).

Apart from the fact that this analysis, once more, demonstrates the disturbing tendency to ride roughshod over inconvenient empirical variations (the public–private dichotomy in China is hardly equivalent to that in the USA), it confirms that there is a pressing need to rethink the terms of political debate. The point is put very well by Lowman *et al.* (1987) who insist that we can no longer draw absolute distinctions between state and civil society; between the 'inside' and the 'outside' of the state: 'It is theoretically fruitless for theories of control to attempt a rigid demarcation of these two domains of authority . . . the state can be located and monitored only through its association with civil society and vice versa' (Lowman *et al.* 1987: 6). Here, their point is that the 'sociologically interesting' problems relate to the interconnections between the dimensions, rather than to the dimensions themselves. Or, in the terms of the previous chapter, to the interactions and intersections between different social and spatial configurations.

CONCLUDING COMMENTS

The resurgence of private policing requires us to address some new issues and to re-address some old issues in new ways. In these final comments I want to suggest three areas in which there is a particular need for further analysis.

The first of these concerns the future research agenda of 'police studies' (which should really be re-named 'policing studies'). Clearly, from what has been said in previous chapters, there are huge gaps in the research base. Very little has been written on private security in Britain. Even less has been written on hybrid forces and vigilante groups. And even when literature does exist (e.g. on some regulatory bodies), there is little attempt to integrate it with other policing research. Needless to say, there is little, if any, comparative research in any of these areas.

It would be relatively easy, then, to construct a shopping list of future research needs. Nevertheless, at this stage, it is probably more useful to think in terms of the direction of future research, than in terms of its specific content. Here, one 'new direction' is worthy of specific mention. In the past, police research has been dominated by a 'productive' focus, emphasis being placed upon the producers of police services (public police forces), rather than upon consumers. The revival of private policing necessitates a change of focus. The 'commodification of security' (Spitzer 1987), which accompanies privatization, opens up unexplored questions about choice and decision making. Why do people make the security choices they do? How is choice constructed and constrained by the market? How are popular fears and needs channelled through relevant social institutions? By what means and in what ways do consumers evaluate security services? Do modes of evaluation differ according to whether security services are provided by public or private means? All of these questions are important to the sociology of policing and, given the recent 'discovery' of the sociology of consumption, there would seem to be a new opportunity for them to be addressed.

A second area concerns the concepts of policing and social control. I have already drawn attention to the problematic relationship between the concepts of 'police' and 'policing', and this book has been, unequivocally, about 'policing' in its broadest sense. Nevertheless, conceptual problems remain. Bayley (1987), in his foreword to Shearing and Stenning's edited volume on private policing (Shearing and Stenning 1987), notes that many contributors use interchangeable terms to elucidate the breadth of the policing function ('ordering', 'regulating', 'controlling', 'governing', etc.). That may be no bad thing – and this book has, certainly, used a number of similar terms. But, in fact, what is being witnessed here is the phenomenon of authors grappling for new, and as yet absent, analytical categories, through which some of this complexity might be articulated.

One common solution to this problem is to invoke the catch-all concept of social control. Hence, the unspoken assumption arises that policing (like capital punishment, education, potty-training, and imprisonment) are all manifestations of the same essential process. Unfortunately, the concept of social control is untenable for several reasons. First, its essentialism causes it to explain everything – and, therefore, nothing. In consequence, it forecloses analysis; for if policing *is* social control there is no more to be said. Second, it precludes understanding of specific forms of such 'control', since essentialism is incompatible with specificity. Third, it makes the tacit assumption that participating agencies actually *achieve* control over their subject populations in some, more-or-less, uncomplicated fashion. All of this is, of course, entirely unacceptable. The problem is, however, that the concept is so ingrained into sociological discourse, nothing will shift it. In particular, as is evidenced from this chapter, one cannot engage in debate with revisionist work on policing (whether historical or contemporary) without being drawn into the terminology. It is all very well to say that alternative terms are preferable (personally, I favour 'social regulation', which avoids some of the above problems), but deploying them, without interminable disruption of the flow of words ('the discourse of "regulation", unlike the discourse of "control", means this, rather than that . . .') is impossible.

For that reason, the important point, whatever terminology is used, is that the shortcomings identified in the revisionist 'self-criticism' (functionalism, teleology, essentialism, formalism, and so on) are avoided. If that is achieved, at some point in the distant future, the concept of social control may simply wither away.

Finally, let us return, again, to the public–private dichotomy. In previous chapters I have suggested that the revival of private policing forces us to reconsider what we understand by the term policing. From what has been said in this chapter, it is equally true that that resurgence also 'forces us to reconsider some of our most fundamental notions about what is "public" and what is "private"' (Shearing and Stenning 1987: 10). Conventional notions of the public–private divide are less and less convincing, and it seems more and more difficult to modify the traditional models, in order to make them conform with existing realities. So, is the solution to dispense altogether with the conceptual distinction between public and private spheres? Shearing and Stenning suggest not. But they add an interesting rider to their qualified retention of the dichotomy. Instead of scrapping the distinction, they say, it may be better to 'explore the ways in which it has been successfully deployed to support political and economic orderings and to see whether it cannot fruitfully be reframed as an analytically useful concept' (Shearing and Stenning 1987: 15).

This notion of 'deploying' the concepts of public and private in support of different political and economic ends is an important one. Public and private spheres should not be seen as distinct 'places' with inherent characteristics, but rather as strategic arenas where political arguments are deployed and where political conflict takes place. The varying boundaries of the public and the private are, in that sense, constituted in political discourse, rather than given in the nature of things. The boundaries change because victories are won and defeats are incurred. They remain pliable because political conflict is enduring. Some of the conflict which occurs in that arena is expressed in the form of ideologies about the alleged virtues of public or private provision. Paradoxically, as I argued in Chapter 2, those ideologies are themselves likely to defend their corners in terms of the inherent (positive or negative) qualities, allegedly attached to a given form of provision. But, as I said before, no political 'outcome' (such as the contraction or expansion of private provision in a given area) should be seen as a simple reflection of the application of its 'corresponding' ideology. Formal ideologies (in the sense of the well-thought-out, clearly articulated positions described in Chapter 2) bear a complex relationship to what goes on in strategic conflict. Ideologies are rarely applied in a coherent and consistent fashion in the messy world of politics. Invariably, the deployment of ideologies involves accommodation to changing social conditions and compromise with other political forces.

A good illustration of the public–private dichotomy having the form of a strategic arena, can be seen in recent debates about active citizenship. Active citizenship is, in fact, a discourse *about* the public–private divide. This is very evident if one reads between the lines of Douglas Hurd's celebrated declaration of principles. Here, Hurd insists that active citizenship does not mean abrogation of the state's responsibilities. The 'massive public services', he says, will continue to function. However, he adds the critical stipulation that 'alongside, and in the gaps between these services, are a myriad of needs which are *not* best met by creating or extending a bureaucratic scheme . . .' (Hurd 1989). Here, in fact, is a wonderful expression of a strategy geared to 'moving the goalposts' on the public–private field of play. Hurd, rightly, sees the dimensions of that field as fluid and open to political manipulation. The mode of political intervention is, in fact, a subtle one, operating at the interstices of public and private spheres (the 'gaps' in between), rather than confronting them head-on. Ostensibly, Hurd's article is about social responsibility. Simultaneously, it is an agenda for reconstructing the boundaries of the public and the private.

That strategy, however, hardly amounts to the coherent expression of some political ideology. Indeed, as Ignatieff (1989) points out, the Conservative discourse on citizenship contains serious contradictions, not least with regard to the concept of freedom. Nor is the impact of that strategy entirely predictable. In circumstances where substantive social inequalities between different categories of citizen remain prevalent, active citizenship is a dangerous political game to play. For it may well expose and politicize conflicts between different sets of 'needs' and 'rights', without offering any just means of resolving them. This suggests that a politics of active citizenship, lacking principles of social justice, may turn out to be explosive. And, if it is true that the effects of deploying this particular strategy are unpredictable, there seems little sense in perceiving the outcome as merely another manifestation of social control.

The example confirms that, at the political level, the public–private dichotomy comprises a complex and changing strategic field. As yet, those involved in the study of policing have failed to capture that complexity in their analytical categories and theoretical concepts. If the rebirth of private policing does nothing else, it should at least ensure that, in future, some of those analytical shortcomings are confronted.

Bibliography

Abrahams, R. (1987) 'Sungusungu: Village vigilante groups in Tanzania', *African Affairs* 86 (343): 179–96.

ACPO (1988) *A Review of the Private Security Sector*, North Wales Police.

Adam, B.D. (1988) 'Neighbourhood democracy in Nicaragua', *Dialectical Anthropology* 13: 5–15.

Albanese, J.S. (1986) 'The future of policing: a private concern?' *Police Studies* Summer: 86–91.

Alderson, J. (1979) *Policing Freedom*, Plymouth: McDonald & Evans.

Alderson, J. (1981) 'How the Chinese deal with juvenile crime', *Police Review* 16 January: 102–4.

Alderson, J. (1988) 'Policing sans frontieres', *Police Review* 1 July: 1382–3.

Allen, M. (ed.) (1988) *The Times 1,000 (1988–9)*, London: Times Books.

Anon (1985) 'Buying and selling in the Middle East', *International Security Review* January/February: 53–7.

Ascher, K. (1987) *The Politics of Privatization*, London: Macmillan.

Ascoli, D. (1979) *The Queen's Peace*, London: Hamish Hamilton.

Ashby, J.F. (1982) 'The private security industry', in A. Rees (ed.) *Policing and Private Security*, Canberra: Australian Institute of Criminology.

Ashworth, J. (1990) 'The big fiddles', *The Times* 19 June.

Ayers, E.L. (1984) *Vengeance and Justice*, New York: Oxford University Press.

Bailey, S. (1988) 'Current trends in the security industry', *Security Surveyor* 19 (3): 22–3.

Bailey, S. (1989) 'Police and the private security industry', *Security Surveyor* September: 13–14.

Bailey, S. and Lynn, G. (1989) *The Private Security Industry – Towards 1992*, Northumbria Constabulary.

Baker, S.R. (1988) 'When boundaries disappear', *Policing* 4 (4): 281–92.

Banton, M. (1964) *The Policeman in the Community*, London: Tavistock.

Barry, N.P. (1979) *Hayek's Economic and Social Philosophy*, London: Macmillan.

Barry, N.P. (1983) 'The new liberalism', *British Journal of Political Science* 13: 93–123.

Bartle, R. (1990) 'Judgement reserved', *Police Review* 31 August: 1725.

Bayley, D. (1987) 'Foreword', in C.D. Shearing and P.C. Stenning (eds) *Private Policing*, California: Sage: 6–8.

Beattie, J.M. (1986) *Crime and the Courts in England, 1660–1800*, Oxford: Clarendon Press.

Bennett, T. (1987) 'Neighbourhood watch: principles and practice', in R.I. Mawby (ed.) *Policing Britain*, Plymouth: Plymouth Polytechnic: 31–51.

Bennett, T. (1989a) 'Factors related to participation in neighbourhood watch schemes', *British Journal of Criminology* 29 (3): 207–18.

Bennett, T. (1989b) 'The neighbourhood watch experiment', in R. Morgan and D.J. Smith (eds) *Coming to Terms with Policing*, London: Routledge: 138–52.

Bennett, T. (1990) *Evaluating Neighbourhood Watch*, Aldershot: Gower,

Ben-Tovim, G., Gabriel, J., Law, I., and Stredder, K. (1986) *The Local Politics of Race*, London: Macmillan.

Birch, R. (1988) 'The way we are', *Police Review* 25: 2445–7, November.

Bittner, E. (1980) *The Function of the Police in Modern Society*, Cambridge Mass: Oelgeschlager, Gunn & Hain.

Blok, A. (1974) *The Mafia of a Sicilian Village 1860–1960*, Oxford: Basil Blackwell.

Boothroyd, J. (1989a) 'Angels with dirty faces', *Police Review* 6 January: 16–17.

Boothroyd, J. (1989b) 'Nibbling away at the bobby's patch', *Police Review* 13 January: 64–5.

Bowden, T. (1978) *Beyond the Limits of the Law*, Harmondsworth: Penguin.

Boyd, M. (1986) 'Security in Nigeria', *International Security Review* July/August: 35–7.

Brewer, J. (1980) 'Law and disorder in Hanoverian England', *History Today* January: 18–27.

Brewer, J. and Styles, J. (1980) *An Ungovernable People*, London: Hutchinson.

Brewer, J.D., Guelke, A., Hume, I., Moxon-Browne, E., and Wilford, R. (1988) *The Police, Public Order and the State*, London: Macmillan.

Bright, J. (1990) *Patrolling the Streets and the Tube: A Job for the Police or Active Citizens ?* Swindon: Crime Concern.

Brogden, M. (1987) 'The emergence of the police – the colonial dimension', *British Journal of Criminology* 27 (1): 4–14.

Brown, M.K. (1981) *Working the Street: Police Discretion and the Dilemmas of Reform*, New York: Russell Sage Foundation.

Brown, R.M. (1975) *Strain of Violence*, New York: Oxford University Press.

Brown, R.M. (1976) 'The history of vigilantism in America', in H.J. Rosenbaum and P.C. Sedeberg (eds) *Vigilante Politics*, Pennsylvania: University of Pennsylvania Press: 79–109.

BTP (1990) *The British Transport Police Annual Report 1989*, London: BTP.

Bunyan, T. (1977) *The History and Practice of the Political Police in Britain*, London: Quartet.

Burrows, W.E. (1976) *Vigilante*, New York: Harcourt Brace Jovanovich.

Butler, A.J.P. (1984) *Police Management*, London: Gower.

Carriere, K.D. and Erikson, R.V. (1989) *Crime Stoppers: A Study in the Organization of Community Policing*, Toronto: University of Toronto, Centre for Criminology.

Castells, M. (1977) *The Urban Question*, London: Edward Arnold.

Cawson, A. (1982) *Corporatism and Welfare*, London: Heinemann.

Chapple, N. (1986) 'The Ministry of Defence Police', *Police Review* 27 June: 1344–5.

CIPFA (Chartered Institute of Public Finance) (1989) *Financial Information Service, Vol. 24. Law and Order*, London: CIPFA.

Clarke, M.J. (1987) 'Citizenship, community and the management of crime' *British Journal of Criminology*, 27 (1): 384–400.

Clarke, M.J. (1989) 'Insurance fraud', *British Journal of Criminology*, 29 (1): 1–20.

Clarke, R. and Hough, M. (1984) *Crime and Police Effectiveness*: Home Office Research Study 79. London: HMSO.

Clayton, T. (1967) *The Protectors*, London: Oldbourne.

Cohen, A. (1988) 'A fellowship of thieves: property criminals in eighteenth century Massachusetts', *Journal of Social History* Autumn: 65–92.

Cohen, P. (1972) *Subcultural Conflict and Working Class Community*, Working Paper in Cultural Studies, Birmingham: Centre for Contemporary Culture, University of Birmingham.

Cohen, P. (1979) 'Policing the working class city', in B. Fine, R. Kinsey, J. Lea, S. Picciotto, and J. Young (eds) *Capitalism and the Rule of Law*, London: Hutchinson.

Cohen, S. (1983) 'Social control talk: telling stories about correctional change', in D. Garland and P. Young (eds) *The Power to Punish*, London: Heinemann.

Cohen, S. (1985) *Visions of Social Control*, Cambridge: Polity Press.

Cohen, S. (1989) 'The critical discourse on "social control": note on the concept as a hammer', *International Journal of the Sociology of Law* 17: 347–57.

Coleman, A. (1985) *Utopia on Trial*, London: Hilary Shipman.

Corns, C. (1987) 'Private policing and the empowerment of crime victims', in *Proceedings of Australian and New Zealand Association of Psychiatry Psychology, and Law Conference'*, Melbourne: 389–414.

Cowdry, Q. (1990) 'Police are obstructing watch plans charity says', *The Times* 22 May.

Cozens, R. (1989) 'Forming a force for the future', *Police Review* 7 July: 1375.

Craig, J. (1989) 'Vigilantes fill police shoes and stop thefts', *Sunday Times* 5 March.

Crenshaw, W.A. (1988) 'Civil aviation: target for terrorism', in I.A. Lipman (ed.) *The Annals of the American Academy of Political Science, The Private Security Industry: Issues and Trends*, California: Sage, Vol. 498, July: 51–9.

Critchley, T.A. (1978) *A History of Police in England and Wales*, London: Constable.

Cronin, J.E. (1984) *Labour and Society in Britain 1918–79*, London: Batsford.

Cunningham, W.C. and Taylor, T. (1985) *Private Security and Police in America* (The 'Hallcrest Report'), Portland: Chancellor Press.

Cutler, J. and Edwards, R. (1988) *Britain's Nuclear Nightmare*, London: Sphere Books.

Davenport, P. (1989) 'Useful chap in an emergency', *The Times* 24 November.

Davenport, P. (1990) 'Ambulance service on road to self-government', *The Times* 12 July.

Davey, B.J. (1983) *Lawless and Immoral*, Leicester: Leicester University Press.

Davies, S. (1989) 'Streets Ahead', *Police Review* 10 November: 2277.

Davis, J. (1989) 'From "rookeries" to "communities": race, poverty and policing in London 1850–1985', *History Workshop Journal*, Spring 27: 66–85.

Deloitte, Haskins, and Sells (1989) *Report on the Practicality of Private Sector Involvement in the Remand System for the Home Office*, London: Deloitte, Haskins & Sells.

Department of Transport (1986) *Crime on the London Underground*. Report of a study by the Department of Transport in conjunction with London Underground, the Home Office, the Metropolitan Police and the British Transport Police, London: Department of Transport.

Dewhurst, H.S. (1955) *The Railroad Police*, Illinois: Charles C. Thomas.

Dilulio, J.J. (1988) 'Private prisons?' *Police* May: 18–19, 34.

Donzelot, J. (1979) *The Policing of Families*, London: Hutchinson.

Draper, H. (1978) *Private Police*, Sussex: Harvester Press.

Eatwell, J. (1979) *The 1945–51 Labour Governments*, London: Batsford.

Edgington, H. (1990) 'Securicor – KGB style', *Mail on Sunday* 7 January.

Efficiency Unit (1988) *Improving Management in Government: the Next Steps*, London: HMSO.

Elliott, N. (1989) *Streets Ahead*, London: Adam Smith Institute.

Emmott, D.A. (1989) 'Stepping out in public . . .', *Police Review* 11 August: 1614–15.

Emsley, C (1983) *Policing and its Context 1750– 1870*, London: Macmillan.

Emsley, C. (1987) *Crime and Society in England 1750–1900*, London: Longman.

Esler, G. (1983) 'The nuclear police: a secret police force with disquieting powers', *Listener* 24 November: 5–6.

Esler, G. and Woolwich, P. (1983) 'The secret police', *Police Review* 9 December: 2304–5.

Ethington, P.J. (1987) 'Vigilantes and the police: the creation of a professional police bureaucracy in San Fransisco 1847–1900', *Journal of Social History* 21 (2): 197–227.

Factor, F. and Stenson, K. (1987) 'At the end of the line', *Youth in Society* January: 18–19.

Fendley, A. (1988) 'Who's guarding who?' *Security Gazette* October: 19.

Fielding, N. (1988) 'Competence and culture in the police', *Sociology* 22 (1): 45–64.

Fijnaut, C. (forthcoming) 'Police co-operation within Western Europe', in F. Heidensohn and M. Farrell (eds) *Crime in Europe*, London: Routledge: 132–54.

Fixler, P.E. and Poole, R.W. (1988) 'Can police services be privatized?' in I.A. Lipman (ed.) *The Annals of the American Academy of Political Science: The Private Security Industry: Issues and Trends*, California: Sage. Vol. 498, July: 108–18.

Flavel, W.R.H. (1973) 'Research into security organizations', paper presented to Second Bristol Seminar on the Sociology of the Police (unpublished).

Fowler, F.J., Jr. and Mangione, T.W. (1986) 'A three- pronged effort to reduce crime and fear of crime: the Hartford Experiment', in D.P. Rosenbaum (ed.) *Community Crime Prevention: Does it Work?* California: Sage: 87–108.

Fraser, R. (1988) *Privatization: the UK Experience and International Trends*, London: Longman.

Friedman, D. (1973) *The Machinery of Freedom: A Guide to Radical Capitalism*, New York: Arlington House.

Fry, G., Flynn, A., Gray. A., Jenkins, W., and Rutherford, B. (1988) 'Symposium on improving management in government', *Public Administration*, Winter 66: 429–45.

Fulton, R. (1989) 'Private sector involvement in the remand system', in M. Farrell (ed.) *Punishment for Profit? Privatisation and Contracting Out in the Criminal Justice System*, London: Institute for the Study and Treatment of Delinquency: 1–11.

Gamble, A. (1979) 'The free economy and the strong state', *Socialist Register*: 1–25.

Gardner, E. (1989) 'Prisons – An Alternative Approach', in M. Farrell (ed.) *Punishment for Profit? Privatisation and Contracting Out in the Criminal Justice System*, London: Institute for the Study and Treatment of Delinquency: 13–17.

Garofalo, J. and McLeod, M. (1988) 'Improving the use and effectiveness of neighbourhood watch programmes', *Research in Action*, Washington DC: National Institute of Justice, US Dept. of Justice, April.

Gay, W.O. (1973) 'Communications and crime: the origins and development of the British Transport Police', *Police Journal* April–June: 109–25.

Geva, R. (1989) 'Cooperation between the police and the private security and investigative industries: the Israeli survey', *The Police Chief* June: 12–17.

Ghezzi, S.G. (1983) 'A private network of social control: insurance investigation units', *Social Problems* 30 (5): 521–31.

Gill, M. (1987) 'The special constabulary: community representation and accountability', in R.I. Mawby (ed.) *Policing Britain*, Plymouth: Plymouth Polytechnic: 52–66.

Gomez-Baeza, R. (1986) 'Spain – the boom years' *International Security Review* January/February:

Gomez-Baeza, R. (1988) 'Spain – too fast too soon?' *International Security Review* September/October: 45–7.

Gordon, P. (1984) 'Community policing: towards the local police state?' *Critical Social Policy* 10: 39–58.

Grant, W. (1985) 'Introduction', in W. Grant (ed.) *The Political Economy of Corporatism*, London: Macmillan: 1–31.

Gray, J. (1986) *Liberalism*, Milton Keynes: Open University Press.

Green, D.G. (1987) *The New Right: The Counter-Revolution in Political, Economic and Social Thought*, London: Harvester/Wheatsheaf.

Green, L. (1989a) 'Industry chief sounds alarms', *Security and Protection Equipment* IFSEC Issue: 16–17.

Green, L. (1989b) 'A Securicor way to the top' *Security and Protection Equipment* July: 10–12.

Green, P. (1989) *Private Sector Involvement in the Immigration Detention Centres*, London: The Howard League for Penal Reform.

Greenberg, M.A. (1978) 'Auxiliary civilian police – the New York experience', *Journal of Police Science and Administration* 6 (1): 86–97.

Grimshaw, R. and Jefferson, T. (1987) *Interpreting Police Work: Policy and Practice in Forms of Beat Policing*, London: Allen & Unwin.

Hamilton, A. (1990) 'Call to privatize Church of England', *The Times* 16 April.

Hargadon, J. (1988) 'Private and commercial security – what is their role in modern day policing?' *International Police Exhibition and Conference Seminar Session 4*.

Haselden, R. (1990) 'Licence to snoop', *Weekend Guardian* September 8–9.

Haviland, L.K. and Haviland, J.B. (1983) 'Privacy in a Mexican Indian village', in S.I. Benn and G.F. Gaus (eds) *Public and Private in Social Life*, London: Croom Helm/New York: St Martin's Press: 341–61.

Hay, D. (1975) 'Property, authority and the criminal law', in D. Hay (ed.) *Albion's Fatal Tree*, Harmondsworth: Penguin.

Hayek, F.A. (1960) *The Constitution of Liberty*, London: Routledge & Kegan Paul.

Hayek, F.A. (1976) *The Road to Serfdom*, London: Routledge & Kegan Paul.

Hayward, D. (1989) 'Beyond the fringe', *New Statesman and Society* 21 July.

Hazelzet, P. (1988) 'France – an exporter's dream?' *International Security Review* March/April: 51.

Heald, S. (1986) 'Mafias in Africa: the rise of drinking companies and vigilante groups in Bugisu District, Uganda', *Africa* 56 (4): 446–66.

Heininger, B.L. and Urbanek, J. (1983) 'Civilianization of the American police 1970–80', *Journal of Police Science and Administration* 11 (2): 200–5.

Held, D. (1987) *Models of Democracy*, Cambridge: Polity.

Henderson, J.W. (1987) 'Public law enforcement, private security and citizen crime prevention: competition or co-operation?' *Police Journal* 60: 48–57.

Hindess, B. (1984) 'Rational choice theory and the analysis of political action', *Economy and Society* 13 (3): 255–77.

Hindess, B. (1987) *Freedom, Equality and the Market*, London: Tavistock.

Hobbs, D. (1988) *Doing the Business*, Oxford: Clarendon Press.

Hobsbawm, E.J. (1959) *Primitive Rebels*, Manchester: Manchester University Press.

Hobson, R. (1990) 'Technology that foils raiders in the street', *The Times* 19 June.

Holdaway, S. (1983) *Inside the British Police: A Force at Work*, Oxford: Blackwell.

Home Office (1979) *The Private Security Industry: A Discussion Paper*, London: HMSO.

Home Office (1983) *Circular 114/83 Manpower, Effectiveness and Efficiency in the Police Service*, London: Home Office.

Home Office (1988a) *Circular 105/88 Civilian Staff in the Police Service*, London: Home Office.

Home Office (1988b) *Private Sector Involvement in the Remand System*, London: HMSO.

Home Office (1988c) *Punishment, Custody and the Community*, London: HMSO.

Home Office (1989) *Immigration Service: Detention Centre Harmondsworth*, Report by HM Chief Inspector of Prisons, London: Home Office.

Home Office (1990) *Crime, Justice and Protecting the Public*, London: HMSO.

Hoogenboom, A.B. (1989) 'The privatization of social control', in R. Hood (ed.) *Crime and Criminal Policy in Europe: Proceedings of a European Colloquium, 3–6 July, 1988*, Oxford: University of Oxford Centre for Criminological Research: 121–4.

Hope, T. (1988) 'Support for neighbourhood watch: a British Crime Survey analysis', in T. Hope and M. Shaw (eds) *Communities and Crime Reduction*, London: HMSO: 146–61.

Horsthuis, T. (1987) 'Holland – an exporter's dream?' *International Security Review* March/April: 57–9.

Hough, M. and Mayhew, P. (1985) *Taking Account of Crime*, Home Office Research Study No. 85, London: HMSO.

House of Commons (1984) *Second Report of the Defence Committee: The Physical Security of Military Instal- lations in the United Kingdom*, 2 vols, Session 1983–4, HC 397–I and II.

House of Commons (1987a) *Third Report of the Home Affairs Committee: Minutes of Evidence*, 1986/7, HC 35–I, London: HMSO.

House of Commons (1987b) *Fourth Report of the Home Affairs Committee: Contract Provision of Prisons*, 1986/7, HC 35–I, London: HMSO.

House of Commons (1989) *Third Report of the Home Affairs Committee, Higher Police Training and the Police Staff College*, London: HMSO.

House of Commons (1990a) *Sixth Report of the Defence Committee. The Physical Security of Military Installations in the United Kingdom*, Session 1989–90, HC 171.

House of Commons (1990b) *Third Report of the Home Affairs Committee 1989–90. Criminal Records*, London: HMSO.

Hulbert, J. (1988) 'Sensitive questions', *Informatics* December: 49–51.

Hurd, D. (1989) 'Freedom will flourish when citizens accept responsibility', *Independent* 13 September.

Hutter, B.M. (1988) *The Reasonable Arm of the Law: the Law Enforcement Procedures of Environmental Health Officers*, Oxford: Clarendon Press.

Hyder, K. (1988) 'Post Office "eyes" go private', *Police Review* 18 Mar: 592–3.

Ianni, E.R. and Ianni, F.A.J. (1983) 'Street cops and management cops', in M. Punch (ed.), *Control in Police Organisation*, Cambridge, Mass: MIT: 251–74.

Ignatieff, M. (1981) 'State, civil society and total institutions': a critique of recent social histories of punishment', in M. Tonry and N. Morris (eds) *Crime and Justice: An Annual Review of Research*, vol. 3, Chicago: University of Chicago: 153–92.

Ignatieff, M. (1989) 'Citizenship and moral narcissism', *Political Quarterly* 60 (1): 63–74, January.

Jacobs, J. (1984) *The Death and Life of the Great American Cities*, London: Peregrine Books.

JCC (Joint Consultative Committee) (1990) *Operational Policing Review*: Avon & Somerset Constabulary, 'Policing in the 1990s'. Devon & Cornwall Constabulary, Home Office Circulars 105/88–106/88. Northumbria Constabulary, 'Efficiency and effectiveness'. Sussex Constabulary, 'Demands and resources'.

Jefferson, T. and Grimshaw, R. (1984) *Controlling the Constable*, London: Muller.

Jepsen, J. (1989) 'Privatisation of social control – four examples from Scandinavia', in R. Hood (ed.) *Crime and Criminal Policy in Europe: Proceedings of a Colloquium, 3–6 July, 1988*, Oxford: University of Oxford, Centre for Criminological Research: 125–33.

Jesperson, A. (1987) 'Who needs a hobby bobby'? *Police Review* 9: 68–9, January.

Johnson, E.H. (1983–4) 'Neighbourhood police in the People's Republic of China', *Police Studies* Winter: 8–12.

Johnston, L. (1986) *Marxism, Class Analysis and Socialist Pluralism*, London: Allen & Unwin.

Johnston, L. (1988) 'Controlling police work: problems of organizational reform in large public bureaucracies', *Work, Employment and Society* 2 (1): 51–70.

Jones, D. (1982) *Crime, Protest, Community and Police in Nineteenth Century Britain*, London: Routledge & Kegan Paul.

Jones, T., MacLean, B., and Young, J. (1986) *The Islington Crime Survey: Crime Victimization and Policing in Inner City London*, Aldershot: Gower.

Jordan & Sons Ltd (1987) *Britain's Security Industry*, London: Jordan & Sons Ltd

Jordan & Sons Ltd (1989) *Britain's Security Industry*, London: Jordan & Sons Ltd.

Judge, T. (1988) 'Is there a profit to be made out of policing?' *Police* December: 12–16.

Kakalik, J.S. and Wildhorn, S. (1972) *Private Police in the United States (The Rand Report)*: Vol. 1. Findings and Recommendations. Vol. 2. The Private Police Industry: Its Nature and Extent. Vol. 3. Current Regulation of Private Police: Regulatory Agency Experience and Views. Vol. 4. The Law and Private Police. National Institute of Law Enforcement and Criminal Justice, Washington: US Dept. of Justice.

Kakalik, J.S. and Wildhorn, S. (1977) *The Private Police: Security and Danger*, New York: Crane, Russak & Company Inc.

Kania, R.E. (1989) 'The French municipal police experiment', *Police Studies* 12 (3): 125–31.

Kay J., Mayer, C., and Thompson, D. (eds) (1986) 'Introduction', in *Privatization and Regulation: the UK Experience*, Oxford: Clarendon Press.

Kelling, G. (1983) 'On the accomplishments of the police', in M. Punch (ed.) *Control in Police Organisation*, Cambridge Mass: MIT: 152–68.

Kenny, D.J. (1986) 'Examining the role of active citizen participation in the law enforcement process', unpublished PhD thesis, Rutgers University.

King, D. (1987) *The New Right: Politics, Markets and Citizenship*, London: Macmillan.

King, J. (1988) 'The raw material', *Security Gazette* October: 16–17.

King, P. (1989) 'Prosecution associations and their impact in eighteenth century Essex', in D. Hay and F. Snyder (eds) *Policing and Prosecution in Britain 1750–1850*, Oxford: Clarendon Press: 171–207.

Kinsey, R., Lea, J., and Young, J. (1986) *Losing the Fight Against Crime*, Oxford: Blackwell.

Kirby, T. (1989a) 'Reserve force proposed as counter to privatisation', *Independent* 17 May.

Kirby, T. (1989b) '"Rock bottom" morale among forensic scientists highlighted', *Independent* 28 February.

Klein, R. (1977) 'The corporate state, the health service and the professions', *New University Quarterly* 31: 161–80.

Klein, R. (1983) *The Politics of the National Health Service*, London: Longman.

Labour Party (1986) *Protecting Our People: Labour's Policy on Crime Prevention*, London: Labour Party.

Laitinen, A. (1987) 'The privatization of police functions in Finland', paper to International Sociological Association Research Committee 29, Montreal Conference, Canada 9–11 November.

Lambert, J. (1970) *Crime, Police and Race Relations*, Oxford: Oxford University Press

Lane, R. (1967) *Policing the City: Boston 1822–1885*, Cambridge Mass: Harvard University Press.

Lea, J. and Young, J. (1984) *What is to be Done about Law and Order?* Harmondsworth: Penguin.

Lee, L. (1962) *Cider With Rosie*, Harmondsworth: Penguin.

LeGrand, J. and Robinson, R. (1984) *Privatisation and the Welfare State*, London: Allen & Unwin.

Leon, C. (1989) 'The special constabulary', *Policing* 5: 265–86, Winter.

Leon, C. (1990) 'A special kind of watch', *Police Review* 13 April: 752–3.

Leppard, D. (1989) 'Transport police lose ferry deal', *Sunday Times* 29 January.

Levi, M. (forthcoming) Developments in business crime control in Europe', in F. Heidensohn and M. Farrell (eds) *Crime in Europe*, London: Routledge: 226–48.

Levitas, R. (ed.) (1985) *The Ideology of the New Right*, Oxford: Polity Press.

'Liao Wang' (1988) 'New security services in Beijing', *Beijing Review* 1–7 August: 24.

Liberty (1989) 'Who's watching you? Video surveillance in public places', *Briefing* no. 16, October.

Lidstone, K.W., Hogg, R., and Sutcliffe, F. (1980) *Prosecutions By Private Individuals and Non-Police Agencies*, Royal Commission on Criminal Procedure, Research Study No. 10, London: HMSO.

Lipman, M. and McGraw, W.R. (1988) 'Employee theft: a $40 billion industry', in I.A. Lipman (ed.) *The Annals of the American Academy of Political Science: The Private Security Industry: Issues and Trends*, California: Sage, Vol. 498, July: 51–9.

Lipson, M. (1988) 'Private security: a retrospective', in I.A. Lipman (ed.) *The Annals of the American Academy of Political and Social Science: The Private Security Industry: Issues and Trends*, California: Sage, Vol. 498 July: 11–22.

Little, C.B. and Sheffield, C.P. (1983) 'Frontiers and criminal justice: English private prosecution societies and American vigilantism in the eighteenth and nineteenth centuries', *American Sociological Review* 48: 796–808, December.

Lock, J. (1979) *The British Policewoman*, London: Robert Hale.

Loveland, I. (1989) 'Policing welfare: local authority responses to claimant fraud in the Housing Benefit Scheme', *Journal of Law and Society* 16 (2): 187–209.

Lowman, J., Menzies, R.J., and Palys, T.S. (1987) 'Introduction: transcarceration and the modern state of penality', in J. Lowman, R.J. Menzies, and T.S. Palys (eds) *Transcarceration: Essays in the Sociology of Social Control*, Aldershot: Gower: 1–15.

Lubans, V. and Edgar, J. (1979) *Policing By Objectives*, Hartford, Connecticut: Social Development Corporation.

McAinsh, S. (1988) 'Security – an investment in failure?' *International Security Review* March/April: 33–8.

McCall, K. (1987) 'Standing by for a crisis', *Police Review* 9 January: 70.

McCarthy, M. (1990) 'Firms braced to meet pollution costs', *Times* 28 September.

McClintock, F.H. and Wiles, P. (1972) 'Introduction', in P. Wiles and F.H. McClintock (eds) *The Security Industry in the United Kingdom: Papers Presented to the Cropwood Round-Table Conference, July 1971*: Cambridge: Institute of Criminology, Cambridge University, 9–11.

McCormick, K., Garrison, C., and Arbogast, D. (1983) 'Public and private law enforcement: the Ohio experience suggests a model for the future', *Journal of Security Administration* 6 (1): 43–52.

McCrie, R.D. (1988) 'The development of the US security industry', in I.A. Lipman (ed.) *The Annals of the American Academy of Political and Social Science: The Private Security Industry: Issues and Trends*, California: Sage, Vol. 498, July: 23–33.

MacDonald, I. (1985) 'The police system in Spain', in J. Roach and J. Thomaneck (eds) *Police and Public Order in Europe*, London: Croom Helm: 215–54.

McLean, A. (1989) 'Private coppers saving pounds', *Police Review* 6 October: 2016–17.

McLynn, F. (1989) *Crime and Punishment in Eighteenth Century England*, London: Routledge.

McMullan, J.L. (1987) 'Policing the criminal underworld: state power and decentralized social control in London 1550–1700', in J. Lowman, R.J. Menzies, and T.S. Palys (eds) *Transcarceration: Essays in the Sociology of Social Control*, Aldershot: Gower: 119–38.

Manning, P. (1979) 'The social control of police work', in S. Holdaway (ed.), *The British Police*, London: Arnold: 41–65.

Marsden, P. (1990) 'In the light of perceived fears of sexually transmitted diseases such as AIDS, to what extent should prostitution be legalised and controlled in garrison towns such as Plymouth?' unpublished dissertation, BA Social and Organisational Studies, Polytechnic South West, Plymouth.

Marshall, G. (1965) *Police and Government*, London: Methuen.
Marshall, T.H. (1950) *Citizenship and Social Class*, Cambridge: Cambridge University Press.
Marx, G. (1987) 'The interweaving of public and private police in undercover work', in C.D. Shearing and P.C. Stenning (eds) *Private Policing*, California: Sage: 172–93.
Marx, G. and Archer, D. (1973) 'The urban vigilante', *Psychology Today* January: 45–50.
Marx, G. and Archer, D. (1976) 'Community police patrols and vigilantism', in H.J. Rosenbaum and P.C. Sedeberg (eds) *Vigilante Politics*, Pennsylvania: University of Pennsylvania Press: 129–57.
Mason, D. (1990) 'Private and public policing: improving the service to the public through co-operation', Brookfield Papers No. 6, Centre for Police and Criminal Justice Studies, Exeter: University of Exeter.
Mason, G. (1987) 'Private eyes in the dock', *Police Review* 2 January: 28–9.
Mason, G. (1988) 'Are civilians second class policemen?' *Police Review* 1 July: 1374–5.
Matthews, R. (1989a) 'Privatization in perspective', in R. Matthews (ed.) *Privatizing Criminal Justice*, London: Sage: 1–23.
Matthews, R. (1989b) 'Privatization in perspective', in M. Farrell (ed.), *Punishment for Profit? Privatisation and Contracting Out in the Criminal Justice System*, London: Institute for the Study and Treatment of Delinquency: 25–9.
May, D. (1979) 'The British Transport police', *Police Review* 23 March: 446–53.
May, J. (1986) 'Britain's nuclear police, a law unto themselves'? *Time Out* 22–9 October: 7.
Mayhew, P., Elliott, D., and Dowds, L. (1989) *The British Crime Survey*, Home Office Research Study No. 11, London: HMSO.
Miliband, R. (1973) *Parliamentary Socialism*, London: Merlin.
Miller, J.P. and Luke, D.E. (1977) *Law Enforcement by Public Officials and Special Police Forces*, London: Home Office, 4 vols.
Mills, C.W. (1959) *The Sociological Imagination*, New York: Oxford University Press.
Millward, R (1986) 'The comparative performance of public and private ownership', in J. Kay, C. Mayer, and D. Thompson (eds) *Privatization and Regulation: the UK Experience*, Oxford: Clarendon Press.
MODP (1989) *Annual Report By the Chief Constable*, London: MODP.
Monkkonen, E.H. (1981) *Police in Urban America 1860–1920*, London: Cambridge University Press.
Moore, J. (1983) 'Why privatize?' in J. Kay, C. Mayer, and D. Thompson (eds) *Privatization and Regulation: the UK Experience*, Oxford: Clarendon Press (published 1986): 78–93.
Morgan, J. (1987) *Conflict and Order: The Police and Labour Disputes in England and Wales, 1900–39*, Oxford: Clarendon Press.
Morn, F. (1982) *The Eye That Never Sleeps*, Bloomington: Indiana University Press.
Nelson, D. (1988) 'Danger – security men at work', *New Statesman and Society* 23–4 September.

Newman, O. (1973) *Defensible Space*, New York: Macmillan.

Newman, S.L. (1984) *Liberalism at Wit's End: The Libertarian Revolt Against the Modern State*, Ithaca: Cornell University Press.

Newton, N. (1987) 'A special kind of watch', *Police Review* 27 February: 430–1.

Nicolaus, M. (1968) 'Sociology liberation movement', in T. Pateman (ed.) *Counter Course: a Handbook for Course Criticism*, Harmondsworth: Penguin: 38–41 (published 1972).

Niskanen, W. (1971) *Bureaucracy and Representative Government*, New York: Aldine Atherton.

Norris, S. (1988) 'Cracking crime together', *Crime Prevention News* July–September: 14–15.

Nozick, R. (1974) *Anarchy, State and Utopia*, Oxford: Blackwell.

Ocqueteau, F. (1987) 'L'irresistible ascension des forces de securité privée, *Actes* 60: 17–19.

Ostrowe, B.B. and DiBiase, R. (1983) 'Citizen involvement as a crime deterrent: a study of public attitudes towards an unsanctioned civilian patrol group', *Journal of Police Science and Administration* 11 (2): 185–93.

O'Toole, G. (1978) *The Private Sector: Private Spies, Rent-a-Cops, and the Police-Industrial Complex*, New York: Norton & Company.

Page, R.W. (1982) 'The growth and control of private security in Australia', in A. Rees (ed.) *Policing and Private Security*, Canberra: Australian Institute of Criminology.

Pahl, R. (1985) 'The politics of work', *Political Quarterly* 56 (4): 331–45.

Pahl, R. and Wallace, C. (1988) 'Neither angels in marble nor rebels in red': privatisation and working class consciousness', in D. Rose (ed.) *Social Stratification and Economic Change*, London: Hutchinson: 127–52.

Painter, R.E. (1988) 'Standing together against crime', *Security Times* February: 77–9.

Pakistani Welfare Society of Waltham Forest (1989) 'Vigilante groups' (Letter to *Independent* 7 February).

Palmer, S.H. (1988) *Police and Protest in England and Ireland 1780–1850*, Cambridge: Cambridge University Press.

Pateman, C. (1983) 'Feminist critiques of the public/private dichotomy', in S.I. Benn and G.F. Gaus (eds) *Public and Private in Social Life*, London: Croom Helm/New York: St Martins Press: 281–303.

Pead, D. (1986) 'The Ministry of Defence Police', *Police Review* 6 June: 1189–91.

Pearce, F. and Tombs, S. (1988) 'Regulating corporate crime: the case of health and safety', paper presented to the American Society of Criminology Conference, Chicago.

Pennell, F.E. (1978) 'Collective vs. private strategies for coping with crime: the consequences for citizen perceptions of crime, attitudes towards the police and neighbouring activity', *Journal of Voluntary Action Research* 7 (1–2): 59–74.

Pennell, S., Curtis, C., and Henderson, J. (1985) *Guardian Angels: an Assessment of Citizen Response to Crime*. US Department of Justice, Washington: Government Printing Office.

Percy, S.L. (1979) 'Citizen co-production of community safety', in R. Baker and F.A. Mayer (eds) *Evaluating Alternative Law Enforcement Policies*, Lexington, Mass: Lexington Books.

Philips, D. (1980) '"A new engine of power and authority": the institutionalization of law-enforcement in England 1780–1830', in V.A.C. Gatrell, B. Lenman, and G. Parker (eds) *Crime and the Law: The Social History of Crime in Western Europe Since 1500*, London: Europa: 155–89.

Philips, D. (1989) 'Good men to associate and bad men to conspire: associations for the prosecution of felons in England 1760–1860, in D. Hay and F. Snyder (eds) *Policing and Prosecution in Britain 1750–1850*, Oxford: Clarendon Press: 113–70.

Pirie, M (1988) *Privatization*, Aldershot: Wildwood House.

Police Advisory Board for England and Wales (1981) *Report of the Second Working Party on the Special Constabulary*.

Pomeranz, F. (1988) 'Technological security', in I.A. Lipman (ed.) *Annals of the American Academy of Political and Social Science: The Private Security Industry: Issues and Trends*, California: Sage, Vol. 498, July: 70–81.

Proctor, I. (1990) 'The privatisation of working class life: a dissenting view', *British Journal of Sociology* 41 (2): 157–80.

Pryke, R. (1986) 'The comparative performance of public and private enterprise', in J. Kay, C. Mayer, and D. Thompson (eds) *Privatization and Regulation: the UK Experience*, Oxford: Clarendon Press.

Punch, M (1985) *Conduct Unbecoming*, London: Tavistock.

Punch, M. and Naylor, T. (1973) 'The police: a social service', *New Society* 24: 358–61.

Randall, W.E. and Hamilton, P. (1972) 'The security industry of the United Kingdom', in P. Wiles and F.H. McClintock (eds) *The Security Industry in the United Kingdom: Papers Presented to the Cropwood Round-Table Conference, July 1971*, Cambridge: Institute of Criminology, Cambridge University: 67–72.

Rau, C. (1989a) 'State warned of crime in security work', *The Age* 14 October.

Rau, C. (1989b) 'Falling victim to "security experts"', *The Age* 14 October.

Rau, C. (1989c) 'Security industry faces a control crisis', *The Age* 16 October.

Rawlings, P. (forthcoming) 'Creeping privatization? The police, the Conservative government and policing in the late 1980s', in R. Reiner and M. Cross, (eds) *Beyond Law and Order*, London: Macmillan.

Reed, J. (1988) 'Policing the UK's nuclear plants', *Law and Order* April: 47–9.

Rees, R. (1989) 'Raising the alarm on time-wasters', *Police Review* 8 December: 2488–9

Reiner, R. (1985) *The Politics of the Police*, Sussex: Wheatsheaf.

Reiner, R. (1989a) 'Thinking at the top', *Policing* 5: 181–99, Autumn.

Reiner, R. (1989b) 'Where the buck stops: chief constables' views on police accountability', in R. Morgan and D.J. Smith (eds) *Coming to Terms with Policing*, London: Routledge: 195–216.

Reiner, R. (forthcoming) 'Chief constables in England and Wales: a social portrait of a criminal justice elite', in R. Reiner and M. Cross (eds) *Beyond Law and Order*, London: Macmillan.

Reiss, A.J. (1988) *Private Employment of Public Police*, Washington: US Dept of Justice, Government Printing Office.

Reith, C. (1952) *The Blind Eye of History*, London: Faber & Faber.

Richardson, J.F. (1970) *The New York Police: Colonial Times to 1901*, New York: Oxford.

Roberts, R. (1973) *The Classic Slum*, Harmondsworth: Penguin.

Rosenbaum, D. (1988) 'A critical eye on neighbourhood watch: does it reduce crime and fear?' in T. Hope and M. Shaw (eds) *Communities and Crime Reduction*, London: HMSO: 126–45.

Rosenbaum, H.J. and Sedeberg, P.C. (eds) (1976) *Vigilante Politics*, Pennsylvania: Univ. of Pennsylvania Press.

Rosentraub, M.S. and Harlow, K.S. (1983) 'Private/public relations and service delivery: the co-production of personal safety', *Policy Studies Journal* 11 (3): 445–57.

Rothbard, M.N. (1978) *For a New Liberty: The Libertarian Manifesto*, New York: Collier Macmillan

Rude, G. (1985) *Criminal and Victim*, Oxford: Clarendon Press.

Ryan, M. and Ward, T. (1988) 'Privatising punishment', *Political Quarterly* 59: 86–90, January–March.

Ryan, M. and Ward, T. (1989a) *Privatization and the Penal System: the American Experience and the Debate in Britain*, Milton Keynes: Open University Press.

Ryan, M. and Ward, T. (1989b) 'The state and the prison system: is there a role for the private sector?' paper to the British Criminology Conference, 1989, Bristol Polytechnic.

Sampson, G. (1984) *An End to Allegiance: Individual Freedom and the New Politics*, London: Temple Smith.

Samuels, R. (1975) '"Quarry roughs": life and labour in Headington Quarry, 1860–1920. An essay in oral history', in R. Samuels (ed.) *Village Life and Labour*, London: Routledge & Kegan Paul: 139–263.

Sansom, E.G. (1978) 'The growth and problems of the British Transport Police', *The Medico-Legal Journal* 2: 47–57.

Saunders, P. and Harris, C. (1990) 'Privatization and the consumer', *Sociology* 24 (1): 57–75.

Savas, E.S. (1982) *Privatizing the Public Sector*, New Jersey: Chatham House.

Schlesinger, P., Tumber, H., and Murdock, G. (1989) 'The media politics of crime, law and justice', paper presented to the British Criminology Conference, Bristol Polytechnic, 17–20 July.

Schmitter, P. (1974) 'Still the century of corporatism? *Review of Politics* 36: 85–131.

Schmitter, P. (1985) 'Neo-corporatism and the state', in W. Grant (ed.) *The Political Economy of Corporatism*, London: Macmillan: 32–62.

Scull, A. (1977) *Decarceration: Community Treatment and the Deviant: A Radical View*, Englewood Cliffs, New Jersey: Prentice Hall.

Scull, A. (1984) *Decarceration: Community Treatment and the Deviant: A Radical View*, Cambridge: Polity Press.

Self, P. (1985) *Political Theories of Modern Government, Its Role and Reform*, London: Allen & Unwin.

Shapland, J. (1988) 'Policing with the public?' in T. Hope and M. Shaw (eds) *Communities and Crime Reduction*. London: HMSO: 116–25.

Shapland, J. and Vagg, J. (1987) 'Using the police', *British Journal of Criminology* 27 (1): 54–63.

Shapland, J. and Vagg, J. (1988) *Policing By the Public*, London: Routledge.

Sharpe, J.A. (1984) *Crime in Early Modern England 1550–1750*, London: Longman.

Shaw, J. (1987) 'James Buchanan and public-choice economics' *Dialogue* 22–5.

Shaw, S. (1989) 'Penal sanctions: private affluence or public squalor?' in M. Farrell (ed.) *Punishment for Profit? Privatisation and Contracting Out in the Criminal Justice System*. London: Institute for the Study and Treatment of Delinquency: 45–52.

Shearing, C.D. and Stenning, P.C. (1981) 'Modern private security: its growth and implications', in M. Tonry and N. Morris (eds) *Crime and Justice: an Annual Review of Research*, Vol. 3, Chicago: University of Chicago Press: 193–245.

Shearing, C.D. and Stenning, P.C. (1983) 'Private security – implications for social control', *Social Problems* 30 (5): 493–506.

Shearing, C.D. and Stenning, P.C. (eds) (1987) *Private Policing*, California: Sage.

Showstack Sassoon, A. (1980) *Gramsci's Politics*, London: Croom Helm.

Shubert, A. (1981) 'Private initiative in law enforcement: associations for the prosecution of felons', in V. Bailey (ed.) *Policing and Punishment in Nineteenth Century Britain*, London: Croom Helm: 25–41.

Silver, A. (1967) 'The demand for order in civil society', in D. Bordua (ed.) *The Police*, New York: Wiley: 1–24.

Sinclair, I. and Miller, C. (1984) *Measures of Police Effectiveness and Efficiency*, London: Home Office Research and Planning Unit, Paper 25.

Skogan, W. (1988) 'Communities, crime and neighbourhood organization', Working Paper: Evanston, Illinois: Centre for Urban Affairs and Policy Research, Northwestern University.

Slinn, T. (1985) 'The Israeli security industry', *International Security Review* March/April: 77–85.

Slinn, T. (1988) 'Holland – the way ahead?' *International Security Review* March/April: 57–9.

Smith, N. (1987) 'Airports – still an easy target?' *International Security Review* May/June: 34–6.

Smith, S.J. (1986) *Crime, Space and Society*, Cambridge: Cambridge University Press.

Smith-Leach, G. (1985) 'The BTP are proper police officers', *Police Review* 8 February: 282.

South, N. (1984) 'Private security, the division of policing labour and the commercial compromise of the state', *Research in Law, Deviance and Social Control* 6: 171–98.

South, N. (1985) 'Private security and social control: the private security sector in the United Kingdom, its commercial functions and public accountability', unpublished PhD thesis, Enfield: Middlesex Polytechnic.

South, N. (1987) 'Law, profit and "private persons"', in C.D. Shearing and P.C. Stenning (eds) *Private Policing*, California: Sage: 72–109.

South, N. (1988) *Policing for Profit*, London: Sage.

South, N. (1989) 'Reconstructing policing: differentiation and contradiction in post-war private and public policing', in R. Matthews (ed.) *Privatizing Criminal Justice*, London: Sage: 74–105.

Spencer, S. (1985) *Called to Account*, London: NCCL.

Spitzer, S. (1987) 'Security and control in capitalist societies: the fetishism of security and the secret thereof', in J. Lowman, R.J. Menzies, and T.S. Palys (eds), *Transcarceration: Essays in the Sociology of Social Control*, Aldershot: Gower: 43–58.

Spitzer, S. and Scull, A. (1977a) 'Privatization and capitalist development: the case of the private police', *Social Problems* 25 (1): 18–29.

Spitzer, S. and Scull, A. (1977b) 'Social control in historical perspective', in D. Greenberg (ed.) *Corrections and Punishment*, Beverly Hills: Sage: 265–86.

Steedman, C. (1984) *Policing the Victorian Community: The Formation of English Provincial Police Forces 1856–80*, London: Routledge & Kegan Paul.

Steel, D. and Heald, D. (1984) 'The new agenda', in *Privatizing Public Enterprises*, London: Royal Institute for Public Administration: 13–19.

Steinberg, A. (1986) '"The spirit of litigation"; private prosecution and criminal justice in nineteenth century Philadelphia, *Journal of Social History* 20: 231–49.

Stenning, P.C. and Shearing, C.D. (1980) 'The quiet revolution: the nature, development and general legal implications of private security in Canada', *Criminal Law Quarterly* 22: 220–48,

Stewart, G.R. (1964) *Committee of Vigilance: Revolution in San Fransisco, 1851*, Boston: Houghton Mifflin Company.

Stewart, J. K. (1985) 'Public safety and private police', *Public Administration Review* 45: 758–65.

Storch, R. (1975) 'The plague of blue locusts: police reform and popular resistance in northern England, 1840–57', *International Review of Social History* 20: 61–90.

Storch, R. (1976) 'The policeman as domestic missionary: urban discipline and popular culture in northern England, 1850–1880', *Journal of Social History* 9 (4): 481–509.

Storch, R. (1989) 'Policing rural southern England before the police: opinion and practice, 1830–56', in D. Hay and F. Snyder (eds) *Policing and Prosecution in Britain 1750– 1850*, Oxford: Clarendon Press: 211–66.

Stronach, A. (1989) 'Parkstone Quay. Has the tide turned?' *Security Times* July: 26–28.

Sundeen, R.A. and Siegel, G.B. (1986) 'The use of volunteers by police', *Journal of Police Science and Administration* 14 (1): 49–61.

Swift, R. (1988) 'Urban policing in early Victorian England, 1835–86: a reappraissal', *History* 73 (238): 211– 37.

Tarlet, C. (1988) 'Private and commercial security – what is their role in modern day policing?' International Police Exhibition and Conference, Seminar Session 4.

Taylor, L. (1976) 'Vigilantes – why not?' *New Society* 4 November: 259–60.

Tendler, S. (1989) 'Street warden call to replace trained bobbies on the beat', *The Times* 28 September.

Thomas, C. (1989) 'Policing public transport throughout the world', *British Transport Police Journal* 2 (24): 41–6.

Thomson, A. (1988) 'Paramilitaries operate a shoot-to-cripple policy', *Listener* 3 March: 7–8.

Thomson, I. (1989) 'A not so clever dick', *Independent Magazine* 29 July.

Tirbutt, E. (1989) 'A share for all seasons', *Security and Protection Equipment* April.

Titmuss, R.M. (1958) *Essays on the Welfare State*, London: Allen & Unwin.

Togliatti, P. (1979) *On Gramsci and Other Writings*, London: Lawrence & Wishart.

Tomkins, L.H. (1986) 'Covert CCTV surveillance techniques', *International Security Review* December: 52–4.

Tucker, W. (1985) *Vigilante: The Backlash Against Crime in America*, New York: Stein & Day.

Tullock, G. (1979) 'Bureaucracy and the growth of government', in S.C. Littlechild, G. Tullock, A.P.L. Minford, A. Seldon, A. Budd, and C.K. Rowley *The Taming of Government*, London: Institute for Economic Affairs.

Tura, P. (1985) 'Intruder alarms – the Italian solution', *International Security Review* March/April.

UKAEA (1989) *Chief Constables Annual Report 1988*, London: UKAEA.

Van Andel, H. (1989) 'Crime prevention that works: the case of public transport in the Netherlands', *British Journal of Criminology*, 29 (1): 47–56.

Van Reenen, P. (1989) 'Policing Europe after 1992: co-operation and competition', *European Affairs* 3 (2): 45–53, Summer.

Veljanowski, C. (1989) *Privatization and Competition: a Market Prospectus*, London: Institute for Economic Affairs, Hobart Paperback 28.

Vines, M. (1988) 'Private and commercial security – what is their role in modern day policing?' International Police Exhibition and Conference, Seminar Session 4.

Waddington, P.A.J. (1989) 'A national police force is the safeguard of civil liberty' *Independent* 7 July.

Warren, R., Harlow, K.S., and Rosentraub, M.S. (1982) 'Citizen participation in the production of services: methodological and policy issues in coproduction research', *South Western Review* 2 (3): 41–55.

Weait, M. (1989) 'The letter of the law? an enquiry into reasoning and formal enforcement in the Industrial Air Pollution Inspectorate', *British Journal of Criminology* 29 (1): 57–70.

Weatherill, S. (1988) 'Buying special police services' *Public Law* Spring: 106–27.

Weatheritt, M. (1986) *Innovations in Policing*, London: Croom Helm.

Weiss, R.P. (1987) 'From "slugging detectives" to "labour relations": policing labour at Ford, 1930–47', in C.D. Shearing and P.C. Stenning (eds) *Private Policing*, California: Sage.

Wheeler, J. (1989a) 'Police accountability and organization', paper

presented to Association of County Council's seminar on Policing for
the Turn of the Century, 12 July.

Wheeler, J. (1989b) 'Who controls the security firms'? *Police* 21 (10): 28–9,
June/July.

Whitaker, B. (1964) *The Police*, London: Penguin.

Whitfield, M. (1990) 'A tale of two ambulances' *Independent* 11 January.

Wildeman, J. (1988) 'When the state fails: a critical assessment of contract
policing', paper presented to American Society of Criminology
Conference, Chicago, November.

Wilkinson, P. (1985) 'European police co-operation', in J. Roach and J.
Thomaneck (eds) *Police and Public Order in Europe*, London: Croom
Helm: 273–86.

Wilson, J.Q. (1968) *Varieties of Police Behaviour*, Cambridge, Mass: Harvard
University Press.

Wilson, J.Q. and Kelling, G. (1982) 'Broken windows', *The Atlantic Monthly*
March: 29–38.

Wolmar, C. (1990) 'Ridley's dream of privatization fails to take off',
Independent 20 April.

Wood, J. (1989) 'The Serious Fraud Office', *Criminal Law Review* March:
175–84.

Wright, E. (1981) 'The Liverpool City Security Force', *International Security
Review* October: 106–12.

Yin, R., Vogel, M.E., Chaiken, J.M., and Both, D.R. (1977) *Citizen Patrol
Projects. National Evaluation Program: Phase One. Summary Report*,
National Institute of Law Enforcement and Criminal Justice. Law
Enforcement Assistance Administration. US Dept. of Justice, January.

Young, D. (1990) 'Even the KGB succumbs to privatization', *The Times* 24
April.

Name index

Subject index

DATE DUE			

DEMCO 38-297